Saint Conan

keep at arms length!

inside a boiler - Otranto

'ng'

back to the boats!

stern bollards - Gracehill

steam steering gear

one less for the pot

Argyll Shipwrecks

PETER MOIR AND IAN CRAWFORD

First published by **Moir Crawford** 1994

Reprinted: 1997

Second edition: June 2003

Copyright: Peter Moir and Ian Crawford

Moir Crawford
1 Cedar Walk
Wemyss Bay
Inverclyde
PA18 6BP

Tel:01475-520141

ISBN 0 9513366 1 4 2nd edition
(Revised and enlarged).

Printed by Cordfall Ltd.
Tel:0141-572-0878

Disclaimer: This book is a catalogue of shipwrecks along the Argyllshire coastline, and is intended for research and reference only. While there are details about the wrecks current condition and location, they are not an invitation to members of the public or other interested parties to dive on any of the sites mentioned. Any individual or group intending to dive on any of the sites included within this book should undertake adequate training, planning and give due consideration to appropriate safety precautions before undertaking any dive.

Cover photographs:
front cover   The Fleetwood trawler *Wyre Majestic* - 1994 Peter Moir
rear cover   Underwater photographs by and reproduced with kind permission of Gavin Anderson Photography - 01577 861881.
L-R: *John Strachan, Hispania and Ospray II.* Sanda Island and Ailsa Craig - Peter Moir.

Contents

Author's Notes

Argyll Shipwrecks was first published in 1994 after an intensive three year period of archive research followed by many enjoyable adventures to the more distant parts of Argyll to locate and dive some of its more remote shipwrecks in often spectacular locations.

Since 1994 we have continued to research and locate new wrecks throughout the area, and have taken the opportunity of a reprint to include a number of new shipwrecks, as well as provide additional details of vessels which have been located since the book was first published.

We continue to provide locations for wrecks both with GPS location and where relevant small chartlets, which give more focused information for divers and fishermen. One change of note is the format for GPS positions. In earlier editions we provided wreck location in degrees, minutes and seconds, this edition gives GPS positions in degrees and minutes to three decimal places. Please note that all Lat/Long positions in the book that are suffixed with (GPS), denotes that the position has been derived using a GPS receiver.

Books such as Argyll Shipwrecks and its companion Clyde Shipwrecks are essentially work in progress, and new finds both above and below the water will always provide further impetus to update and add to the current edition. New diving technologies and techniques are now allowing the suitably trained amateur diver to go to depths previously unattainable by the amateur diver breathing compressed air. These advances have opened up a whole new field of wrecks throughout the Argyll area, but especially along the southern boundary in the North Channel. In recent years wrecks such as the *Tuscania, Justicia, Calgarian,* HMS *Audacious* and in the Sound of Mull the SS *Buitenzorg* have all been visited by experienced teams of divers wishing to explore and photograph these wrecks in challenging conditions.

Argyll Shipwrecks has proved very popular, with a wide readership. The book has helped to publicise and open up areas and sites to the diving public previously unexplored, or only by a very few amateur divers. We will continue to catalogue shipwrecks in the area and welcome any additional information which the reader can provide to build a more complete record of shipwrecks within the region.

for
Joyce and Sheila

Photo Acknowledgements

Author's Collection - all uncredited photographs.
Mr. J.G. Addison, Cullen - 55.
Mr. Gavin Anderson - 191.
Campbeltown Courier - 32 (Empire Ace).
Mr. Terry Clutton, Tarleton - 75, 93.
Mr. Wilf Dodds, Bridgwater - 51, 52, 76, 78, 83, 98, 194(S).
East Dunbartonshire Council, Information and Archives - 22, 23, 30.
Glasgow Herald - 40, 41, 110, 123, 141, 189.
Glasgow Museums and Art Galleries - 21, 37, 97, 149, 150, 198.
Glasgow University Archives - 20.
Mr. Mike Hughes and Mr. George Holleyman - 174.
Mr. Peter Horsley, Fleetwood - 53,.
Imperial War Museum - 87, 175, 197.
McLean Museum and art Gallery - 57.
Memory Lane, Hull - 167, 168.
The Mitchell Library, Glasgow City Council - 14, 44, 60, 61, 86, 91, 94, 95, 146, 147, 194.
National Maritime Museum, London - 58, 89, 90, 102, 134, 144, 164.

Mr. Richard McCrory - 179.
Mr. Robert Preston, Paisley - 32 (Erskine).
Scottish Daily Record and Sunday Mail - 25, 26, 80, 115, 199, 200.
Mr. Loet Steeman - 129.
Swan Hunter, Newcastle - 186.
Mr. Philip Thomas & Mr. Charles Waine - 163
Mr. Urbain Ureel - 47 (x2).
World Ship Society - 18, 19, 48, 50, 68, 73, 85, 105, 107, 109, 114, 137 151, 158, 161, 171, 177, 182, 187, 196.

Acknowledgements

Both prior to its initial publication in 1994 and in subsequent revisions, many people have helped with the preparation of this book and we would like to thank those listed below for their particular contribution.

For their invaluable assistance and detailed local knowledge:

Donald Fairgray (Campbeltown), Gus and Iain Newman (Islay), Neill McNeill (Islay), Chris Oldfield (Tiree).

General information and assistance while researching and diving:

Wilf Dodds, Rod Macdonald, Cliff Parsons(World Ship Society), Joe Quinn, Willie Lee, Ewan Rowell, Lord Strathcona, Stan Simpson, Tom Lang, Ian Whittaker and Gavin Young (Gourock) for photographic services. A special mention must go to the members of Irvine Branch SS-AC who have helped out on many of our diving expeditions.

For their assistance during research through archive material:

Andrea Mullen (DOT Marine Library), Robert Tweedie (Caledonian Newspapers), the staff of the Mitchell Library-Glasgow, the staff of the Guildhall Library-London, Mr John McNeill (Scottish Daily Record and Sunday Mail).

Symbols and Abbreviations

Tonnage

dt	Displacement tonnage
nt	Net tonnage
gt	Gross tonnage
bn	Burden

Hull Material

I	Iron
S	Steel
W	Wood

Type of Vessel

SS	Steamship
PS	Paddle steamer
S. Tr	Steam trawler
A. Tr	Admiralty trawler

Type of Vessel (contd)

A. Dr	Admiralty drifter
S. Tug	Steam tug
P. Tug	Paddle tug
Syt	Steam yacht
LCV	Landing craft
Drg	Dredger
A/c	Aircraft
S	Sailing ship, fully rigged
Bk	Barque
Bkn	Barquentine
Bg	Brig
Bn	Brigantine
K	Ketch
Sk	Smack
Sl	Sloop
Sr	Schooner
Yt	Yacht

Cause of Loss

A/c	Aircraft
S	Stranding
F	Foundering
C	Collision
T	Torpedo
M	Mine
S/f	Stranded on fire

Clyde Shipwrecks

Also available in the Scottish Shipwreck series:

Clyde Shipwrecks...................

the highly popular book and definitive history of shipwrecks along the coast of Scotland's most important seaway. Contains details of over 400 shipwrecks, many accompanied by details of their current location and condition. This unique catalogue of shipwrecks also includes a rare collection of photographs recording many of the vessels either before or after their loss.

Clyde Shipwrecks written by divers, for divers, sea anglers, shipping historians and anyone interested in the local history of the region.

**PETER MOIR
AND
IAN CRAWFORD**

CHAPTER KEY

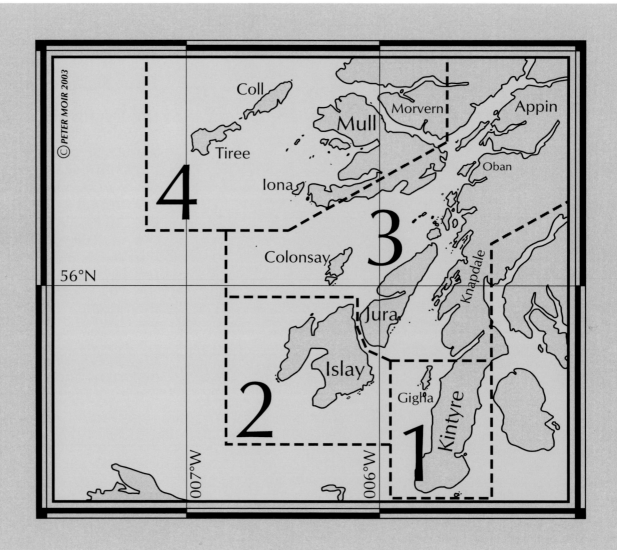

© PETER MOIR 2003

Coll

Mull

Morvern

Appin

Tiree

4

Oban

Iona

3

Colonsay

56°N

Jura

Knapdale

2

Islay

1

Gigha

Kintyre

007°W

006°W

MAIN INTRODUCTION

The varied region of Argyll spreads across an area covering many miles of the west coast of the Scottish mainland and dozens of islands of the Inner Hebrides. From the Mull of Kintyre in the south to Mull and Coll in the north, the coastline is scattered with hundreds of shipwrecks dating from earliest times, when the Vikings invaded and made many of the islands their own, through the days of the Spanish Armada and the Jacobite rebellions and into modern times, where both World Wars and the continual flow of trading vessels between the islands added further to the underwater collection of shipping history.

The area's proximity to the North Channel, the main artery of shipping between the Western Approaches and the main west coast ports of the Clyde and northern England, the unpredictable tides around many of the islands and the prevailing south west winds have taken a terrible toll on ships from the age of sail, steam and still even on today's modern motor driven vessels.

This book provides the history, details and locations of over three hundred of those wrecks. While written substantially for sub-aqua divers the stories provide interesting reading for shipping historians and steamer enthusiasts alike and provide a fascinating insight into the lives of the local communities on the islands of the Inner Hebrides and the part they played in the rescue of many of the unfortunate seamen driven ashore on the rugged coastline of the region.

The book is divided into four chapters, each covering a geographical area from the Mull of Kintyre north to Ardnamuchan. Each chapter is prefaced by a map showing the approximate location of each major wreck and ends with a list of smaller and older wrecks which could form the basis for further research by the interested reader. Many of the wrecks were removed or have been heavily salvaged but have been included for completeness with details, where known, of the salvage.

While every effort has been made to establish the exact details of each ship and incident, it is impossible to guarantee the exact accuracy of every detail as the records of many are vague or misleading. The authors have visited the sites of all of the major wrecks shown making this the most complete and accurate record of the dive sites in this area ever written. Where possible the positions given have been established using the GPS satellite location system and are indicated as such. We hope you enjoy the book as much as we have enjoyed researching it!

Peter Moir and Ian Crawford
April 2003

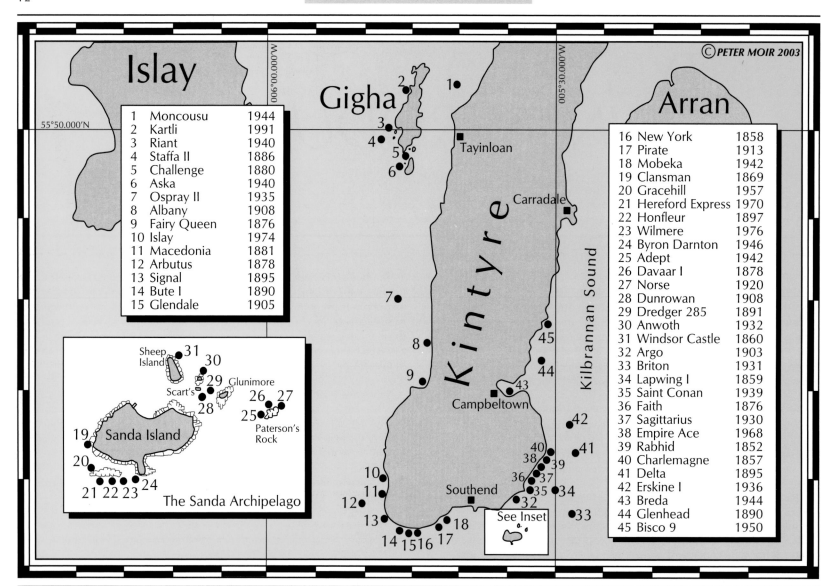

© PETER MOIR 2003

Islay

Gigha

Arran

55°50.000'N

Tayinloan

Carradale

Kintyre

Kilbrannan Sound

Campbeltown

Southend

See Inset

1	Moncousu	1944
2	Kartli	1991
3	Riant	1940
4	Staffa II	1886
5	Challenge	1880
6	Aska	1940
7	Ospray II	1935
8	Albany	1908
9	Fairy Queen	1876
10	Islay	1974
11	Macedonia	1881
12	Arbutus	1878
13	Signal	1895
14	Bute I	1890
15	Glendale	1905

16	New York	1858
17	Pirate	1913
18	Mobeka	1942
19	Clansman	1869
20	Gracehill	1957
21	Hereford Express	1970
22	Honfleur	1897
23	Wilmere	1976
24	Byron Darnton	1946
25	Adept	1942
26	Davaar I	1878
27	Norse	1920
28	Dunrowan	1908
29	Dredger 285	1891
30	Anwoth	1932
31	Windsor Castle	1860
32	Argo	1903
33	Briton	1931
34	Lapwing I	1859
35	Saint Conan	1939
36	Faith	1876
37	Sagittarius	1930
38	Empire Ace	1968
39	Rabhid	1852
40	Charlemagne	1857
41	Delta	1895
42	Erskine I	1936
43	Breda	1944
44	Glenhead	1890
45	Bisco 9	1950

Sheep Island

Glunimore

Scart's

Sanda Island

Paterson's Rock

The Sanda Archipelago

KINTYRE AND GIGHA

Chapter 1

SANDA TO WEST LOCH TARBERT

The long peninsula of Kintyre, stretching some fifty miles from Tarbert in the north to the Mull in the south, forms a substantial protective barrier for the Firth of Clyde from the worst extremes of the Atlantic swells.

On the east side the scenery is gentle, escaping the onslaught of the prevailing wind and weather from the south west and west. It is on this coast that the main town of the region - Campbeltown - nestles around the sheltered shores of its famous loch. The seabed offshore here drops fairly steeply into the deep channel of Kilbrannan Sound. The west coast on the other hand, for most of its length, has sand beaches and a gently shelving seabed. This and its exposure to the prevailing winds, make it a spectacular place with massive rollers breaking over sand and rocks leaving a mist of sea spray hanging in the air ashore even in relatively calm weather.

At the north end of the peninsula lies the picturesque, but often windswept, islands of Gigha and Cara but it is at the south, around the dramatic cliffs of the Mull and close to the small island of Sanda, that the area shows its real character. The tides in this vicinity can be fierce. The lighthouse on the Mull, first lit in 1788, looks down on a wild scene where, in bad weather and often even in comparatively calm conditions, gigantic seas build as the currents of the Atlantic, the Clyde and the Irish sea meet in the narrow North Channel. It is these tides and the area's location as the first major landfall in Scotland for shipping from the Western Approaches that has caused the majority of the areas many shipwrecks.

Kintyre and Gigha offer some of the best dive sites in the west of Scotland, especially those on the west side open to the clearer waters flooding in from the Atlantic. The peninsula itself also gives the diver visiting the area the advantage of a lee shore dependant on the prevailing weather conditions.

Dive sites within the area of this chapter can be split into three basic categories. Firstly the east side, here wreck sites offshore tend to be less affected by tide and are generally protected from the prevailing westerly winds. Secondly, the south coast from Sanda round to the Mull lighthouse. This is an area of strong tides, rich and colourful sealife, with sightings of porpoise and dolphins not uncommon. Finally the west coast of Kintyre and the islands of Gigha and Cara provide excellent conditions with offshore wrecks often having 10-15 metre visibility. Tidal flows in this area are not as strong as the Mull of Kintyre, but still provide enough movement to promote colourful growth on most wrecks, again making this an excellent location for underwater photography.

ADEPT

630grt. Steel rescue tug.
Built by J. Cochrane and Son, Selby.
Launched August 1941.

Dimensions   156.5' x 35.0' x 16.5'

The *Adept* joined a host of other vessels that have been wrecked in this location when she ran aground on the northwest corner of Paterson's Rock on the 17th March, 1942. The *Adept* had run aground in thick fog and at high tide and was well over on the reef. A tug, the *Zwarty Zee*, was immediately sent to the scene along with the Campbeltown Lifeboat, the lifeboat managed to rescue all the crew and returned to Campbeltown. A salvage steamer was also sent for, but attempts to refloat the *Adept* failed and as with many of her unfortunate predecessors wrecked on the same rock. The vicious tides, often wild weather experienced in the area, no doubt contributed to her final loss. The *Adept* has also been commercially worked by a salvage team, but the remians still merit a dive in this remote and scenic location.

Naval Rescue Tug *Adept*.

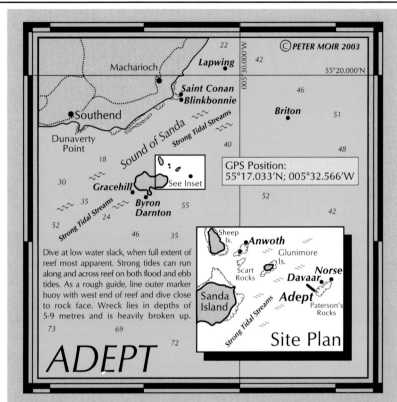

© PETER MOIR 2003

GPS Position:
55°17.033'N; 005°32.566'W

Dive at low water slack, when full extent of reef most apparent. Strong tides can run along and across reef on both flood and ebb tides. As a rough guide, line outer marker buoy with west end of reef and dive close to rock face. Wreck lies in depths of 5-9 metres and is heavily broken up.

Site Plan

ADEPT

The wreck of the *Adept* lies on the southwest corner of Paterson's Rock in approx position 55°17.083'N, 005°32.584'W (GPS). The rock itself is easiest to locate at low tide as it is completely submerged at high water. The wreck is well dispersed, due probably to extensive salvage and rough weather. The most striking feature is the huge boiler lying in around 9 metres, but there is also a lot of other wreckage scattered around. Extreme care must be taken when diving any of the wrecks here as the tidal flows can be very strong making good boat cover essential. However the reward is a dive on a shallow wreck covered in colourful sealife with at least two other wrecks, the SS *Davaar* and *Norse*, lying close by, making a single dive on all three wrecks the best way to experience this site.

ALBANY

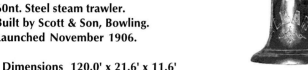

60nt. Steel steam trawler.
Built by Scott & Son, Bowling.
Launched November 1906.

Dimensions 120.0' x 21.6' x 11.6'

In the late afternoon of 29th December, 1908, the *Albany*, trawler No 42 from Fleetwood, was returning to her home port after a successful trip to the fishing grounds off the west coast of Scotland when she was caught in a storm and blizzard off the Mull of Kintyre. Captain Courtney turned north to try to find some shelter from the dreadful weather but ran aground 150 yards from the shore at Tangytavil, just north of Machrihanish, in zero visibility. In a few minutes the decks were awash and the trawler was being pounded by huge seas, which quickly carried off the ship's boat and any other moveable items above deck. Eight of the now helpless crew took refuge in the wheelhouse with the remaining two clinging to the engineroom casing fully exposed to the wrath of the wind, snow and the sea. Even the shelter of the wheelhouse was quickly diminished as huge waves smashed the windows leaving the men inside little better off than their colleagues.

Three other trawlers stood by offshore until the morning, but could not get close enough to assist and eventually sailed off leaving the trawlermen to their fate. The crew hung to their shattered ship throughout the following day but still no help arrived, although they did see some signs of life ashore in the late afternoon. Soon however, darkness fell and they were left to spend another freezing night aboard the wreck.

Meanwhile ashore, the alarm had been raised but the Campbeltown lifeboat was disabled and was therefore useless. The brave lifeboat crew tried to reach the wreck scene overland but, finding the road blocked by snow, were forced to take to the fields and scramble through deep snowdrifts towards the wreck. Many of the locals had assembled on the shore but could find no way of getting a line to the trawler. Despite his now freezing condition, the captain attempted to swim ashore with a line but the breakers were too much for him and eventually

he was hauled back aboard, exhausted and badly bruised. The crew tried many times to float a lifebuoy ashore before finally, after two and half days on the wreck, they managed to get a line to the shore. They were then hauled, one by one, through the surf and the rocks to the safety of the beach. Thankfully they all survived their ordeal and within a few days had recovered and had been sent home to Fleetwood. The trawler became a total wreck. There is a small amount of wreckage still existing in approximate position 55°29.666'N 005°42.850'W; lying in 3 to 8 metres with the remains of the boiler being the most visible item. The site is extremely exposed from the west and as a result is only diveable in flat calm weather or when an east wind is blowing.

The trawler **Albany** ashore.

ANWOTH

92nt. Steel steam trawler.
Built by J. Cran and Co, Leith.
Launched 1915.

Dimensions 115.9' x 22.0' x 11.9'

The *Anwoth* was registered in Leith and owned by Messrs Thomas Scales and Sons of Newhaven. Her voyage from the fishing grounds off the Hebrides in April 1932 was to start in triumph but to end in tragedy. She had gone to the assistance of the trawler *Ratapiko*, which had developed engine trouble off the Butt of Lewis, and had successfully managed to get a line aboard and tow the disabled vessel to safety in Oban. She then set off herself on her return to her homeport. On the 3rd of April, as she rounded the Mull of Kintyre, she ran ashore near Sheep Island, Sanda. Initially the weather was calm but, as the wind rose, her six crew were brought ashore in a local farmer's boat when she developed a list to port and the stern settled beneath the surface. Soon waves were breaking over her and she was abandoned as a total wreck. There is wreckage of a steam trawler on the northeast side of Big Scart Rock in position 55°17.491'N, 005°33.766'W (GPS), and although not confirmed as such, it is thought that this wreckage marks the final resting place of the *Anwoth*.

Sitting over the wreck of the **Anwoth**, with Big Scart in foreground and Sanda Harbour beyond.

ARBUTUS

336nt. Iron steamship.
Built by A & J Inglis, Glasgow.
Launched 1875.

Dimensions 209.7' x 28.1' x 14.4'

The Laird & Co. steamship *Arbutus* left Londonderry for her homeport of Glasgow on Wednesday 17th April, 1878. She had a general cargo aboard, mainly of farm produce, plus 209 head of cattle and around sixty passengers well looked after by Captain Aitken and his crew.

At first the voyage went well but, when off Moville, Northern Ireland, they encountered dense fog. The captain slowed his ship to around seven knots and for several hours, as they crossed the North Channel, he continually fired the signal gun and blasted the ship's foghorn. Despite the weather the passengers were relaxed and unaware of the danger that lurked, hidden in the fog, just ahead of their ship.

Shortly after midnight, when most of the passengers had retired to their cabins, the ship ran onto a rock north of the Mull of Kintyre lighthouse. The strong tidal streams offshore had combined with the slow speed of the *Arbutus* to push her west of her intended course. Panic broke out aboard the ship. Many passengers rushed on deck in their nightclothes and, for a short while, they believed the vessel was about to sink. After they were given a final shock as the ship lurched to one side then the other, she settled on an even keel and an orderly evacuation of the ship got underway. The passengers and crew disembarked into the *Arbutus's* four lifeboats, which were easily rowed ashore in the calm conditions, two reaching the lighthouse and the other two continuing round the coast to Southend. Shortly after they left, the ship slipped off the rock and sank in a reported depth of around 30 fathoms amid the tide rips off the Mull and became a total loss.

ARGO

584nt. Wooden barque.
Built by J. Gran, Bergen.
Launched 1868.

Dimensions 154.3' x 33.1' x 18.1'

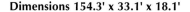

The Norwegian barque *Argo*, under the command of Captain N J Ellefsen and with a crew of eleven, was en route from Wilmington, North Carolina to London with a cargo of resin when she came ashore at Macharioch just south of the Arranman's Barrels in the early hours of the morning on 27th February, 1903. The sea was very rough at the time and, with the waves crashing over her, it was obvious that the vessel would soon break up. Three of the crew managed to get ashore in the ship's boat and raise the alarm. Two of them and a local man then put back out to sea to return to their ship but were unfortunately swept away and lost. Their empty boat was washed ashore at Davaar two weeks later.

The Southend lifeboat was called out but, as it was too rough to launch, a message was sent to Campbeltown calling for the assistance of the lifeboat from there. The signal gun was fired at 9am and by 9:45 the lifeboat, *James Stevens II*, was on its way. She was assisted by the Clyde Shipping Company's tug *Flying Dutchman* which towed the lifeboat much of the way to the wreck significantly reducing the travelling time from Campbeltown. This assistance probably saved the lives of the crew because, when they arrived at the wreck site, the situation for the nine remaining crew members clinging to the rigging had become critical as their ship was breaking up beneath them. Indeed, as the lifeboat pulled alongside the masts crashed into the sea. Thankfully they were able to pluck the crew from the wreck but only in the nick of time for, as they sailed away towards Campbeltown, she settled deeper into the water, rolled over onto her port side and broke up. The lifeboat cox, George McEachran, and the lifeboat crew were later awarded medals and diplomas by the King of Norway for their bravery in rescuing the shipwrecked crew.

ASKA

3995nt. Steel steamship.
Built by Swan Hunter, Newcastle.
Launched August 1939.

Dimensions 444.6' x 61.2' x 25.2'

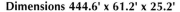

The *Aska*, owned by the British India Steam Navigation Company, was a beautiful cruise liner built to carry passengers in its 200 cabins, looked after by a crew of 180, on its regular route between Calcutta and Rangoon. In addition it could carry over 2,000 deck passengers on this busy and profitable route.

However, with the outbreak of war later in 1939, like many of her counterparts, she was hired into government service to be used as a troop carrier. It was on this service that she left Freetown in West Africa in September 1940. On the 7th she called at Bathurst and then set sail for Liverpool. She had on board fifty British troops, three hundred French troops plus nine other passengers and her crew of one hundred and eighty four, mainly Indians, plus a cargo of six hundred tons of cocoa. She was a fast ship, capable of 17 knots, and believing her speed to be her best defence, did not sail in convoy. She sped safely though the dangerous waters of the east Atlantic, patrolled by the German U-boat packs, and north past the west coast of Ireland to turn finally into the killing ground of the North Channel between Ireland and the Mull of Kintyre. As the war progressed many other vessels were to meet their doom in this narrow deep channel, which was to become a favourite hunting ground of the German U-boat commanders. The *Aska*'s end however was to come from the skies rather than beneath the waves.

On the 16th September at 2:30am, while between Rathlin and Maiden Rock, she was attacked by a German bomber, which scored direct hits with two heavy bombs in or near the engine room, killing six officers and six of the crew instantly. Shortly afterwards another bomb wrecked the forecastle and in no time the vessel was a floating inferno. The passengers and crew abandoned the *Aska* in the ship's boats in a position reported as 55°24'N, 06°05'W. They were picked up by HMS *Hibiscous* and HMS *Jason* and a small fleet of trawlers that had raced

SS *Aska*.

to the scene. It was some time before the tally of survivors could be completed, as they were landed at various ports in Northern Ireland, Scotland and the north of England over the next two days but, thankfully, apart from the casualties resulting directly from the bomb hits, the remainder of the passengers and crew got safely ashore.

Meanwhile the burning and twisted hull of the once beautiful liner was drifting northwest towards the Scottish coastline. She eventually came ashore, still ablaze, on the northwest side of Cara, a small island lying south of Gigha close to the Kintyre coast. A report on 23rd September, from salvage teams standing by, stated that she was still burning and had as yet not been boarded. Even when the fire finally burned itself out it was still impossible to get aboard the grounded vessel for some time as she was pounded by a huge swell but it was obvious, even without close examination, that the vessel was a total loss.

She lay on an irregular rocky bottom in around 20 feet of water with a 14 degree list to port. Only because the stern and bow were reasonably intact was it possible to see that she was pointing NNW because the middle section of the ship was totally destroyed with superstructure gone and all her holds and engine room awash. She was abandoned as a total wreck and was heavily salvaged for scrap during subsequent years.

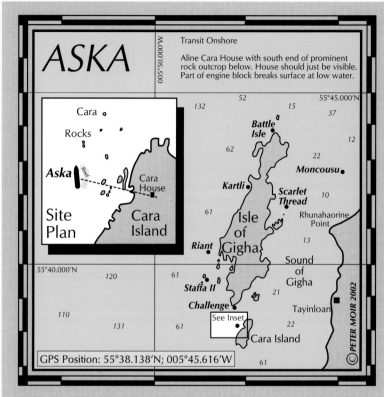

The remains of the *Aska* lie in position 55°38.183'N, 005°45.616'W (GPS), which is at a reef called Cara Rocks situated half a mile from the northwest coast of Cara Island. As already stated the wreck has been heavily salvaged over the years but a fair amount of wreckage still remains at the above position scattered among rocks and seaweed in depths between 5 and 10 metres making it an interesting second dive after returning from the deeper wrecks around Cath Sgeir. At most states of the tide the top of the remains of the engine are visible above water making location of the wreck easy except at extreme high tide. The wreck site is very exposed to wind and subject to huge swell and as such, with the shallow depth, care is required both in mooring close by and when diving the wreck.

BISCO 9

5218nt. Steamship.
Built by Fred Krupp, Keil.
Launched 1908.
(ex COLONIAL ex ASSYRIA ex YPIRANGA)

Dimensions 449.8' x 54.9' x 27.8'

The sad final journey of most ships is to the breaker's yard to be taken apart piece by piece and returned to the metal plates and girders from which she had once been assembled. After a career with the Anchor Line and a period sailing under Portuguese ownership the *Colonial*, renamed *Bisco 9* for her last voyage, was indeed to be broken up but not without one last adventure to be added to her long history of more than forty years of voyages all over the world.

The last chapter in her story began in Lisbon when she left for the Clyde and the Dalmuir yard of the shipbreaking firm W H Arnott Young and Co. As she entered the outer reaches of the Firth of Clyde on September 19th, 1950, under tow by the tug *Turmoil*, she was caught in a violent gale with winds gusting to 90 mph. The huge hawsers holding her on course repeatedly snapped like

SS *Colonial* - later *Bisco 9*.

threads as she pitched and heaved in the mountainous seas whipped up by the gale force winds. Four times the hawser broke and four times she was successfully brought under control again but, as the hawser snapped for the fifth time, the crews aboard the tug and the *Bisco* knew that they were beaten. By now they were close to Ailsa Craig. Campbeltown lifeboat arrived on the scene in answer to the *Bisco's* radio distress calls but could only stand by as she was swept north in ever increasing seas. For nine hours she was pushed before the wind, missing the rugged south coast of Arran to be swept into Kilbrannan Sound and north past Campbeltown Loch and Davaar Island.

The *Bisco 9* ashore.

She finally made landfall between Black Bay and Kildonald Point, some four miles north of Campbeltown. The lifeboat and tug crews could only watch helplessly as she crashed ashore. As soon as she grounded the lifeboat came alongside and fired a line aboard. Before they could rig up a breeches buoy the rocket brigade from Campbeltown also arrived on the scene and quickly set up their own breeches buoy from the beach with which the six crew and Captain Painter were lifted safely ashore. The *Bisco* was later broken up where she lay finally succumbing to her fate after her last exciting voyage.

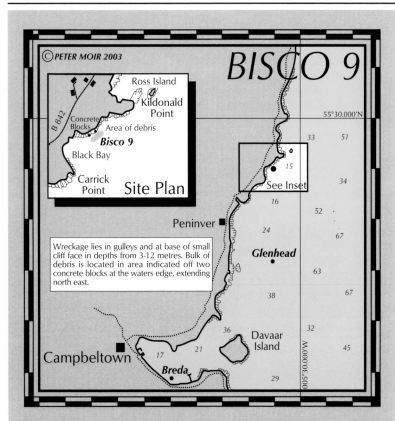

© PETER MOIR 2003

BISCO 9

Ross Island
Kildonald Point
Concrete Blocks
Area of debris
Bisco 9
Black Bay
Carrick Point

Site Plan

See Inset

Peninver

Glenhead

Davaar Island

Campbeltown

Breda

Wreckage lies in gulleys and at base of small cliff face in depths from 3-12 metres. Bulk of debris is located in area indicated off two concrete blocks at the waters edge, extending north east.

Despite the almost total salvage of the vessel the site still makes an interesting shallow dive with substantial quantities of discarded material still littering the seabed. The site lies on the north side of Black Bay in position 55°29.079'N, 005°31.063'W (GPS) and is easily located as there are still four large concrete blocks, presumably the remains of the salvage work, among the rocks inshore of the site. Underwater the seabed drops from a shallow reef some 3 metres deep to a sandy seabed at around 12 metres. The debris from the salvage operation extends around 100 metres along the top and side of the reef with small metal fittings and hundreds of discarded floor tiles scattered among the rocks.

HMS *BREDA*

546nt. Steel steam yacht.
Built by J. Brown and Co Ltd, Clydebank.
Launched 1912.
(ex SAPPHIRE)

Dimensions 285.0' x 35.2' x 14.0'

The *Sapphire* was built by John Brown's yard in Clydebank for the Duke of Bedford and was a magnificent vessel. She was manned by a crew of forty-nine and had every comfort imaginable for her rich owner to enjoy. She was mainly used by the Duchess of Bedford on ornithological trips round the Hebrides, Orkney and Shetland. During the First World War the *Sapphire*, like many of her luxurious counterparts, was requisitioned for war service and, after being fitted with one four inch gun and a twelve pounder, she served out the war as an auxiliary patrol vessel. Unlike many of the other steam yachts forced into national service, she survived the First World War and was returned to her owner and to her normal use as a private yacht.

Steam Yacht *Sapphire*

At the beginning of the Second World War she was again called-up. This time she was given a new name - HMS *Breda* - and was fitted out for use as a submarine tender. She operated safely through the first years of the war but, on the night of the 17/18th February, 1944, she was in collision with another, unknown HM vessel and badly damaged, barely staying afloat with a large hole in her hull. She was brought to Campbeltown on February 18th and beached on the south side of the loch. Later that same day she was refloated to be to taken away for repairs but she immediately filled with water and sank again, this time in deeper water. Initially it was expected that she would be raised, but a report in Lloyd's records on 2nd April states that, on that date, salvage operations were to be discontinued.

The wreck of HMS *Breda* lies in position 55°24.966'N, 005°34.993'W (GPS), about 400 metres from the south shore of Campbeltown Loch. The bow of the vessel points directly towards the shore and lies in around 9 metres. The wreck lies down a gentle, muddy slope reaching 14 metres under the stern. Forward of midships the wreck is a mass of tangled metal, the result of the initial plunge to the seabed and subsequent efforts to salvage the large quantities of non ferrous metal that are used to fit out these beautiful

HMS *Breda* sunk in Campbeltown Loch, circa 1954.

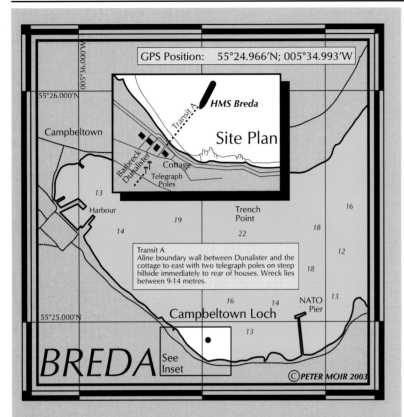

GPS Position: 55°24.966'N; 005°34.993'W

HMS Breda

Site Plan

Campbeltown

Balbreck
Dunalister
Cottage

Transit A

Telegraph
Poles

13

Harbour

14   19

Trench
Point

22

16

18

12

18

Transit A
Aline boundary wall between Dunalister and the
cottage to east with two telegraph poles on steep
hillside immediately to rear of houses. Wreck lies
between 9-14 metres.

16   14

NATO
Pier

13

Campbeltown Loch

13

55°25.000'N

BREDA See
Inset

©PETER MOIR 2003

yachts. However, the dramatically undercut stern is still almost intact and provides the most impressive and interesting area of the wreck. Conditions for diving the wreck are generally good as she lies in a sheltered location and is not affected by tides. Indeed the very lack of movement in the water, combined with the deep mud of the seabed and the silt that covers the wreck, are the only drawbacks as the visibility, which can be good at the start of an exploration, quickly reduces as the seabed is stirred up by passing fins. It is possible to dive this wreck from the shore by swimming out on the transit shown, then following the contour of the seabed at 12 metres until you reach the wreck.

Launch of the SS **Briton** at Kirkintilloch.

BRITON

34nt. Iron steamship.
Built by J & J Hay, Kirkintilloch.
Launched 1893.

Dimensions 65.6' x 18.0' x 8.2'

The *Briton* was built and owned by J & J Hay of Kirkintilloch and was a typica Clyde puffer used to convey cargos around the Clyde and to the west coast c Scotland. She was named after Hay's tradition of using tribal names, with he sister ships of *Celt*, *Saxon* and *Norman* all being launched in 1894. These sma vessels, sized to navigate the Crinan and Forth and Clyde canals were built a Hay's yard on the banks of the canal at Kirkintilloch and were often side launche as can be seen from the photograph of the *Briton's* launch on 30th Novembe 1893.

The launch party

Like most 'puffer' type vessels, she is very simple in design, with a large central hold, still full with the cargo of limestone, engine room to the rear and a small forecastle cabin for the crew. Visibility in the area is generally good, the site seems to provide better conditions on high tide. The wreck is subject to strong tidal flow, and we would advise that you plan your dive for slack water, as diving mid tide is probably impossible. As a result of the tidal flow the wreck is carpeted in large orange and white plumose anemones and soft corals.

Finally a word of caution. This wreck is only for the most experienced dive teams, due to its exposed location, tidal conditions and depth. Anyone considering decompression dives on this wreck should carefully plan their dive, have preferably two boats for cover and all divers should carry delayed SMB's.

BUTE I

39nt. Iron steamship.
Built Scott & McGill, Bowling.
Launched 1879.

Dimensions 95.1' x 19.0' x 9.2'

The *Briton* was lost on the evening of Wednesday 18th March, 1931 after being in collision with the Fleetwood trawler *Ernesta* approximately 4 miles east of Sanda Island. At the time, the *Briton* was inward bound from Carnlough to Glasgow with limestone. The weather at the time was clear and calm and the crew had barely time to abandon ship before she sank. The *Briton's* master, Angus McMillan, and her crew were later landed at Campbeltown by a local motor vessel the *Eagle*; they travelled onto Glasgow the following day.

The wreck of the *Briton* lies upright in 52 metres of water in position 55°18.765'N, 005°27.786'W (GPS). The wreck is almost completely intact with only the simple wooden superstructure missing from on top of the engine casing which is the shallowest part of the vessel at 48 metres. She lies with bows facing south east, on a gently sloping muddy seabed, which drops away to greater depths to the northwest.

Another vessel to be lost on the treacherous coast close to the Mull of Kintyre was the small steamship *Bute I* belonging to Mr John Rogers of Largs. She left Runcorn on Wednesday 24th December, 1890 with a cargo of salt for Stornoway under the command of Captain Hugh McCallum but when she approached the coast of Kintyre she was caught in a blinding snowstorm. In the moderate southeasterly gale and driving snow the visibility was reduced to almost nil and, as a result, she ran ashore close to the Mull lighthouse. Captain McCallum at first reversed his engines but quickly changed his mind and ran ahead again and further onto the rocks to avoid foundering in deeper water. This action probably saved the lives of his six crew. They stayed aboard their vessel until first light when they came ashore in the ship's boat. The vessel became a total wreck.

BYRON DARNTON

7176gt. Steel Liberty ship. Built by Bethlehem-Fairfields, Baltimore, USA. Launched December 1943.

Dimensions 441.0' x 57.0' x 27.0'

The vessels that became known as Liberty ships were designed as basic cargo carrying vessels, mass produced to meet the desperate needs of the war. The programme started in September of 1941 and by the end of the war some 2710 ships, built from the original British design, had been constructed. The design had many critics but there is no doubt that the success of the programme was a major contributor to the Allied victory. The design provided simple, fast construction (the record time from keel laying to launch was four days fifteen and a half hours for the *Robert E Perry*) and then speedy shipment of large bulk cargoes. The *Byron Darnton* was one of these ships.

Launched from the Bethlehem Fairfields yard in 1943, she had a successful war career surviving voyages to Murmansk and the Phillipines. In March of 1946, under the management of Denholm and Co Ltd of Greenock, she left Copenhagen for New York, via the Clyde, in ballast. She had on board fifteen passengers, including nine women, and a crew of thirty nine.

A typical liberty ship.

As Captain Robert King navigated his vessel round the Mull of Kintyre and into the Firth of Clyde on the evening of 16th March, the weather was foul with strong winds driving the heavy rain and sleet, which had reduced the visibility to almost zero. It was 10:50pm and the passengers were settling themselves for their last evening aboard before the stop over at Greenock. Without warning there was a terrible grinding and tearing noise as the ship crashed onto Boiler Reef just below the lighthouse on the island of Sanda. There was no panic, as it was obvious that those aboard were in little immediate danger, but the crew fired distress flares as they feared that the ship could soon succumb to the pounding of the huge waves that were smashing into her starboard side. The flares were spotted by the coastguard at Southend who immediately called out the lifeboat from Campbeltown.

The lifeboat, *Duke of Connaught*, reached the scene later that night but was unable to approach in the darkness. She anchored in the sheltered lee north of the island of Sanda until dawn then came round to attempt the rescue. The vessel was lying in a very difficult position aground on the reef with her bow facing the lighthouse. She was lying along the reef with her port side facing shorewards making access to that side for the lifeboat extremely dangerous. Her starboard side was being pounded by mountainous seas making any approach from the seaward side impossible.

The lifeboat coxswain, Duncan Newlands, made three attempts to ease his small craft alongside the stricken ship between the towering walls of the hull, now heeling over dangerously towards the shore, and the treacherous rocks of the reef. On the third attempt he succeeded, taking off everyone on board some fourteen hours after the ship had run aground. The brave radio operator, who had stayed at his post continuously since the stranding, was the last to leave. Their adventure was not quite over for, as they sped north towards Campbeltown, the lifeboat engine flooded off Johnston's Point and they had to proceed for the next five miles under sail. The engineer managed to deal with the problem and eventually the engines were restarted allowing them to reach Campbeltown safely.

The rescue had come just in time for only two hours later the ship broke in two forward of the bridge and her stern section started to slip off the reef. By the following day the two sections had slipped deeper into the water on opposite sides of the reef. The captain was able to board the stern section and salvage a

few items of the passengers' luggage but it had developed a severe list to starboard and would soon disappear beneath the surface. The ship was to be heavily salvaged in the autumn of 1953 but until this time the bow section, lying on top of the reef, was to be a visible reminder of the loss of the *Byron Darnton*.

The remains of the *Byron Darnton* lie on the east end of Boiler Reef, Sanda in position 55°16.416'N, 005°35.116'W (GPS). Due to the extensive salvage carried out the majority of the wreckage is unrecognisable although sizeable portions still remain. The bow section lies on top of the reef near the lighthouse about 100 metres from the shore and is visible above the surface at most states of the tide. The larger parts of the wreckage are further out to sea, in

a southwesterly direction from the lighthouse, on the south side of the reef. Here the wreckage lies in depths of between 9 and 16 metres with the largest pieces rising some 5 metres from the seabed. At this point the wreckage is complete enough to swim through. As the site is very exposed to wind and swell care is required both when diving and when approaching by boat. Boat access from the landward side is particular hazardous with many unseen rocks just below the surface making study of the relevant chart an essential preparation for a safe visit.

View of the *Byron Darnton* ashore below Sanda Lighthouse.

CHALLENGE

1255nt. Wooden barque.
Built by Patton & Co, Quebec.
Launched 1863.

Dimensions 197.2' x 35.5' x 23.9'

The barque *Challenge*, owned by Messrs. Adam and Company of Greenock, set sail from Quebec, Canada on 20th October, 1880. Captain Campbell and his crew of twenty three were bound for their home port of Greenock with a cargo of timber. Unknown to the captain or crew, three stowaways had also slipped aboard unseen. As they made their way across the North Atlantic they were continuously battered by storms, but they had managed well in the severe weather although the voyage was taking much longer than expected. A full month later, as she was nearing the Scottish coast, they ran into yet another severe gale from the southwest. This time the ship could take no more and on Thursday 25th November she became unmanageable as her sails were torn away by the violent winds. As she drifted, out of control, towards the rocky west coast of Kintyre, the crew laboured on the rain lashed decks to rig up new sails. These were hauled up the masts but no sooner were they unfurled than they too were torn to ribbons by the ever increasing wind.

The ship's last chance for survival had vanished and, as the morning of Friday 26th dawned, the crew prepared themselves for the worst. In the growing light they could see that they were being swept towards the shallow waters on the southwest corner of the island of Gigha. Sometime between ten and eleven o'clock that morning the ship struck the rocks at Leim Point and immediately began to break up with huge waves sweeping over her. Within two hours she had been smashed to pieces, littering the shores for miles around with bits of wreckage and cargo.

A brave crew member tied a rope round his waist and attempted to swim to the shore but he was lost after he was hit by a floating log. The remaining crew and the unlucky stowaways had no choice but to risk the swim to the shore. The position of the vessel and the boiling surf had made it impossible to launch the ship's boats. The hazardous swim was made even more dangerous by the hundreds of logs from the ship's cargo deposited into the sea as the she broke up. Five more of the crew and one of the stowaways, a young lad called Thomas Mornan of Greenock, were lost as they tried to reach the shore, either drowned or crushed by the timber logs as they were tossed around in the huge swell.

The survivors were cared for by the residents on the island until they could be transferred to the mainland when the storm had abated. Before they departed they attended a burial service at the Gigha Burial Ground for the four members of the crew whose bodies had been recovered. They arrived at Greenock on the SS *Chevalier* on the 30th to be met by an anxious crowd desperate for news of the dead and the survivors.

The Wreck Today

Metal wreckage including parts of an old winch lie in 5-6 metres, 100 metres east of Leim Point in position 55°38.738'N, 005°45.621'W (GPS). The site is heavily overgrown with kelp making detailed investigation difficult, especially during summer months. Debris can also be found in shallow rock gullies and below larger boulders, the gullies no deeper than 1-2 metres run north to south, perpendicular to the shoreline. Debris has also been found on the south west side of reefs southwest of Gigalum Island, these rocks show at most states of the tide, although nothing of substance or immediately recognisable was found.

CHARLEMAGNE

1014bm. Iron sailing ship.
Built by Alexander Stephen, Kelvinhaugh.
Launched March 1857.

Dimensions 195' x 30' x 21'

The *Charlemagne* was on her maiden voyage when disaster struck and she ran aground on Johnston's Point near Feochaig Farm in the early hours of the morning of 20th March, 1857. She had left Greenock on Thursday 19th bound for Melbourne, Australia with a general cargo including four valuable horses and some breeding sheep and ten passengers aboard. The vessel and cargo were insured for £100,000, an enormous sum in 1857. Captain Reid used the services of a tug and a pilot until he was clear of Pladda at the south end of Arran, which he passed at 11pm in the evening. Two hours later his new ship was on the rocks south of Campbeltown, destined to become a total wreck. He was later to blame the error that led to her loss on a faulty compass.

The passengers and crew were quickly taken the short distance to the shore in the ship's boat but, inexplicably, he made no attempt to save the valuable livestock that unfortunately perished. A report the following morning stated that she had seven feet of water in her hold and was lying, leaning towards the sea in an exposed position. Three days later she was reported as a total wreck breaking up during an easterly gale on the 23rd. By this time a good deal of the cargo had been salvaged either officially or otherwise. There is a report of one local youth who had to be carried to the nearby farm and attended by the doctor after some unofficial salvage of some of the liquor included in the cargo.

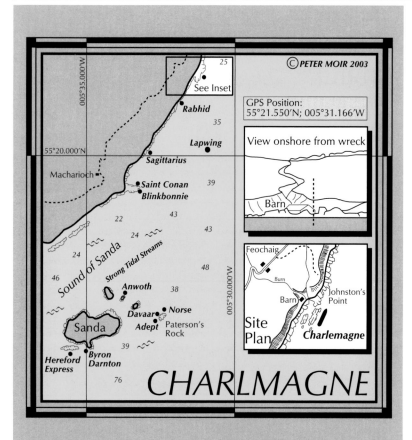

The wreck of the *Charlemagne* lies in shallow water in position 55°21.550N, 005°31.166W (GPS). The remains lie about 100 metres from the shore in depths of 8 to 12 metres. The rock and shingle seabed is littered with broken pottery, bottles and hundreds of shattered clay pipes. On the top of the reef, in around 5 metres, there are some larger sections of hull material and other metal remains. The site is fairly sheltered and is only affected by winds from easterly or south easterly direction. In this situation the shallow exposed nature of the site would make it unsafe.

CLANSMAN

414gt. Iron paddlesteamer.
Built by J. & G. Thomson.
Launched June 1855.

Dimensions 192' x 26' x 13'

The Hutchison owned paddlesteamer *Clansman* reached the Mull of Kintyre en route from Stornoway to the Clyde with a general cargo on 20th July, 1869 but was unfortunate to be caught in thick fog as she approached Sanda. The first officer was in charge on the bridge at the time but, worried about navigating blind in this vicinity, called Captain Sinclair on deck. The captain steamed on at his slowest speed feeling his way through the murk but, although he took every possible precaution, his ship ran aground on rocks at the west end of Sanda.

As all efforts to get the steamer off the rocks using the engines failed, word was sent for another steamer to come to her aid. Some of the passengers were taken off by the small steam coaster *Celt*, passing on her outward trip to Islay, but others stayed aboard awaiting the arrival of the owner's ship sent to help. Lloyd's agent, Baillie Dickson, arrived on the scene later in the afternoon but, just after he arrived aboard the steamship *Swan*, the *Clansman* slipped alarmingly deeper into the water by the stern and it was decided to remove everyone else from the wreck. The *Clansman* was now submerged from her stern forward to midships and was clearly in a dangerous position. After taking the passengers ashore to safety the *Swan* returned to the wreck and successfully salvaged most of the cargo aboard. A newspaper report two weeks after she ran aground indicated that she had broken into three pieces and was considered to be a constructive total loss.

Wreckage has been found inshore of the reef at Clach Point in approximate position 55°16.732'N, 005°35.959'W. The wreckage appears to consist of broken iron or steel frames and general debris, and is heavily concreted into the seabed. The remains may belong to either the *Clansman* or the paddlesteamer *Windsor Castle* and until an item is discovered to confirm identity, it's origin remains a mystery.

DAVAAR

268nt. Iron steamship.
Built by Campbeltown Shipbuilding Co Ltd.
Launched October 1878.

DUNSMUIR & JACKSON
GOVAN ENGINE WORKS.
GLASGOW.

Dimensions 165' x 24' x 11'

After sea trials and setting her compasses at Garelochead the *Davaar* made her way up river to Glasgow for her maiden voyage for her owner, Matthew Louden of Glasgow. She had been chartered by McPhail and Co Ltd, Broomielaw for a voyage to Limerick in Ireland. Also on board the vessel, which was under the command of Captain George Prior, were two passengers and the crew of twelve. She departed from Glasgow on the morning of 9th December, 1878 with a 300 ton general cargo and stopped at Greenock to pick up 180 tons of sugar before proceeding down river into the open waters of the Firth of Clyde.

By 8pm she was abreast of Pladda at the south tip of Arran, on a hazy calm evening steaming at her cruising speed of eight and a half knots. The captain steered WNW for twenty minutes before turning onto a course west by south calculated to clear Sanda light. He then handed over to Mr McKinnon, a master mariner hired by the charterers to look after their cargo during the voyage, before retiring to his cabin instructing McKinnon to call him when Sanda light was spotted. McKinnon became nervous about the course, fearing they were too close to the Kintyre shore, and made a small adjustment. He was then shaken by a shout from the lookout telling him that there was land on the starboard bow. He steered the ship hard to port but almost immediately the ship ran aground on Paterson's Rock, which lies east of Sanda, and there it remained stuck fast.

The night was calm and as such there was no problem in getting the passengers and crew off safely in the ship's boat but the vessel was left sitting in a very exposed position with her bows high out of the water on the rock. Some of the cargo was transferred onto steamer *Seamew* and the steam lighter *Pelican* before the ship slipped off and sank. She was sold at auction where she lay on 7th January, 1879 and was later heavily salvaged. The subsequent enquiry into the

loss was to find that the master had steered a wrong course when leaving Pladda and that he should not have left McKinnon in charge. In his defence the captain stated that the mate, J Martin, had been drunk and could not be left in charge although the mate strongly denied this.

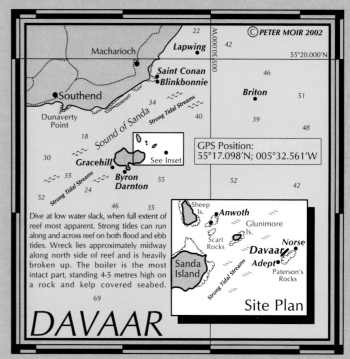

Dive at low water slack, when full extent of reef most apparent. Strong tides can run along and across reef on both flood and ebb tides. Wreck lies approximately midway along north side of reef and is heavily broken up. The boiler is the most intact part, standing 4-5 metres high on a rock and kelp covered seabed.

GPS Position:
55°17.098'N; 005°32.561'W

Site Plan

DAVAAR

The wreck of the *Davaar* lies on the north side of Paterson's Rock in approximate position 55°17.098'N, 005°32.561'W (GPS). Due to the salvage activities the only large item of wreckage is the huge boiler which rears up from the otherwise scattered and flattened debris which remains at the wreck site. The wreckage lies in general depths of 12 metres and makes an interesting dive particularly because of its proximity to the wrecks of the *Adept* and the *Norse* that can be visited on the same dive. The site is very exposed to wind, swell and is subject to fierce tides demanding extreme care both in the water and by boat handlers.

DELTA

32nt. Iron steamlighter.
Built by J & J Hay, Kirkintilloch.
Launched 1881.

Dimensions 65.5' x 17.5' x 7.5'

The *Delta*, a Clyde puffer, was built and owned by J & J Hay of Glasgow. She was a typical example of this small, reliable workboat and she, like dozens of similar craft, plied up and down the Clyde with small cargoes for the many ports and shallow anchorages around the estuary. The smaller puffer type vessel was sized to navigate the locks and network of the Forth and Clyde canal, as many of these craft were built and launched at Hay's yard in Kirkintilloch.

The *Delta* was lost off Ru Stafnish, Kintyre on 27th March 1895 while on a trip from Glenarm to Forth & Clyde Canal with a cargo of limestone. The *Delta* apparently sprang a leak in moderate easterly winds, and sank in 5 minutes, fortunately the crew managed to escape in the ship's boat, eventually arriving in Campbeltown.

Many hands make light work!

The *Delta* at Kirkintilloch.

The Wreck Today

The wreck of the *Delta* lies upright in 38 metres of water in position 55°21.716'N, 005°28.333'W (GPS) which is about 2 miles ESE of Ru Stafnish. The wreck has fallen to pieces although the stern section remains partially intact. She lies, facing west, on a level shingle and mud seabed and rises no more that 1.5 metres at her vertical boiler. At the stern, remains of her rudder, propellor and engine can still be found, inhabited by small shoals of haddock and bib. The bow area is characterised by the prominent pile of her cargo of limestone; a few pieces of hull lie to the side, the bow and winch lie just forward of this.

Visibility on the wreck is variable, but in good conditions this makes a pleasant dive with no tidal problems to worry about unlike the wrecks closer to Sanda. However, this is a very exposed piece of water and conditions can change very quickly, so good boat cover and delayed SMB's are strongly recommended.

DREDGER No. 285

195gt. Steam dredger.
Built by William Simons, Renfrew.
Launched 1891.

Dredger 285 was a brand new steam dredger and was en route to Blyth in Northumberland from Renfrew with a planned passage through the Caledonian Canal when she went aground on the Scart Rocks, Sanda on 29th August, 1891. She had a crew of fourteen aboard and was under the command of Captain John Robertson. Later Captain Robertson stated that he had mistaken Sheep Island for the mainland in poor visibility and this error had caused him to put the ship ashore on the rocks.

The first reports from the scene were not alarming as, although the forward compartment was full of water, the rest of the ship was dry and there were high hopes that she would be refloated successfully. Salvage tugs were quickly dispatched from the Clyde to assist but, as is often the case on this exposed part of the coast, the weather was to take a hand when, the following day, a gale sprang up and the dredger slipped off the rocks and sank in deep water. As far as the authors can ascertain the wreck has not yet been located.

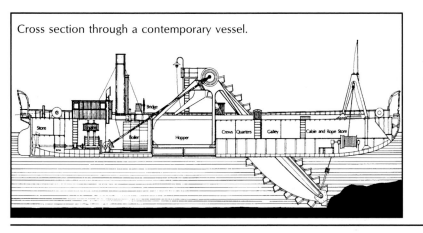

Cross section through a contemporary vessel.

DUNROWAN

56nt. Steel steamship.
Built by J McArthur & Co, Paisley.
Launched December 1898.

Dimensions 100.0' x 20.1' x 8.3'

The small coastal steamer *Dunrowan* left Irvine for Kinlochleven with a cargo of coal around noon on the 8th October, 1908. She proceeded west towards the Mull of Kintyre until later that same evening when Captain Wilson was forced to reduce speed to dead slow as they ran into a thick haze. He knew that they were now in the treacherous waters off Sanda as he could feel the pull of the fierce tides on her tiller. Suddenly, as they peered through the darkness and the mist, they were jolted as the *Dunrowan* ran onto Steamboat Reef off Sheep Island.

The ship was badly gashed on the port side but she held firm on the rocks. The six crew quickly gathered together some clothing and a few personal belongings and clambered into the ship's boat. As the sea was calm they rowed around until first light waiting to board the vessel again and try to get her off the reef. The next morning they tried to pull her off using her own engines but it was obvious that the assistance of a tug would be required to refloat her. They therefore decided to go ashore and telegraph for help. The crew spent the next night at a local farmhouse but, when they returned to their stranded ship the following morning, they found that she had slipped off the rock during the night and had sunk in deep water. The only task remaining for the Clyde Shipping Company tug *Flying Limit* when she arrived, was to take the shipwrecked crew of the *Dunrowan* aboard and convey them to Greenock.

Wreckage of a small steamship has been found to the south of the south reef which forms the Scart Rocks in position 55°17.258'N, 005°33.878'W. The wreckage lies in 22-25 metres and may be the remains of the *Dunrowan*.

The *Empire Ace* ashore at Glenhervie.

EMPIRE ACE

275 grt. Steel tug.
Built by Cochrane and Sons, Selby.
Launched December 1942.
(ex EMPIRE ACE ex DILIGENT)

Dimensions 118.0' x 28.5' x 12.4'

The Ministry of Defence tug *Empire Ace* ran aground at Glenhervie on the 11th November, 1968 in high winds and rough seas. The Campbeltown lifeboat was called out but by the time they reached the scene the twelve man crew of the tug had made it safely to the shore in the ship's boat and liferaft. The position of the tug made successful salvage unlikely but the boom defence ship *Mandarin* stood by for a number of days hoping to take her off and pumps were put on board to keep her free of water. This continued for almost a month when, with weather closing in for the winter, they were forced to give up. They left the tug to its fate and the mercies of the winter gales. The ship was pounded by storms during the following months but eventually, in June 1969, she was successfully refloated. By this time she was too badly damaged to be economically repaired and she was towed to Campbeltown where she was broken up for scrap.

ERSKINE No. 1

34nt. Steel steam chain ferry.
Built by John Reid & Co., Whiteinch.
Launched 1903.

Dimensions 55.0' x 38.5' x 4.5'

This vessel was originally a steam chain ferry working the narrows at Erskine in Renfrewshire, and ran a regular service between the north and south banks. The *Erskine* worked the crossing from 1903 until her sale in 1935 to work at Kessock Ferry. It was during her trip north that she foundered while under tow by the tug *Flying Cormorant*, south of Davaar Island on 28th February 1936, fortunately without loss of life.

The wreck of the *Erskine* lies approximately 3.5 miles south east of Davaar Island in position 55°23.355'N, 005°28.105'W (GPS). The wreck is almost completely intact and lies upright in 35 metres of water, oriented along a north

The chain ferry *Erskine I.*

south axis. The wreck rises approximately 1.5-2 metres above the surrounding muddy seabed, and beware if visibility is poor as a large fishing net hangs above the north end of the wreck by a further 4 metres. The net actually makes the wreck easier to find with an echo sounder, providing a larger target.

Like many of the wrecks in the area, the *Erskine* is coated in colourful sealife, which, at times masks the true shape and form of the wreck. Shoals of small haddock can often be found in April or May swimming above the wreck, seeking refuge within the folds of the old fishing net.

The site is exposed to wind from most directions and good boat cover is required due to distance offshore. Fortunately tide is not a problem when diving this wreck.

FAIRY QUEEN

366gt. Iron steamship.
Built by Gourlay Bros., Dundee.
Launched 1860.

Dimensions 175.3' x 23.0' x 12.6'

The *Fairy Queen* left Stornoway, under the command of Captain Munro, on Tuesday 13th November, 1876 en route from Thurso to Liverpool with a cargo of 750 sheep plus 18 passengers. She was owned by Messrs John Langlands and Sons and registered in Glasgow. The screw steamer was usually employed on the east coast but made the occasional trip to Liverpool. By the afternoon of the 14th she was running down the west coast of the Kintyre peninsula when dense fog enveloped her reducing visibility to almost nil. Shortly afterwards she ran ashore in Machrihanish Bay and despite all efforts remained fast. The passengers and crew were taken off safely although two of the crew had a lucky escape when the ship's boat capsized throwing them into the sea. The following day, after jettisoning her cargo of limestone and salt and throwing the sheep into the sea to swim for their lives to the shore, she was safely towed off by the tugs *Flying Squall* and *Flying Tempest* and had sustained only minor damage.

FAITH

609nt. Wooden barque.
Built by P. Valin, Quebec.
Launched 1856.

Dimensions 161.5' x 30.3' x 18.7'

The *Faith* was owned by a Mr Samson of Irvine and had left Troon for Pensacola, USA on the afternoon of 11th November, 1876 with a cargo of coal and pig iron and a crew of sixteen aboard. Captain Gemmell set a course for the Mull of Kintyre, expecting to clear it later in the day before setting off across the North Atlantic.

As the ship approached the east coast of Kintyre night began to fall and a strong south easterly breeze got up. The breeze pushed the vessel north of its intended course and the captain realised that he was not going to clear Sanda. He put about but could not make headway into the strong wind and so he decided to anchor and await a more favourable wind before attempting to round the Mull. He set two anchors but almost immediately the chains parted and the ship was driven ashore in Polliwilline Bay.

Some members of the crew launched one of the ship's boats and attempted to get ashore but it capsized and they had to be rescued by the local residents who had rushed down to the beach to render assistance. The remaining crew then managed to float a line ashore. Two of them did get ashore using this line but both were almost drowned in the process. Finally a boat was launched from the shore and safely took the rest of the crew off the stricken vessel. The *Faith* became a total wreck.

PS *Glendale* ashore at Sron Uamha.

GLENDALE

252nt. Iron paddlesteamer.
Built by J Elder & Co, Glasgow.
Launched 1875.
 (ex LA BELGIQUE ex FLAMINGO ex PARIS)

Dimensions 220.0' x 25.2' x 11.0'

The first thirteen years of the *Glendale's* career were spent plying between Newhaven and Dieppe under the name *Paris* but in 1888, as she had become too slow to compete on this route, she was sold back to her builders (now the Fairfield Company) and reboilered. She then moved onto the tourist route from Liverpool to North Wales, now named *Flamingo*, before spending a further period abroad first in Germany, then in Belgium named *La Belgique*. Finally in 1902 she was purchased by D MacBrayne, renamed *Glendale* and set to work on various West Highland routes.

Her career for her final owners was destined to be a short one. At 5:20pm on Thursday 20th July, 1905 she left Greenock bound for Port Ellen, Islay under the command of Captain J McKechnie and with thirteen passengers plus the crew aboard. She was going to the island to pick up holidaymakers there and return them to Glasgow. As she passed Pladda she was enveloped in a thick fog. At 11:10, while rounding the Mull of Kintyre, she ran aground at Cove Point at speed and stuck fast on a reef just a short distance from the rocky shore. She was badly holed but settled upright and in no immediate danger. As a precaution the passengers were taken ashore in the ship's boats and spent the night on the rocks. Next morning they were able to reboard the *Glendale* to take off their possessions before being rowed round to Southend. The *Glendale* was to become a total wreck.

The Wreck Today

The wreckage lies in shallow water approximately 50 metres from the shore between it and the reef on which the ship went aground in position 55°17.316'N, 005°45.552'W (GPS) which is about 100 metres east of the point, named Sron

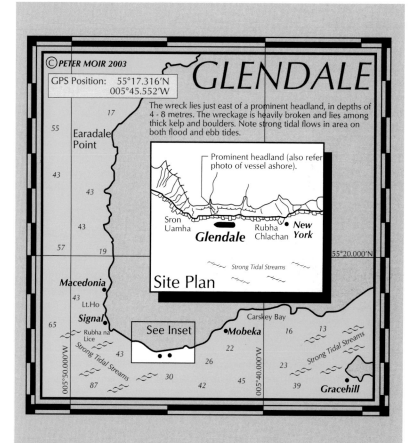

Uamha on the chart of the area. It is possible that further wreckage exists outside the reef but the tides in the area make a dive outside the reef extremely difficult except at slack water. Even inside the reef the tide can be a hazard. The wreck has obviously been subjected to heavy salvage, as little remains except some plates and pipes among the rocks in depths from 4 to 8 metres. The site is also very exposed to wind and swell and can only be dived in very good weather conditions and with good boat cover.

GLENHEAD

34nt. Iron steamlighter.
Built by Scott and Son, Bowling.
Launched 1887.

Dimensions 66.0' x 17.5' x 6.4'

The *Glenhead* was owned by John Turnbull of Glasgow and was a typical example of this small, reliable workboat, dozens of which plied up and down the Clyde with small cargoes for the ports of the estuary.

At 3:30pm on Sunday 23rd March, 1890 she left Glasgow, under the command of Captain McCulloch, bound for Campbeltown with a cargo of 80 tons of coal. Her route took her down river past Greenock, south to Toward where she turned west to pass through the Kyles of Bute and then south again into Kilbrannan Sound. All through the Sunday afternoon and evening and into the early hours of 24th March the weather was calm and fine and the crew relaxed as they looked forward to their arrival in Campbeltown early in the morning.

As they steamed on south the welcoming flash of Davaar Lighthouse appeared out of the darkness but, as they cleared Kildonald Point and Ross Island, the light north east wind veered steadily to the southeast and soon the sea became rough and the night unpleasant. When the *Glenhead* was within a mile of the lighthouse she was struck on the port side by a large wave and began, quickly, to capsize. She sank within three minutes giving the four men on board only just enough time to jump into the ship's small boat and cut the painter to avoid going down with her. The crew rowed ashore and landed safely at Ardnacross to make their way sadly to Campbeltown arriving at seven o'clock in the morning.

The wreck of the *Glenhead* lies upright in 36 metres of water in position 55°27.233'N, 005°31.216'W (GPS), which is about 400 metres north northwest of the cardinal marker buoy at Otterard Rock. The wreck is almost completely intact with only the simple wooden superstructure missing from its original

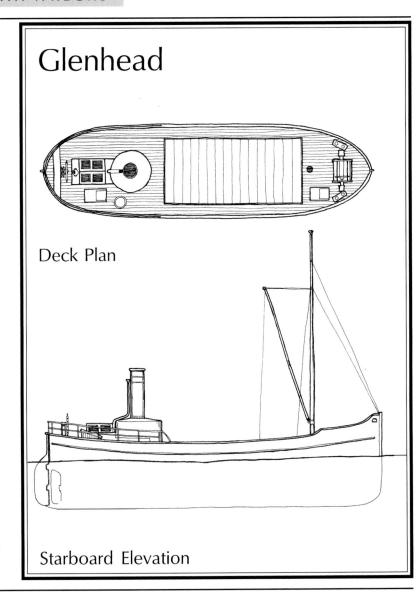

Glenhead

Deck Plan

Starboard Elevation

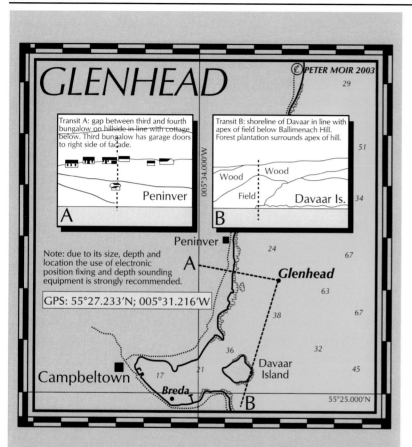

GLENHEAD

© PETER MOIR 2003

29

Transit A: gap between third and fourth bungalow on hillside in line with cottage below. Third bungalow has garage doors to right side of facade.

Peninver

A

Transit B: shoreline of Davaar in line with apex of field below Ballimenach Hill. Forest plantation surrounds apex of hill.

51

Wood   Wood

Field   Davaar Is.   34

B

005°34.500'W

Note: due to its size, depth and location the use of electronic position fixing and depth sounding equipment is strongly recommended.

GPS: 55°27.233'N; 005°31.216'W

Peninver ■

24   67

A   Glenhead

63

38   67

36   32

Davaar
Island   45

Campbeltown ■

17   21

Breda

B   55°25.000'N

condition. She lies, facing southwest, on a gently sloping mud and shingle seabed. The only damage to the hull is in the bow area, probably caused by the impact with the seabed as she plunged down from the surface. She is a very simple vessel with a large central hold, still full with the cargo of coal, engine room to the rear and a small forecastle cabin for the crew. The visibility in the area is generally good and, as she lies deep, the wreck is not subject to the same difficulties of swell and current experienced on many of the other wrecks in the area.

GRACEHILL

172nt. Steel steamship.
Built by Forth Engineering & SB Co, Alloa
Launched 1918.

Dimensions 162.0' x 25.2' x 12.4'

At 9:53pm on the evening of 8th March, 1957 the radio operator at Portpatrick Radio Station received the first message indicating that the Belfast coaster *Gracehill*, en route from Londonderry to Ayr, had gone aground in dense fog at Sanda west of the Lighthouse on the notorious Boiler Reef. Captain James Smith and his nine crew on the *Gracehill* were in no immediate danger but required the urgent assistance of the lifeboat.

Aboard the ship there was no panic but they soon realised that they were far from safe with their ship being pounded heavily by the swell as it surged over the shallow reef. The *Gracehill* had hit the western end of Boiler Reef that lies about a quarter of a mile from the Sanda shore. She had run almost over the top

SS *Gracehill*.

Wreck of the *Gracehill* on Boiler Reef, Sanda.

of the reef and was now lying with bow submerged and stern high on the rocks. A quick inspection by the captain found that the engine room was flooded. As a precaution he ordered his men into the lifeboat to wait alongside the ship for the arrival of the lifeboat, now speeding south towards them. By 2am they were all safely back in Campbeltown none the worse for their adventure but their ship was lost.

The captain returned to his ship the next day but it was clear that salvage would be extremely difficult. The following day a more thorough inspection was made which found that the ship was flexing badly in the swell and that the boiler had already shifted indicating severe damage to the hull. The starboard side was also badly damaged and rudder and propeller were smashed. She was declared a total wreck.

The Wreck Today

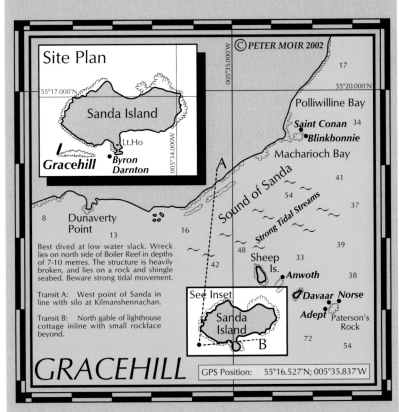

© PETER MOIR 2002

Site Plan

55°17.000'N

Sanda Island

Lt.Ho

Gracehill • *Byron Darnton*

17

55°20.000'N

Polliwilline Bay

Saint Conan 34
• *Blinkbonnie*

Macharioch Bay

Sound of Sanda

41

54

37

Strong Tidal Streams

8 Dunaverty Point 13   16   39

48   42

Sheep Is. 33

• *Anwoth* 38

Davaar Norse

Adept Paterson's Rock

See Inset

Sanda Island   72   54

B

A

Best dived at low water slack. Wreck lies on north side of Boiler Reef in depths of 7-10 metres. The structure is heavily broken, and lies on a rock and shingle seabed. Beware strong tidal movement.

Transit A: West point of Sanda in line with silo at Kilmanshennachan.

Transit B: North gable of lighthouse cottage inline with small rockface beyond.

GRACEHILL

GPS Position: 55°16.527'N; 005°35.837'W

As with all of the wrecks in this vicinity the activity of both salvors and the prevailing weather have reduced the wreck of the *Gracehill* to an unrecognisable tangle of metal. The wreckage lies on the north side of Boiler Reef in position 55°16.527'N, 005°35.837'W (GPS). The boiler and engine are the most recognisable items but there is a lot of other wreckage strewn around in depths of between 7 and 10 metres. The site is very exposed and undiveable with any wind from a southerly direction.

HEREFORD EXPRESS

217nt. Steel steamship.
Built by E J Smit, Westerbroek.
Launched June 1950.

Dimensions 218.8' x 31.4' x 11.8'

In the newspaper headlines the day after the wreck of the Dutch coaster *Hereford Express* off Sanda on October 29th, 1970 the fate of the 250 cattle aboard overshadowed the loss of the ship itself and even the ordeal of the nine man crew. The story of the loss began when the ship, en route from Londonderry to Glasgow, ran aground on a reef a mile from the Mull of Kintyre. The crew worked frantically to free her from the rocks and, despite serious damage to her hull, they got her afloat and, with the aid of her pumps, she was taken in tow by the German coaster *Hope Isle* which had sped to the scene in response to the *Hereford Express's* distress calls. The crew of the disabled ship were taken aboard the *Hope Isle* as a precaution as they set off towards Ardrossan.

The weather was not going to be kind and the continual pitching and rolling of the ship in the heavy swell caused the tow line to break a number of times as they struggled eastwards. Campbeltown lifeboat stood by and a tug was called from Ardrossan to assist. The line broke one last time as they passed Sanda and the *Hereford Express* drifted onto Boiler Reef south west of the island lighthouse. She stuck fast and took on a heavy list to port but there was nothing that the *Hope Isle* or the lifeboat could do either for the ship or for the terrified cattle aboard the grounded ship. The tug *Ardnell* arrived from Ardrossan too late to save the ship and could only take the crew aboard and return to her homeport. In the confusion of the wrecking many of the cattle had broken out of their pens and were rampaging about the ship. Initially it was hoped that many of the cattle could be saved but the day after the stranding the ship took on a severe sixty-degree list and it was clear that they were doomed. RSPCA Inspector Alec Miller was winched aboard the *Hereford Express* and had the unpleasant job of humanely destroying those that had not already drowned.

The Wreck Today

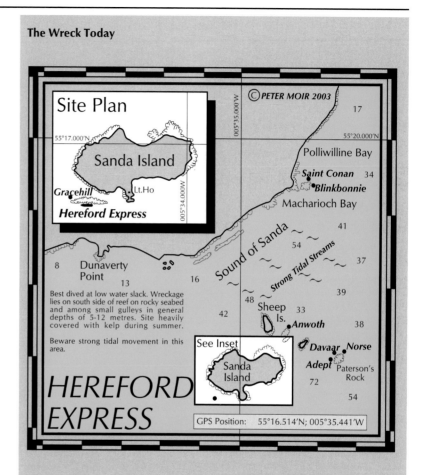

The wreck of the *Hereford Express* was heavily salvaged and as a result very little of interest remains. There are still a large amount of steel plates and girders at the site lying in 5-12 metres in position 55°16.514'N, 005°35.441'W (GPS) on the south slope of Boiler Reef. As with all of the wrecks in the area the site it very exposed to prevailing wind and swell and care is needed when diving.

The **Hereford Express** ashore on Boiler Reef, Sanda.

HONFLEUR

194nt. Iron steamship.
Built by Gourlay Brothers, Dundee.
Launched 1875.

Dimensions 150.4' x 20.9' x 11.7'

The *Honfleur*, formerly owned by the London Brighton & South Coast Railway Company, had been purchased by Paton & Hendry of Glasgow to carry cargoes from the Clyde to Northern Ireland. It was on a voyage from Sligo to Ardrossan in ballast that she ran aground on 23rd June, 1897 on Boiler Reef, Sanda in dense fog. Captain McMillan and his crew got safely ashore although one of the crew fell down a hatchway when the ship struck and broke several ribs. A salvage team with pumps and other equipment was quickly on the scene but close examination of the ship, which was continually bumping on the reef in the heavy swell, showed that she was badly damaged beneath the water line and she was declared a total wreck.

ISLAY

25gt.   58' long steel motor fishing vessel. Built 1968.

The four crew of the clam boat *Islay* were very lucky to survive after their vessel developed a problem with its fuel in the wild waters off the Mull of Kintyre on 2nd October, 1974. She was helpless and was driven ashore in a position reported at Lloyd's as 55°21.300'N, 005°47.933'W which is some distance north of the Mull. The weather at the time was poor with a heavy swell as she went ashore at the foot of a 700 feet high cliff. Forced to take to their raft the outlook for the crew was not good but luckily one huge wave swept the liferaft ashore and the men jumped for their lives. One of the men fell back into the boiling sea but again the swell came to his rescue as he was lifted back onto the rocks with the next wave to be grabbed by his shipmates. With difficulty they then scrambled up the cliff and started the long walk to the lighthouse. Two hours after going ashore they met the Southend rocket brigade who had set out for the scene of the wreck.

MFV *Islay* aground.

KARTLI

1900t. Steel factory ship.
Built by Veb Volkswerft, Stralsund.
Launched 1966.

Dimensions 79.8 x 13.2 x 5.2m

The plight of the disabled Russian fish factory ship off the west coast of Islay in December 1991 sparked a huge rescue effort which involved an RAF Nimrod plane, four RAF helicopters from Gannet, Lossiemouth and N Ireland, the Royal Navy Fleet Auxiliary vessel *Olna*, The Royal Navy Auxiliary tug *Roysterer*, the British tanker *Drupa* and the Islay lifeboat.

The *Kartli*, with fifty-one crew aboard under command of Kaptain Vladimir Gayduk, had finished her fishing trip in the fishing grounds west of Shetland and was homeward bound to Bulgaria. Nine miles off the west coast of Islay she was caught in a violent storm and disabled when a gigantic, freak wave smashed her bridge and flooded her engine room. Local residents on Islay later described

Devastation within the bridge area.

the conditions on the night of the accident as the worst they had seen. The terrible weather and the strong tides that sweep the west coast of Islay no doubt combined to throw up the massive thirty foot wave which crashed onto the bridge and tore the aluminium structure as if it were paper. Three of the crew, including one of the three females aboard, were killed instantly as the structure caved in beneath the huge wave. A fourth died in hospital later.

The ship's distress flares were first answered by the *Drupa* which stood by and calmed the crew while help, in the form of the RAF and the Navy, rushed to the scene. Despite this, six of the crew left the ship in a boat but luckily they were picked up later suffering from hypothermia but alive. The remaining crew were airlifted to safety by the helicopters to be transferred either to the *Olna* or directly to hospital in Scotland.

Stern trawler **Kartli** ashore Port Ban, Gigha.

The abandoned ship drifted westward in the continuing gale and, despite efforts by the naval tug *Roysterer* eventually came ashore on the north west side of Gigha. For many months there were various stories of impending salvage but the ship gradually broke up and slipped beneath the surface. In the early days after running ashore she was the subject of some looting, particularly of the electronic goods that the crew had acquired to take home to their eastern Europe homeland.

When the authors first visited the wreck she lay ashore at Port Ban on the north west side of Gigha parallel to the shore, port side towards land with a heavy list to starboard. Even then her stern was gradually sinking beneath the surface but it was still possible to board her and wander around the hastily

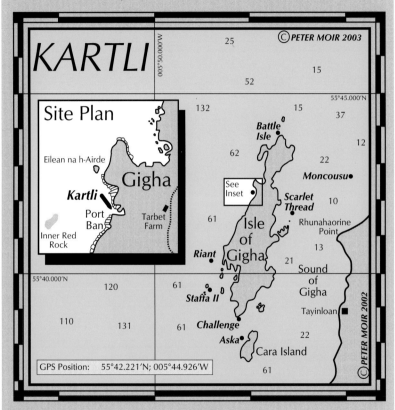

KARTLI

N 000'05.500

© PETER MOIR 2003

25

52

15

132

15

55°45.000'N

37

Site Plan

Battle Isle

62

12

See Inset

Moncousu●

Eilean na h-Airde

Gigha

22

Scarlet Thread

10

Kartli

61

Rhunahaorine Point

Port Ban

Tarbet Farm

Isle of Gigha

13

Inner Red Rock

21

55°40.000'N

Riant

Sound of Gigha

120

61

Staffa II

© PETER MOIR 2002

Tayinloan ■

110

131

61

Challenge

22

Aska●

Cara Island

GPS Position: 55°42.221'N; 005°44.926'W

61

abandoned ship. However, during the gales of the winter of 1993 the rusting ship finally succumbed to the incessant pounding of the sea and broke up. Wreckage is no longer visible above water except for a few pieces inshore among the rocks, and exploration is now substantially an underwater exercise in depths of up to 5 metres in position 55°42.221'N, 005°44.926'W (GPS).

The crumpled aluminium wheelhouse where the wave hit.

PS *Cygnet* sistership of the ***Lapwing***.

LAPWING

**Iron paddlesteamer.
Built by John Reid & Co., Port Glasgow.
Launched 1848.**

Dimensions 77.5' x 14.5' x 10.0'

The *Lapwing* was a small coastal cargo passenger vessel that plied the west coast route between Glasgow, Oban, Fort William and Inverness. It was on such a trip on 22nd February, 1859 that she was lost after coming into collision with the steamer *Islesman* off Glenhervie, near Sanda.

Both vessels had left Glasgow the preceding afternoon bound for west coast ports and it would appear that when they reached Sanda in poor weather conditions the skipper of the *Lapwing* decided to turn back, only to turn into the path of the *Islesman* which was following. The *Lapwing* was holed just forward of her starboard paddlebox and was so badly damaged that she sank within 3 minutes. Most of those aboard the *Lapwing* managed to scramble aboard the *Isleman* with the exception of a woman passenger and the ship's cabin boy who were below at the time, and were unfortunately drowned.

The Wreck Today

The wreck lies in position 55°20.067'N, 005°31.116'W (GPS), in general seabed depths of 36 metres. The wreck is oriented NW/SE with stern to the shore, the central section rises a maximum of 2.5 metres above the seabed.

The wreck sits within a 2 metre scour, approximately 30 metres in diameter, which is no doubt created by the strong tides running over and around the engine and boiler. The main section of wreck remaining is the central section of machinery and main paddlewheel hub, this area is festooned with whelk creels and associated ropes so be careful when diving around this area. The remainder of the wreck has fallen away and in many areas has been absorbed into the surrounding seabed. However, this strong tidal movement constantly changes

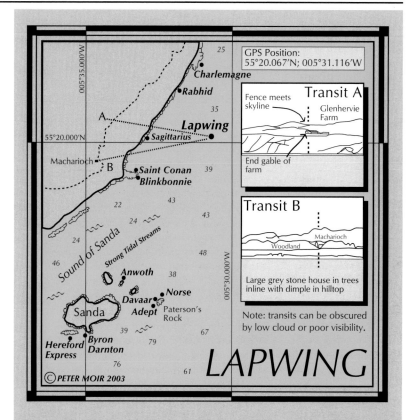

the shape and depth of the coarse coraline sandy seabed and parts of the wreck continually disappear and reappear on successive visits. The main hazard is tide, this is a slack water dive and the tidal window varies somewhere between 30 to 80 minutes dependant on phase of the tide. As a precaution we would recommend that all divers carry delayed surface marker buoys.

This is a very picturesque wreck site, visibility is generally excellent, and the wreckage is inhabited by a colourful and varied selection of sealife. Infact it is not uncommon for large shoals of small haddock to circle above the wreck, a silvery shroud that parts to show the wreck as you descend.

MACEDONIA

1454nt. Iron steamship.
Built by Malcolmson, Waterford.
Launched 1864.

Dimensions 315.0' x 34.0' x 24.2'

The Anchor Line steamer *Macedonia* was en route from New York to Glasgow with a general cargo and a large number of cattle when, on Monday 30th May, 1881, she encountered dense fog as she tried to make her way through the dangerous North Channel and round the Mull of Kintyre. Unfortunately for Captain Martin and his sixty-three crew they misjudged their position in the poor visibility and treacherous tides and ran ashore north of the Mull of Kintyre lighthouse. The weather was calm at the time and, as a result, all of the crew and the four cattlemen aboard to look after the animals, escaped safely in the ship's boats and landed at Southend.

The cliffs north of the Mull are very high and steep making any approach to the wreck from the land extremely difficult but at first there were high hopes of getting the ship off the rocks and saving her. Salvage equipment was sent for from Ardrossan but, by the time it arrived, hope was fading. The *Macedonia* was lying broadside to the rocks and, although the weather remained calm, she was swept by the tremendous tides that affect the area at most times and was rolling badly on the rocks. The day after the grounding, on the ebb tide, a tug managed to get along side and take off 80 head of cattle, a valuable horse and the ship's silverplate, papers and materials. Inspection of the ship determined that the hull was already holed by the continual rolling on the rocks caused by the rushing tide and she was declared a total wreck. The salvage tugs departed for Glasgow later in the day. Soon the ship's cargo was washing out through the holes in the hull and bags of flour were washed ashore as far north as Gigha and Islay. The wreck and cargo, valued at approximately £17,000, were sold at auction in Glasgow on 8th June for £10, the very low value of the wreck resulting from the very difficult access making successful salvage almost impossible.

The wreck of the *Macedonia* lies in 8 - 10 metres of water approximately half a mile north of the Mull of Kintyre Lighthouse in position 55°19.168'N, 005°48.058'W (GPS). There are still fairly substantial amounts of wreckage to be found although it is completely smashed and mostly unrecognisable. The wreckage is spread among the rocks and boulders at the base of the cliff and, at the outer edge, is partly submerged in the white sand of the seabed. The most impressive aspect of the wreck is that some of it is under massive boulders that must have been moved around by the power of the sea after the shipwreck.

The site is totally exposed to the prevailing wind and swell and just offshore is subject to very strong tides although close to the shore on the wreck itself the tide is less strong. She can only be dived in good conditions or it could be dangerous. Approach by boat from the east takes you through the tide race off the Mull and again care is required, as the unpredictable surface conditions can be treacherous for small boats.

MOBEKA

3512nt. Steel motor vessel.
Built by Flensburger Schiffsb.
Launched August 1937.

Dimensions 426.5' x 55.7' x 25'

The *Mobeka* ashore.

As the *Mobeka* lay off the Mull of Kintyre in the early hours of the morning of the 19th January, 1942 awaiting a Royal Navy convoy escort a drama was unfolding inshore that was ultimately to result in the loss of the Belgian motor vessel. A trawler called *Annie Marie*, with a six-man crew aboard, had run aground near Carskey Bay and had fired distress flares to attract the attention of the coastguards at Southend. As the coastguards set out to attempt a rescue of the crew of the trawler the *Mobeka* also headed for the scene, it was later confirmed

The *Moreno* sistership of the *Mobeka*.

that the captain of the *Mobeka* had mistaken the distress flares for a signal to join the convoy. The crew aboard the trawler tried to warn them off by firing more flares but by the time the captain of the *Mobeka* realised his error it was too late. At 8:05am the *Mobeka* ran aground just west of Carskey Bay and a second rescue began. Lines were secured ashore and the ship's boats were launched but unfortunately only one made it ashore with six passengers and three crew aboard. Two other boats were smashed to pieces as they were lowered to the water. The remaining forty-four crew members stayed aboard the *Mobeka* until the lifeboat arrived to take them off safely. Close by, five of the six crew aboard the grounded trawler were drowned that morning.

The exposed position of the *Mobeka* made salvage unlikely but the Liverpool and Glasgow Salvage Association was called to the scene. On January 22nd they reported her back was broken and she was lying broadside to the shoreline and very exposed to the prevailing weather. By the time the weather allowed them to board her for a detailed examination on the 26th the hull was badly buckled and there was water in every compartment. The salvage of the cargo was possible and this was started immediately - there was even still some hope that the ship could be saved. On the 9th February a diver was sent down for a further examination revealing very extensive damage to the hull, keel and bilges. She became a total wreck.

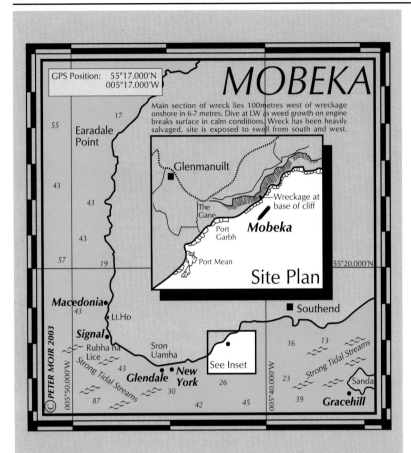

GPS Position: 55°17.000'N
                 005°17.000'W

MOBEKA

Earadale Point

Main section of wreck lies 100metres west of wreckage onshore in 6-7 metres. Dive at LW as weed growth on engine breaks surface in calm conditions. Wreck has been heavily salvaged, site is exposed to swell from south and west.

Glenmanuilt

The Gane

Wreckage at base of cliff

Port Garbh

Mobeka

Port Mean

55°20.000'N

Site Plan

Macedonia

Lt.Ho

Southend

Signal

Rubha na Lice

Sron Uamha

See Inset

Strong Tidal Streams

Glendale •**New York**

Sanda

Gracehill

© PETER MOIR 2003

The Wreck Today

The wreck has been heavily salvaged over the years but there is still a substantial amount of wreckage lying in general depths less than 10 metres in position 55°17.964'N, 005°42.322'W (GPS). Sections of hull and parts of the engine are still visible near the shore and items from her cargo of military equipment also litter the seabed.

MONCOUSU

862nt. Steel steamship.
Built by Mackay Brothers, Alloa.
Launched 1912.
(ex NESTOR)

Dimensions 235.2' x 36' x 16.3'

The wreck of the *Moncousu* in the shallows of the Sound of Gigha has its origin in the port of Plymouth. She had been requisitioned by the Ministry of Shipping for war service and was used as an ammunition storage ship in that port. Plymouth was one of the key British ports on the English Channel and was often the target of German air raids. In the darkness of the night of April 28/29th, 1941 during one of these raids the *Moncousu* was badly damaged and as a result she foundered the following day at Bull Point.

SS *Moncousu*.

The *Moncousu* left Plymouth in tow on October 14th and was moored near Gigha a few days later. For some months she was used as a target for live bombs and by January 5th, 1944 was so damaged that she was reported to be sinking. It was hoped that she could be beached and repaired enough to continue as a floating target but, before the tug sent to tow her ashore into Gigha's East Tarbert Bay arrived, she settled and sank. It was decided to leave her where she lay as the water was shallow and she could still be used as a target. The hulk was in continual use for the remainder of the war and was then salvaged for scrap after the conclusion of the hostilities.

The Wreck Today

The small amount of wreckage that remains of the *Moncousu* lies in shallow water between Gigha and the west Kintyre coast in position 55°42.657'N, 005°39.879'W (GPS). The depth here is 9 metres. Only a few pieces of tangled metal have survived lying on a sand/silt seabed. The wreckage is covered in dead men's fingers and populated by some large, friendly wrasse but the silty nature of the seabed means that the visibility quickly diminishes as the diver explores the area.

This wreck is best kept for days when weather conditions preclude the west side of Gigha. Having said this, when sea conditions are rough from the west, visibility in the area tends to be poor close to the shore and in the shallows, so perhaps this wreck is best left for the armchair!

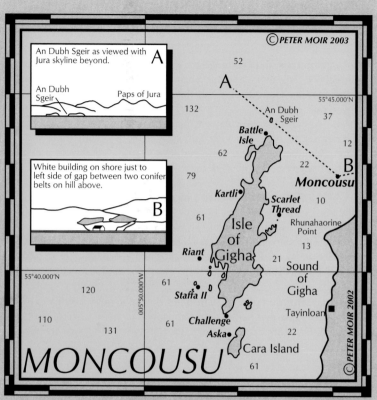

The majority of the ammunition aboard was recovered soon after and it was expected that the ship itself would soon be raised. She was to lie underwater for almost two years, as it was not until February 1943 that she was finally brought to the surface. She was then towed to shallow water where she was allowed to settle down again in fifteen feet of water. After some repairs she was pumped out and, on 23rd March, she was finally refloated again. Unfortunately, due to the pressure of the war on the port, no dry dock could be found to bring her ashore for proper repairs and so, on April 10th, it was decided that she should be towed north and used as a target for bombing practice.

NEW YORK

2050gt. Iron steamship.
Built by Tod and MacGregor, Glasgow.
Launched August 1854.

Dimensions 283.2' x 40.5' x 14.4'

The *New York* was the third vessel of this size built for the New York Steamship Company by Tod & MacGregor at Partick. She entered service in 1854 and was immediately chartered to the French Government for troop transport to the Crimea. The *New York* commenced her intended service of regular transatlantic crossings in the late summer of 1856, and provided a few years of active service before her untimely loss.

The *New York* steamed down the Clyde on the evening of 12th June, 1858. The passengers promenaded on the deck of the beautiful steamship enjoying the warm, calm summer's evening. Many of them gazed a little sadly at the picturesque Clydeside shoreline for the last time before heading for a new life in the Americas. She was bound from Glasgow to New York and had two hundred and twenty two passengers aboard in addition to her eighty crew, under the command of Captain McWilliam, a native of Campbeltown and an experienced transatlantic navigator.

As they passed Arran and Pladda the passengers were beginning to settle for the night, although many were still about or below decks sketching, singing and talking about the adventure that lay ahead in the New World. Their adventure was to start long before they reached the other side of the Atlantic. Just after 10pm, the ship passed Sanda and the crew took a last bearing, setting course to take them safely past the Mull of Kintyre. They did not know it but a defect in the ship's compass put the course towards the rocks near the Mull instead of safely off shore as her Captain had planned. As she passed Sanda lighthouse the night was still clear but, as she approached the Mull, a thick fog came down and soon the flashing light of Sanda was lost. Despite the fog, she was steaming at about eleven knots and, at about 12:15am she crashed bow first, onto the rocks at Rubha Clachan. Her bow rose up into the air and she listed heavily to

starboard but luckily did not capsize. The captain tried to reverse engines but to no avail, although it is probably just as well as she had been severely damaged on impact and would most likely have sunk in deep water if she had come off.

As it was, the crew and frightened passengers rushed on deck, many of them in their night-clothes, expecting the worst. At first many of the crew panicked and threatened to abandon ship but the captain's good sense prevailed and soon everyone was calm and an orderly preparation for getting ashore was under way. As the night was calm and the vessel, after her initial lurch, had now settled safely on the reef, they waited until daybreak before attempting to reach the shore. Next morning the crew rigged a series of lines that were used to pull boatloads of passengers, with their belongings, to the rocky shore.

The scene ashore was almost like a picnic, as the passengers sat in the sun, among the rocks, eating a hearty breakfast and discussing the adventure of the previous evening. As they waited to be picked up and taken to Campbeltown, they watched the ship gradually settle, by the stern until, by the time they were picked up by the steamship *Celt*, the back half of the ship was almost under the surface and the starboard gunwales were awash for her full length.

The subsequent court of enquiry held that there had been a problem with the ship's main compass that had caused the captain to steer a wrong course and he was absolved of any blame in the matter. The *New York* quickly became a total wreck.

SS *Edinburgh,* sister ship to the *New York.*

The Wreck Today

© PETER MOIR 2003

NEW YORK

GPS Position: 55°17.322'N
005°45.050'W

The wreck lies close into the shore on the east side of the reef, which provides a degree of shelter from westerly swell and the flood tide. Wreckage lies among boulders, rock and kelp. Depths range from 5-18 metres.

Earadale Point

Sron Uamha · **Glendale** · Rubha Chlachan · **New York**

Strong Tidal Streams

Site Plan

Macedonia
Lt.Ho.

Signal
Rubha na Lice

Strong Tidal Streams

See Inset

Carskey Bay

Mobeka

Strong Tidal Streams

Gracehill

The wreckage of the *New York* lies to the east of the reef at Rubha Clachan in position 55°17.322'N, 005°45.050'W (GPS), in depths ranging from 7 metres to 18 metres. The wreckage, which is well broken, is spread among the boulders on the side of the reef and down onto the white shingle seabed at the base. A section of the stern at the shallowest part of the wreck and a

huge crankshaft, lying almost on top of the reef, are the most recognisable items, but there is still a great deal of wreckage to explore with many broken pieces of crockery and other remnants of the ship's cargo or gear, particularly at the deeper part of the wreck. The reef is visible at most states of the tide as the swell breaks over it. The tide sweeps past the outer edge of the reef and the combination of tide and swell make it an "interesting" site, not for the novice. Also boats must be handled with great care to avoid joining the *New York* on the reef although a small boat can normally be safely anchored inside the shelter of the reef itself.

The trawler *Norse*

NORSE

125nt. Steel steam trawler.
Built by J. Duthie, Aberdeen.
Launched January 1915.

Dimensions 135.9' x 23.1' x 12.4'

The third of the trio of wrecks lying on Paterson's Rock is the Fleetwood steam trawler *Norse*. She ran aground on the rock on the evening of 17th September, 1920 while en route from Glasgow to Northern Ireland. The weather at the time was fairly clear and the sea relatively calm. The crew managed to reach Southend safely in their own boat.

The next day the ship could be seen sitting high and dry on the rock at low tide but she was badly holed. A tug arrived on the scene to assist in salvage attempts but, as work proceeded over the next few days, it was clear that the first spell of bad weather would probably result in the loss of the ship. On the 27th the feared storm arrived and, after the ship had shifted and started to settle into the water, the would be salvors gave up their attempts. By the 3rd October the ship had broken up completely and vanished.

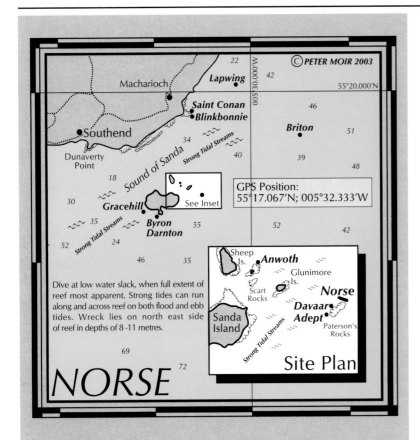

© PETER MOIR 2003

GPS Position:
55°17.067'N; 005°32.333'W

Dive at low water slack, when full extent of reef most apparent. Strong tides can run along and across reef on both flood and ebb tides. Wreck lies on north east side of reef in depths of 8-11 metres.

Site Plan

NORSE

The trawler *Norse* ashore on the east end of Paterson's Rock.

The Wreck Today

The *Norse* is the most northerly of the three wrecks lying on Paterson's Rock lying in approximate position 55°17.067'N, 005°32.333'W (GPS) along the north east side of the reef. She is well broken although there is still a considerable amount of wreckage to be seen in depths of 8 to 11 metres. The most recognisable feature is the bow structure, which is basically still intact, facing towards the wreck of the *Davaar*. Conditions for the site are as detailed in the descriptions of the *Davaar* and *Adept*.

OSPRAY II

114nt. Steel steam trawler.
Built by Smith's Dockyard, Middlesborough.
Launched March 1911.

Dimensions 130.0' x 23.0' x 13.2'

The Fleetwood trawler *Ospray II*, with skipper Kelly in charge of his ten crew, was bound for the fishing grounds off the west coast via the Sound of Jura on April 6th, 1935. Another trawler from the same port, the *Caldew* under skipper Harris, was engaged in fishing operations off the west coast of Kintyre when, for some unexplained reason as the weather was calm and clear at the time, the two fishing boats collided with each other around 8:30am. The *Caldew* crashed into the *Ospray* amidships and tore a huge hole in the side of the vessel. One of the crew of the *Ospray* later said that the hole was so big that a stream of coal poured out of it into the sea.

The stern of the *Ospray II*

The main winch.

S.T. OSPRAY II

The *Caldew* quickly took the *Ospray* in tow in an attempt to pull her to the nearest land and beach her but this was nearly ten miles away. The skipper of the *Ospray* ordered the boat lowered as a precaution which was just as well because, as the *Caldew* started to tow the *Ospray*, it was clear that she was already starting to sink lower in the water. The crew bravely manned the pumps until the water was swirling around their waists but it was obvious that their efforts were in vain. With the fires extinguished and the ship sinking beneath them the crew were forced to jump for their lives and, less than an hour after the collision, the *Ospray* sank in 20 fathoms in a position reported at the time to be approximately two miles from Ballochantuy shore.

The Wreck Today

The wreck of the *Ospray II* was found by Gus and Ian Newman from the Islay Dive Centre in 1995, and lies in position 55°31.016'N, 005°45.612'W (GPS). The wreck is oriented 330/150 degrees, with stern to the north and lies in general seabed depths of 33-34 metres. Her stern, which is fast breaking up, rises 2 metres above the seabed. It is sometimes possible, when the tide has scoured out the shingle seabed around the propeller, to swim between the prop and the rudder, this area is very colourful with all surfaces carpeted in orange and white anemones and soft corals.

Although the wreck is heavily broken up, this is an excellent wreck dive with normally very clear conditions during the summer months. Sealife on and around the wreck is very colourful, it is normal to see bib, ling, conger as well as lythe. Tides do run over a knot on springs at mid tide, so delayed SMB's and good surface cover are recommended.

A diver explores the bow section.

PIRATE

69nt. Iron steamship.
Built by Scott and Co, Bowling.
Launched 1884.

Dimensions 130' x 21' x 9.9'

The regular voyages of the steamer *Pirate* between Campbeltown, Glasgow and Stranraer made her a well known sight in many of the harbours of the Firth of Clyde and provided a profitable trade for her owners Messrs James Little and Co. of Glasgow. In August of 1909 she had a scrape with disaster when she was run down by the SS *Princess Maud* while anchored in Loch Ryan. She sank immediately but was successfully raised, returning to service the following month.

In October of 1913 she made one of her rare trips outside the Clyde estuary when she steamed to Islay to pick up a cargo of sheep to be shipped to Ayr for the autumn sales. All went well and she docked in Campbeltown on Friday 3rd to discharge some of the general cargo on board for the outward trip. At about 1am on the Saturday morning she steamed out of Campbeltown Loch and south to round the Mull of Kintyre. As she passed Sanda on her starboard beam a dense fog enveloped the ship. Two hours after leaving Campbeltown she ran ashore, apparently at full speed, on the rocks below Feorlan between Southend and the Mull. The ship was badly damaged but luckily the crew and the single passenger aboard, a shepherd on board to look after the sheep on the return voyage, managed to reach the safety of the rocky shore.

The following day a team of salvage experts, including a diver arrived on the scene but after three frustrating days of poor weather they gave up and returned to Glasgow to await better weather. The wreck was reported a total loss two weeks later. The author's have looked for the remains of the *Pirate* but without success, we conclude that the wreck was probably removed shortly after her loss.

RABHID

Iron paddle tug.
Launched 1841.

The *Rabhid* was reaching the end of a long, difficult voyage from North Shields to the Clyde when she was wrecked on the east coast of Kintyre in the early hours of 11th January, 1852. She left her home port on 30th December, 1851 intended by her owner, Mr George Fenton, to take up her trade as a tug on the Clyde. She had to fight her way through storms off North Berwick to head north past Aberdeen and Rattray Head before escaping, for a time, into the shelter and calm of the Caledonian Canal. She steamed out of the south end of the canal on the 8th January but was to encounter bad weather yet again when she was 15 miles north of Gigha. She lay for two days at Crinan before continuing her journey south and round the Mull of Kintyre.

Once again the weather deteriorated and this, combined with a strong ebb tide, forced them to anchor under the lee of the Mull to await the flood. As the tide turned they got up steam and started off again. They were now in a perilous situation steaming along slowly during a stormy night, in the dangerous waters around Sanda. The pilot aboard, Mr Alex Muir from Lochgilphead, who knew the area well, repeatedly suggested they take shelter until morning but the master, Andrew Jacobsen refused. Their situation became hopeless when the pumps became blocked, allowing water to rise in the boiler room, which finally extinguished the fire. A staysail was quickly rigged and they ran for the shore.

The *Rabhid* struck, bow on, at Legdhu Coves, three miles north of the Arranman's Barrels. Almost immediately she was smashed broadside onto the rocky shore by huge waves which, within minutes had washed away the ship's boat, the funnel and broken off the ship's bow. The five men on board were left to fight for their lives in the foaming seas around the wreck. Only the pilot managed to reach the shore alive.

RIANT

40nt. Steel steam drifter.
Built by Colby Brothers, Lowestoft.
Launched 1920.
(ex. HMD Green Sea, Gladys & Violet (A.639))

Dimensions 86.2' x 13.4' x 9.25'

Although completed after the end of World War I, the *Riant* was built to the order of the Admiralty as HMD *Green Sea*. Later the same year she was sold to the Fisheries Board for Scotland and registered at Aberdeen as A.639. The following year she was sold to private owners and re-named *Gladys & Violet*, and again in 1924 she was sold, re-named as *Riant* and registered at Inverness. At the outbreak of World War II she was requisitioned by the Admiralty, in whose ownership she remained until her loss. Not much detail is known about her loss other than she foundered off Gigha during a storm on 25th January, 1940 after hitting rocks.

HM Naval drifter *Riant*.

The wreck of the *Riant* lies approximately 0.5 miles west of Carraig Mhor off the west side of Gigha in position 55°40.303'N, 005°46.926'W (GPS). The wreck lies on the south side of a reef in general seabed depths of 35-37 metres with least depth over the wreck of 32-33 metres. She lies upright and canted over on her port side, and although at date of writing remains intact, it is clear the bow section is beginning to distort and will eventually fall away.

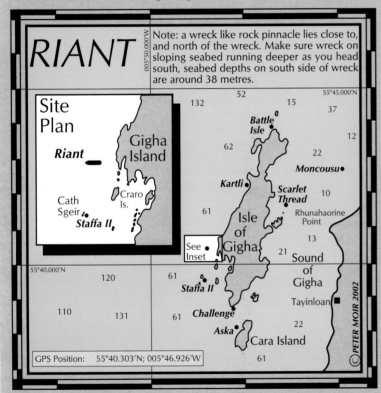

RIANT

Note: a wreck like rock pinnacle lies close to, and north of the wreck. Make sure wreck on sloping seabed running deeper as you head south, seabed depths on south side of wreck are around 38 metres.

Site Plan

Riant

Gigha Island

Cath Sgeir

Staffa II

Craro Is.

Battle Isle

Kartli

Moncousu

Scarlet Thread

Isle of Gigha

Rhunahaorine Point

See Inset

Sound of Gigha

55°45.000'N

Staffa II

Challenge

Aska

Cara Island

Tayinloan

© PETER MOIR 2002

GPS Position: 55°40.303'N; 005°46.926'W

She lies, facing west, on a gently sloping rock and boulder seabed, the reef to the north actually shields her and can be confused as the wreck on an echo sounder. This is another very scenic wreck, ideal for video and stills photography with clear water, and as the wreck acts as an extension of the reef it attracts all types of marine life.

SAGITTARIUS

90nt. Iron steamship.
Built by Earles Shipbuilding Co., Hull.
Launched 1887.

Dimensions 119.1' x 20.2' x 10.6'

Even as late as the 1930s it was not unusual for the steamships plying the waters of the Firth of Clyde to run aground and in most cases they escaped with only a few scrapes on the hull of the vessel and some minor embarrassment for the captain in charge. When the *Sagittarius* ran aground between Polliwilline and Glenhervie in the early hours of the morning of 19th June, 1930 there was very little alarm and, after the passengers had been safely ferried to the shore and taken care of, Captain Miller and his seven crew settled down to wait for a tug to arrive to pull them off. She had been en route from Glasgow to the Hebrides with six passengers heading for a holiday in the Western Isles and a general cargo for her owners, Jack Brothers of Kingston Dock, Glasgow when she ran aground in dense fog. The sea was flat calm and the tide was almost at its highest when she struck. She ran aground so gently that the passengers aboard hardly felt her hit and there was very little damage to the ship's hull.

Her owners quickly dispatched one of their other vessels, *Challenger*, to pull her off but this plan was changed and the Glasgow and Liverpool salvage tug *Flying Kite* was sent to assist. She arrived on the scene at 7:45pm on the 20th but by then the fate of the *Sagittarius* had been sealed. She had run aground at high tide that made any approach at other states of the tide impossible. The second bit of bad luck was that, unusually for the time of year, the flat calm of the night of her stranding changed to a stiff breeze and then to a full gale. By the time the *Flying Kite* arrived at the scene she was being pounded by a heavy swell. The master of the tug reported her listing forty-five degrees to port with her stern completely submerged at high tide. Already much of her cargo and gear was being washed ashore along the nearby beach. The tug departed almost immediately leaving the ship and what remained of her cargo to be sold where she lay, some weeks later.

View onshore, wreck site in foreground.

The SS *Sagittarius* ashore at Creanan's Cave below Glenehervie Farm.

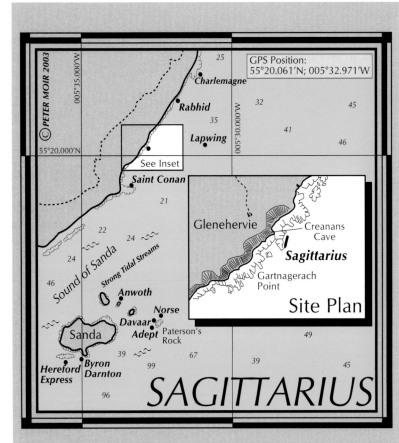

GPS Position:
55°20.061'N; 005°32.971'W

See Inset

SAGITTARIUS

Site Plan

The wreckage of the *Sagittarius* lies on the north side of a reef off Creanan's Cave, below Glenehervie Farm. The main wreckage can be found in position 55°20.061'N, 005°32.971'W (GPS), in depths ranging from 2 metres to 8 metres. The wreckage, which is well broken, is spread along the north side of the reef and down onto the white coarse sand seabed at the base of the rock shelf. A section of the bow lies in shallow water within a gulley in the middle of the reef.

SAINT CONAN

272nt. Steel steamship.
Built by J P Renoldson, South Shields.
Launched August 1917.
(ex Princetown).

Dimensions 188.5' x 28.7' x 11.1'

The circumstances surrounding any wreck often result in controversy at the subsequent inquiry with arguments on who was to blame for the incident. In the case of the *Saint Conan*, the blame for the wrecking was unequivocal. The ship, which was owned by J & A Gardner and Co, Clyde Street, Glasgow and registered at Port Glasgow, had sailed from Ayr bound for Sligo with a cargo of 600 tons of coal at 10:30pm on 29th August, 1939. She was commanded by Mr Donald Carmichael and he took charge of her as they steamed out of Ayr and set a course west by half south which would take them past Pladda where he then planned to turn towards Ireland. At midnight the captain handed over command of the vessel to the mate, George Moore, leaving instructions for him to change course to west south by three quarters south as they passed Pladda and to stream the log. On reaching Pladda around 12:15am, Moore went below to fetch the log and failed to return to the bridge. After the ship ran aground he was found lying, asleep, on the settee in the chartroom.

SS *Saint Conan* - as *Princetown*.

The night was fine and calm and, as the *Saint Conan* steamed on at nine knots, the lights on the east coast of Kintyre were clearly visible to the crew on board. Two hours later the mate still had not returned to the bridge and the vital course change, instructed by the captain, had not been made. At 2:15am the ship ran ashore. It is not clear why John McVeigh, able seaman, who was actually steering the vessel, did not take any action to avoid the stranding, although he later testified that he thought he was steering the correct course. After the ship went ashore the mate was found lying, asleep, on the settee in the chartroom. It is therefore certain that, despite his testimony to the contrary, he had not ordered the change of course that would have taken them safely on their way and as such he was fully to blame for the loss of the vessel. The mate attempted to explain his lengthy absence from the bridge by a heart seizure but this was not supported by medical evidence. The court suspended his certificate for 12 months.

Like may other ships before her the *Saint Conan* had run aground on the treacherous reef of Arranman's Barrels which extends more than half a mile from the shoreline. She ran onto the reef at full speed and the bow reared up over the top of it so far that, the following day, it was possible to row a small boat under the keel. She was lying at an angle of forty five degrees with her bow high in the air and her stern under water. The crew got safely ashore but the vessel was doomed. There were a number of unsuccessful attempts to pull her off, both under her own power and by tugs, but it was hopeless. For a few days it was hoped that the cargo could be off-loaded and then another salvage attempt made but, later in the week, when the weather worsened she settled onto the reef and the vessel and cargo became a total loss.

The story surrounding the wreck of the *Saint Conan* was completed in October of 1939 when the steam lighter *Kinsol* ran onto the reef while working on the salvage of the wreck. She was badly holed and abandoned by her crew - she sank a few hours later.

The Wreck Today

The remains of the *Saint Conan* lie in approximate position 55°19.414'N, 005°33.495'W on the north side of the Arranman's Barrels. The wreck was heavily salvaged in situ and this, plus the effects of the weather and tides, means that she is well dispersed. However substantial quantities of wreckage still

remain at the site. Her boiler, lying on the seabed at the bottom of the reef in around 12 metres, is the largest recognisable item. The rest of the wreck lies scattered around the boiler, on a shingle seabed, to maximum depths of 14 metres and along the side and even on top of the reef with the shallowest parts in less than 5 metres. The site, which is easiest to locate at low water, is fairly exposed to wind and swell and careful boathandling is required to make sure that your boat doesn't join the long list of casualties on the Arranman's Barrels.

The PS *Signal* at anchor in Oban Bay.

SIGNAL

174nt. Steel paddlesteamer.
Built by Caird & Co., Greenock.
Launched 1883.

Dimensions 160.1' x 25.1' x 11.5'

The *Signal* was owned by the Commissioners of the Northern Lighthouses and was on one of her regular trips as a tender to the Commissioners' steamer *Pharos*, which carried provisions and relief keepers to the lighthouses in the Western Isles, when she left McArthur's Head, Islay at 3:15am on 28th September, 1895. She had a crew of twenty-two, under the command of Captain Ewing, plus eight passengers aboard. At first, the weather was clear and the night was calm but, around 5am, they ran into a bank of thick fog. Captain Ewing was not alarmed although he could hear the two pitch blasts of the fog signal at the Mull of Kintyre sounding every four minutes in the distance. He estimated it to be two miles to the ENE and, as a result, at 5:55am he made his planned course alteration to the SSE. This change of direction was to be his undoing. As a precaution he slowed from his cruising speed of 10 knots to around 5 knots.

At 6:10am the lookouts suddenly spotted breakers close to the port bow and the captain ordered an emergency turn away from the danger but, before this could be executed, the ship ran aground on a sunken rock three quarters of a mile south of the lighthouse and stuck fast. The engines were run full speed in reverse for fifteen minutes in an attempt to pull her off but she would not move. She was bumping heavily on the rock in the westerly swell and was soon found to be taking water. The captain reluctantly abandoned ship and took the passengers and crew by boat to Carskey Bay. The crew returned to the wreck to remove personal effects and the ship's papers but did not stay aboard fearing that she would slip off and sink.

Later that day a salvage tug arrived but could not find the *Signal* in the fog. On the 29th she reached the wreck and began salving what could be removed as it was quickly concluded that the ship would become a total wreck. During the following night the *Signal* broke in two with the stern section slipping off into deep water leaving only the bow section partly visible above water the next morning. At the Court of Inquiry the captain was absolved of blame for the wreck, which was blamed on the thick fog, although he was criticised for not sounding with lead when he neared the danger area. They also recommended that the four minute interval between signals from the Mull foghorn should be shortened as, in their opinion, a shorter interval would make judgement of distance from the shore easier.

The Wreck Today

The authors have located remains of a steamship approximately 150 metres north of the Mull foghorn in position 55°18.009'N, 005°48.092'W (GPS). Although not positively identified as such we believe this to be the remains of the *Signal*. The wreckage extends over a reasonable area of rock and boulder seabed between 5 and 17 metres, although the bulk of the wreckage lies in the shallows. The site is also overgrown with kelp down to around 15 metres.

This is an exposed site and only diveable in calm conditions. Strong tidal streams run off the point south of the wreck (Rubha na Lice) especially on the ebb, although the wreck site is sheltered from the main flow.

STAFFA II

154nt. Iron steamship.
Built by J & G Thomson.
Launched 1863.

Dimensions 148.3' x 23.1' x 11.2'

The MacBrayne's steamer *Staffa* left Glasgow on Monday 23rd August, 1886 on her usual route, round the Mull of Kintyre, north up the Scottish west coast and through the Caledonian Canal to Inverness, with a general cargo and more than twenty passengers aboard. Captain McKinnon was relaxed on this familiar trip but, as they sailed north along the coast of Kintyre in the darkness, the night became hazy and, at around 2am, they ran aground at full speed on Cath Sgeir, a small rocky outcrop lying half a mile off the west coast of Gigha.

The sleeping passengers were rudely awakened by the terrible grinding noises as the ship crashed over the top of the rocks and stopped dead. It was quickly

SS *Staffa II.*

obvious that they were in no immediate danger and, after the initial shock, everyone was calm and a disciplined evacuation of the ship was quickly completed as the passengers and crew were taken by ship's boats to Dubh Sgeir, another rocky outcrop nearer to the Gigha shore. They spent the night there and then; at around 10am in the morning, the steamer *Fingal* arrived on the scene, took them aboard and conveyed them to Tarbert. By the time they left the *Staffa* had settled with water now between her decks and she had

a heavy list to starboard. During the next two days the wreck was battered by gales and she gradually sank beneath the surface. By the Thursday only the masts and a small portion of her funnel were visible and she was abandoned as a total wreck.

The wreck of the *Staffa* makes an interesting dive. It lies in position 55°39.616'N, 005°47.299'W (GPS) on the east side of Cath Sgeir with the stern the shallowest part of the wreckage in around 6 metres and the rest of the wreck lying among the rocks on a steep slope down to 15 metres. She is well broken up but there is still a lot to see. Her propeller and boiler are the most obvious items but large quantities of other wreckage are packed into an almost vertical gully. The wreckage is surrounded and covered by interesting encrusting sealife and there are always lots of fish about as well. The only hazard on the site is the swell which often crashes over the rocks which themselves only rise up a couple of metres above sea level. Care is therefore required with boathandling near the rocks. The remains of the coaster *Leven* lost in 1901 are also to be found on the reef and lie slightly north of the *Staffa* in shallow water.

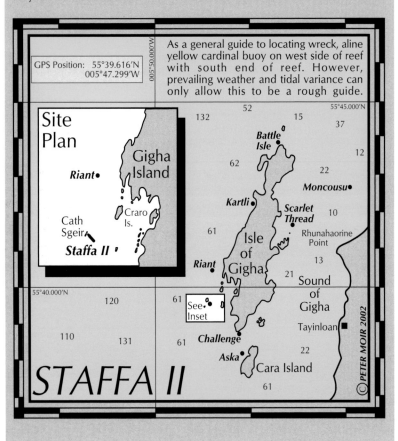

GPS Position: 55°39.616'N
005°47.299'W

As a general guide to locating wreck, aline yellow cardinal buoy on west side of reef with south end of reef. However, prevailing weather and tidal variance can only allow this to be a rough guide.

Site Plan

Gigha Island

Riant●

Cath Sgeir

Staffa II

Craro Is.

Riant ●

Isle of Gigha

Battle Isle

Kartli

Scarlet Thread

Moncousu●

Rhunahaorine Point

Sound of Gigha

Tayinloan ■

Challenge

Aska●

Cara Island

55°45.000'N

55°40.000'N

© PETER MOIR 2002

See Inset

STAFFA II

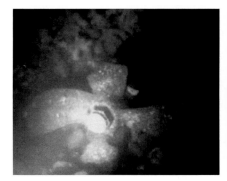

The twisted remains of the **Wilmere's** propellor.

WILMERE

Steel motor vessel.

Dimensions 95' long

The *Wilmere* was a small motor coaster, which sank on 13th August, 1976 while being used to salvage scrap metal from the wreck of the *Byron Darnton* at Sanda. It appears that her mooring broke and the tide took her onto the adjacent reef, she later sank some 50-75 metres west of the *Byron Darnton*.

The Wreck Today

The wreck of the *Wilmere* lies in position 55°16.367'N, 005°35.189'W (GPS), parallel to the main reef which runs east west. Lying in general seabed depths of 17-18 metres the vessel remains intact, including her metal wheelhouse, the wreck rises approximately 2-3 metres above the rock seabed, although her mast rises slightly higher just forward of the main hold at the bow. Tidal streams run along the south side of the reef between 2-3 knots at spring tides, even faster where the reef shallows. In short, this is a slack water dive unless you are willing to drift along the outside of the reef. You never know what you may find.

WINDSOR CASTLE

Iron paddlesteamer.
Built by Caird & Co.
Launched 1859.

Dimensions 191' x 20'

The *Windsor Castle* had only been in service for two seasons when she and her sister ship, *Rothesay Castle*, were sold by their owners for service in India. Both ships were taken out of service on 4th September, 1860. After removal of the engines and paddle boxes and strengthening of the hull with metal stringers they were rigged as three masted schooners for the long voyage east.

The *Windsor Castle* set off on its final voyage on the morning of 27th September in a gentle northeast breeze. Captain Walker slowly made his way down the Kintyre coast and at 11pm, after 19 hours on deck; he went below for some sleep leaving the mate in charge to take the ship through the treacherous Sound of Sanda. Here the strong tidal flows pushed the ship ever closer to the shore and eventually, around 1:30am, she grounded. Initially the crew remained aboard as they were in no danger but, as the heavy swell began to work the ship on the rocks, they left her and made their way easily ashore. The ship, weakened by the removal of her engines and paddle boxes, quickly began to buckle and before long broke her back and became a total wreck.

Diving the **Byron Darnton** below 'The Ship' Lighthouse, Sanda

KINTYRE

Listed below are a selection of 65 smaller vessels wrecked within this area. This list is included as a basis for further research. Names suffixed by (S) denote extensive salvage work or total removal subsequent to date of loss.

NAME	BUILT	TONNAGE	HULL	TYPE	LOST	CAUSE	LOCATION
Abigail	1833	138nt	W	Bg	24.01.1883	S	Arranman's Barrel
Active	1817	55nt	W	Sr	30.08.1888	F	Off Sanda
Albatross	1884	40nt	I	Slt	31.03.1901	F	2 Miles off Mull of Kintyre
Ann	1850	77nt	W	Sr	07.02.1883	S	Coldryan
Anna	-	350t	W	Bk	19.04.1878	S	Sanda Island
Battle Isle	1885	44nt	I	SS	18.01.1890	S	Gigha
Ben Nevis I	1824	45nt	W	PS	10.08.1831	S	Carskey
Black Eagle	1867	36nt	I	SS	04.08.1892	S	Machrihanish Bay
Blairbeg(S)	1917	2202nt	S	SS	21.06.1935	S	Sanda Sound
Blinkbonnie	1874	96nt	W	Sr	14.11.1880	S	Arranman's Barrel
California	1849	480bn	W	Bk	09.04.1859	S	Dunaverty
Chieftain	1845	26bn	W	PS	08.03.1854	S	Cour, Kilbrannan Sound
Christiana	1818	276bn	W	Bgn	02.12.1825	S	Paterson's Rock, Sanda
Chrysolite	1868	65gt	I	SS	27.03.1873	F	4mls SSW Sanda
Clyde	1861	191nt	W	Sr	10.12.1868	S	Glenhervie
Craigs	-	1148gt	W	Bk	13.03.1881	S	Glenhervie
Cyclops	1852	48nt	W	Sr	29.11.1866	F	Near Davaar Is.
Despatch		51nt	W	Sr	05.05.1841	S	Glunimore, Sanda
Dotterel	1887	168gt	I	SS	17.02.1923	S	Ru Stafnish
Drumsyne	-	20nt	I	SS	23.04.1889	S	Carskey
Duchess	1932	1375dt	S	Des	12.12.1939	C	8.6mls WNW Mull of Kintyre
Eagle	1859	68nt	W	Sr	21.02.1907	Fr	Davaar Island
Elagh Hall	1883	126nt	I	SS	30.07.1892	S	2.5mls N Mull of Kintyre
Elizabeth(S)	-	524gt	-	SS	02.11.1935	S	Johnston's Point
Ella	1856		W	Bgn	04.01.1867	S	Carradale
Esperance	1862	167nt	W	Bg	15.03.1893	F	Near Gigha
Ethel	-	300gt	I	SS	07.12.1887	S	Sheep Island
Falcon	1860	389gt	I	SS	05.01.1867	S	Machrihanish
Fastnet	1881	85gt	I	SS	09.05.1894	F	5m SW Gigha

NAME	BUILT	TONNAGE	HULL	TYPE	LOST	CAUSE	LOCATION
George Lamb	1854	62nt	W	Sr	19.07.1886	S	Limestone Point
Gertrude	1874	99nt	W	Sr	29.02.1884	S	West Sanda
Gnome	1892	48nt	S	SS	15.11.1902	F	Between Sanda and Mull of Kintyre
Golden Fleece	1932	20gt	-	MFV	18.03.1958	F	300m E Pluck Pt.
Golden Gleam	1853	111nt	W	Bn	03.03.1886	S	Paterson's Rock
Helena	1869	33nt	I	SS	23.07.1877	F	3mls NE Davaar Is
Jeune Heloise	-		W	Bg	24.01.1868	S	Entrance Campbeltown Loch
Kinsol	1909	89gt	S	SS	30.09.1939	S	Arranman's Barrels
Lady Inez	1917	45gt	S	Myt	08.06.1921	S	S. end Cara Island
Leo	1881	31nt	I	SS	10.01.1890	S	Saddell
Leven	1895	120gt	S	SS	07.09.1901	S	Cath Sgeir, Gigha
Lidskjall	1855	265nt	W	Bk	14.10.1879	S	Paterson's Rock
Lincoln	-	171gt	W	Bn	13.12.1888	-	Near Campbeltown
Loch Etive	1877	104gt	I	SS	29.09.1906	S	0.5ml S Tarbet
Lyra	1880	100gt	I	SS	08.03.1903	F	8mls SW Sanda
Madelaine Ann	1867	108nt	W	Bn	22.12.1894	S	Caldrine Bay
Morell	1871	137gt	W	Bgn	14.12.1893	F	Arranman's Barrels
Myrtle I	1853	590gt	I	PS	04.08.1854	S	Baron Reef Sanda
Neanthes	1858	187nt	W	Bn	06.01.1867	C	3mls S Sanda
Niels Rossing Parelius	1882	354nt	W	SS	10.05.1894	S	Arranman's Barrels
Nordale	1903	71nt	S	Str	12.01.1942	S	Borgadale Point
Parrsboro	-	144nt	W	Bg	17.11.1864	F	Kildalloig Bay, S Davaar Is.
Primrose	1907	87gt	W	SDr	30.05.1933	S	Glenhervie Point
Priscilla	1866	141nt	W	Bn	03.01.1906	S	Torrisdale Bay
Quesada	1938	39t	S	MV	23.05.1966	F	East of Davaar
St Kilda I	-	185nt	-	SS	19.11.1892	S	Sanda
Sirdar	1885	25nt	S	SS	17.06.1900	F	12mls S Mull of Kintyre
Sovereign	1877	97nt	W	Sr	25.12.1899	S	Boiler Reef Sanda
Stately	1904	72gt	S	SDr	12.09.1927	S	North end Sheep Is., Sanda
Tina	1891	215gt	I	SS	18.09.1898	F	3mls off Mull of Kintyre
U-482	-	871dt	S	S	16.01.1945	DC	6mls NW Machrihanish
Udea	1873	82nt	I	SS	08.04.1894	S	Cath Sgeir, Gigha
Victoria	1866	31nt	I	SS	07.03.1894	S	Pluck Point
Victoria	1897	55nt	-	Str	07.11.1940	S	W end Sanda
William	1851	47nt	I	Sltr	24.09.1878	S	Inniemore

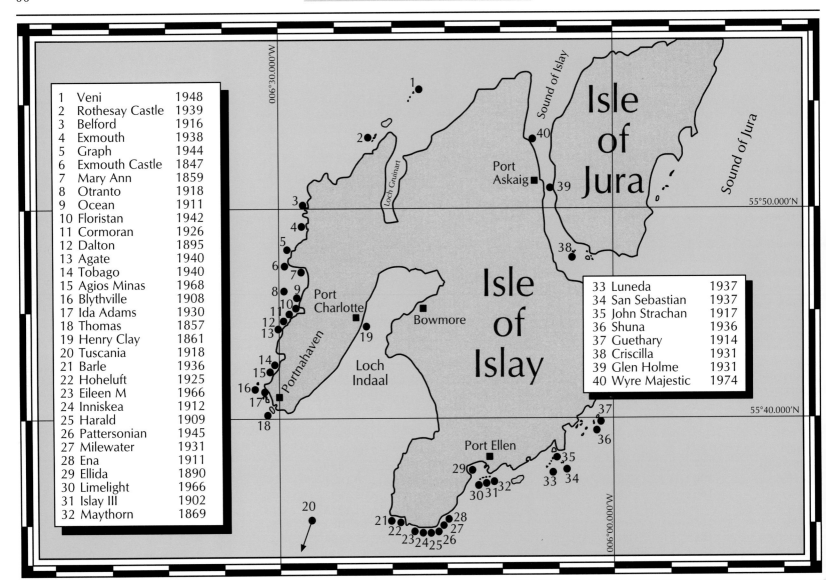

1	Veni	1948
2	Rothesay Castle	1939
3	Belford	1916
4	Exmouth	1938
5	Graph	1944
6	Exmouth Castle	1847
7	Mary Ann	1859
8	Otranto	1918
9	Ocean	1911
10	Floristan	1942
11	Cormoran	1926
12	Dalton	1895
13	Agate	1940
14	Tobago	1940
15	Agios Minas	1968
16	Blythville	1908
17	Ida Adams	1930
18	Thomas	1857
19	Henry Clay	1861
20	Tuscania	1918
21	Barle	1936
22	Hoheluft	1925
23	Eileen M	1966
24	Inniskea	1912
25	Harald	1909
26	Pattersonian	1945
27	Milewater	1931
28	Ena	1911
29	Ellida	1890
30	Limelight	1966
31	Islay III	1902
32	Maythorn	1869

33	Luneda	1937
34	San Sebastian	1937
35	John Strachan	1917
36	Shuna	1936
37	Guethary	1914
38	Criscilla	1931
39	Glen Holme	1931
40	Wyre Majestic	1974

Isle of Jura

Isle of Islay

Sound of Islay

Sound of Jura

Loch Gruinart

Port Askaig

Port Charlotte

Bowmore

Loch Indaal

Portnahaven

Port Ellen

55°50.000'N

55°40.000'N

6°00.000'W

6°00.000'W

6°00.000'W

ISLE OF ISLAY

MULL OF OA TO RUBHA A MHAIL

Chapter **2**

The island of Islay (pronounced Isla by local residents) is probably best known for the output of its seven famous distilleries which produce malt whisky of the highest standard. In the world of diving it is equally famous for its incredible concentration of shipwrecks.

The island's position, lying to the north east of the North Channel, and the prevailing on-shore south west winds, have made it the final resting place of hundreds of vessels from the earliest to modern times. The west coast, with its sweeping beaches and sand dunes interspersed by some imposing cliffs is a desolate place when the weather is bad and the wind is from the west or south west. The ferocious tides which sweep past the Rhinns and the Mull of Oa add another hazard for passing ships. In the narrow sound between Islay and Jura the tides race through at up to five knots at spring tides yet another difficulty in navigating round the island's coast. Finally the south coast has hundreds of hidden rocks and reefs which guard the entrance to Port Ellen, the island's main port. In all, it is not an area for the inexperienced or careless seaman.

The main centres of population are spread round the coast at Bowmore, Port Ellen and Port Charlotte but picturesque Portnahaven and Port Wemyss are an essential stop-off on a tour round the island. Inland the scenery is fairly barren with the centre of the island dominated by a huge peat bog still the source of

heating fuel for many of the islanders. However, the unusual variety of geology and habitats dunes and cliffs, peat bogs and mud flats make Islay a paradise for bird watchers.

The chart opposite clearly illustrates the most dangerous areas being those of strong tidal movement and exposed coastline. Islay is also blessed with clear waters, rich with colourful sealife. There are a number of sites around the headlands at the Rhinns, the Mull of Oa and also in the middle Sound of Islay where exciting drift dives can be experienced, provided you have adequate boat cover. Many of wrecks around Islay lie inshore on exposed coastlines and have been reduced to piles of wreckage although wreck sites such as the *Otranto, Thomas, Agate* and *Belford* all provide excellent dives in good conditions.

There are also a number of wrecks located to the west of Islay, which are beginning to be visited by more experienced dive teams. These wrecks are found in deep water below 50 metres. We have dived an as yet unidentified wreck of a twin engine vessel on the 007° longitude line, some 15 miles west of Portnahaven. Here clear water and coraline sand provide perfect underwater conditions. Planning and safety must be paramount in any expedition to these sites.

AGATE

397nt. Steel steamship.
Built by Scott and Son, Bowling.
Launched May 1917.

Dimensions 199.4' x 30.1' x 11.9'

The British steamship *Agate* was en route from Goole to Belfast with a cargo of coal for her owner, Mr William Robertson when she ran aground in fog at Cairns Point near Tormisdale on the west coast of Islay at 4:30am on 30th December, 1940. Captain Humphries and his crew were taken off by the Islay lifeboat but the following day the ship broke her back and became a total wreck. By the 4th of January she had broken up and was completely submerged. Lloyd's agent reported her sunk in 10 fathoms.

The remains of the *Agate* lie just north of the point at Rubha Ghlamraidh on the west coast of Islay in position 55°44.202'N, 006°29.835'W (GPS). There is a prominent 'sharks fin rock' lying approximately 20 metres off the rocky coastline with a deep gully running between. The remains of the *Agate* lie in the gully;

SS *Agate*.

depths in the gully range from 15 to 5 metres at the east end close to shore. The site is over shadowed by the prominent headland directly inshore; the whole area is very exposed to heavy swell from the west and on such occasions makes the site off limits.

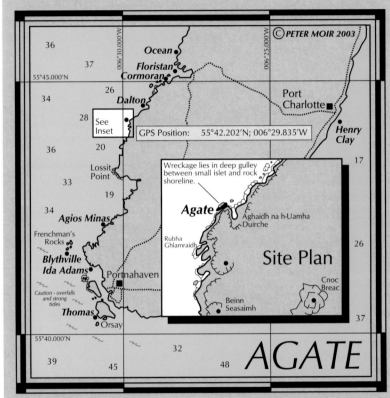

The wreckage is located in the base of the gully and consists of a four bladed propeller, engine parts, prop shaft and ferrous and non-ferrous debris either loose or fused into the seabed. The remains are testament to the power of the sea, with the prop shaft and engine components bent and distorted by winter storms. The site also provides an interesting dive along the steep sided gully with varied and colourful sealife.

AGIOS MINAS

1395nt. Steel steamship.
Built by Atel. & Ch. de la Seine Maritime, France.
Launched 1940.
(ex EGEE ex ASIMI)

Dimensions 307.5' x 43.6' x 19.1'

The weather on the morning of the 8th September, 1968 was clear and the sea calm. It can only be assumed that the captain of the Liberian registered *Agios Minas*, en route from Archangel to Sharpness with a cargo of £250,000 worth of timber, made an error in identification of the light at Orsay because, at 6 am that morning a message crackled from the radio at Malin Head: " aground Islay Island two miles north of Oversay Light; require tug assistance."

The tug *Cruiser* was immediately called out from Greenock and raced to the scene. The Islay lifeboat was also launched to stand-by as a precaution. The ship had run straight ashore and was lying with her bows high on the rocks beneath a steep cliff at Cill Cleit north of Frenchman's Rocks. Later the same day the tug arrived and stood by during the night to attempt to pull her off at high tide the next day. The crews of the three vessels listened anxiously to their radios that night as the shipping forecast ominously predicted that the weather would deteriorate with a southeast gale moving in from the Atlantic. Early the next morning, with the ship gradually listing to port and settling by the stern, sixteen of the crew were taken off by the lifeboat leaving only the captain aboard. An inspection by the Lloyd's surveyor later that day revealed holes in number 1 and 2 holds and water in 3 and 4. The sea round the ship was already covered in floating timber as some of her deck cargo was washed off by the waves now pounding her. Attempts by the *Cruiser* to pull her off failed and the captain reluctantly abandoned his ship by the end of the day.

With the ship declared a total loss, work began on salvaging her valuable cargo. This work proceeded, on and off as weather allowed, for most of the winter and then work began to dismantle the ship herself for scrap. She had been well stripped before she broke up in a series of gales in the winter of 1969.

SS *Agios Minas*.

SS *Agios Minas* ashore near Portnahaven.

The Wreck Today

GPS Position: 55°42.116'N; 006°30.785'W

Wreckage lies at base of rock and boulder slope between 17-20 metres. Wreck has been extensively salvaged, and little remains standing more than 1-1.5 metres above the seabed.

Site Plan

AGIOS MINAS

The remaining wreckage of the *Agios Minas* lies among deep rocky gullies and on a sloping rocky seabed close to the foot of the cliffs at Cill Cleit in position 55°42.116'N, 006°30.785'W (GPS). The wreckage lies in depths of 17-20 metres and although there is a fair amount scattered in the gullies inshore the larger pieces lie deeper, on the rocky slope, with some standing well above the seabed. The site is very exposed and subject to heavy swell from any westerly direction.

BARLE

120nt. Steel steam trawler.
Built by Cochrane and Son, Selby.
Launched 1914.

Dimensions 135.2' x 23.5' x 12.2'

The graphic story of the loss of the Fleetwood trawler *Barle* only came to light when the 10 crew arrived back in their home port aboard another trawler the *Collena*. The *Barle* had been fishing off the west side of Islay on Wednesday 1st April, 1936 when she encountered poor visibility, hauling her nets she made slow progress probing the thick fog but unfortunately ran aground approximately 1 mile south east of the Mull of Oa on Sgeirean Buidhe.

Steam trawler *Barle* ashore.

The *Barle* was badly holed and quickly became waterlogged, the boiler fire was extinguished and as a result power to the wireless soon faded. Rockets were fired to try and raise help. The crew eventually abandoned ship although it was not until the following morning that they found they were only a few boat lengths offshore below 300 foot high cliffs.

Site Plan

© PETER MOIR 2003

Laggan Bay

Kintra

Dun Athad

Port Ellen

Port an Eas

Sgeirean Buidhe

Barle

Limelight

Islay III

Wreckage on beach maybe from *Hoheluft*

Wreckage lies in gulley between rocks off point and outermost rock. Note tide runs through this gulley at some stages, site also exposed to swell.

Milewater

Pattersonian

Eileen M Harald

See Inset

Caution - overfalls and strong tides

GPS Position: 55°34.944'N
006°18.825'W

BARLE

The crew struggled up near vertical sheep paths and finally reached the cliff top. It took them a further 2 mile walk to reach a farm where they were given food and were able to dry off and warm up. A few hours later they retraced their steps to the cliff top and managed to attract the attention of one of her home fleet, the *Collena*, which they later boarded, before returning to Fleetwood.

The Wreck Today

The wreck of the *Barle* lies below the prominent headland at Sgeirean Buidhe. A small rock lies no more than 20 metres to the south of the point, the wreck lies between the rock and the point and there can be no more than 8-10 metres between them.

This can be a spectacular dive in the right conditions, slack water and good visibility. The wreck lies in a very exposed location in position 55°34.944'N, 006°18.825'W (GPS) with depths ranging from 4-11 metres. Strong tides run parallel to the coastline on both ebb and flood tide, this coupled with swell often makes the site undiveable. In good conditions this is an excellent dive, the watchful eye of a seal is not unusual.

BELFORD

2076nt. Steel steamship.
Built by J. Priestman, Sunderland.
Launched July 1901.

Dimensions 325.0' x 47.0' x 25.6'

TURBINE STEAMERS LIMITED

The exact cause of the loss of the steamship *Belford* is not known, although it is possible to surmise, from the evidence of the wreck, the possible cause. She had been on a voyage from Barry Dock to New York, in water ballast, under the command of Captain J H Marshall with a crew of twenty-four aboard.

She was reported drifting off the Scottish west coast on January 30th, 1916 with no one on board. When she finally came ashore on the 9th of February on the north west coast of Islay near Ballinaby it was reported by a local who visited the wreck that the propeller was gone. It seems likely therefore that she lost her propeller, perhaps by running aground somewhere, and as a result her crew abandoned the helpless ship and made for land. They must have been swept away and lost in the strong tidal currents that exist off the west coast of Islay. Meanwhile the *Belford* herself drifted towards the Islay coast finally coming ashore at Poll an Dubhaidh just north of Smaull.

SS **Belford** ashore near Smaull.

A dive through the narrow shallow gully is only for the most experienced diver except on one of the rare, perfectly calm days. Normally, when the swell surges through the gully, the diver has to cling to pieces of wreckage to

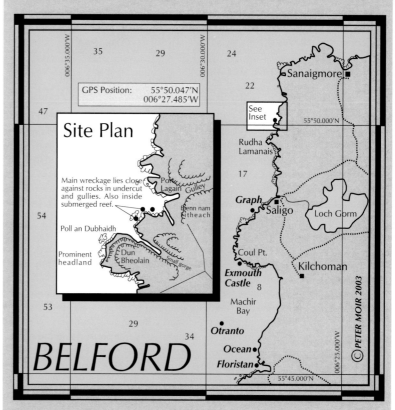

The wreck, standing upright on rocks under the cliff, was visited by the local agent of Lloyd's on the 11th who immediately declared the vessel a total wreck due to her position wedged between the cliff and a reef. When he returned on the 15th he found that she had vanished, smashed to pieces by the huge Atlantic swell that pounds the Islay coast, sometime during 12/13th. The only trace of the large steamship was an engine skylight, a few hatches and a couple of lifeboats washed ashore.

The Wreck Today

The wreck of the *Belford* is one of the least visited of the Islay wrecks due to the distance from suitable boat access and to the same Atlantic swell that wrecked her in the first place. The wreckage lies mainly in a shallow gully 6 metres deep, between a reef which breaks the surface and the base of the cliff in position 55°50.047'N, 006°27.485'W (GPS). At the north east end of the gully the boiler is the largest single intact item and the white sand seabed is strewn with metal plates, ribs and other items of wreckage.

prevent being swept, out of control, backwards and forwards among the jagged metal. The dramatic effect of the swell can be seen in the rock formation, which is undercut two metres on the shore side, and on the wreckage itself where the gleaming items of brass provide evidence of the abrasive effect of the waves and suspended seabed particles sandblasting it as it surges through.

BLYTHVILLE

898nt. Iron steamship.
Built by W. Gray, West Hartlepool.
Launched July 1877.

Dimensions 248.0' x 32.1' x 18.4'

At 11am on June 2nd, 1908 the *Blythville* left Stornoway in water ballast for a short voyage south along the Scottish west coast and through the Irish Sea to Swansea. Her route took her through the Minch and she passed Barra as darkness began to fall. The weather at first was fine and the sea calm but as they sailed south fog began to sweep over the vessel. By midnight the crew could hear the Skerryvore explosive fog signal sounding off the port bow and at 1am Captain James Stephen ordered her course changed to south half east. This course was calculated to take her five miles west of Islay but, in the thickening fog, failed to take account of the strong tidal streams off Islay's west coast.

By 5:30am the captain was getting worried and he slowed his speed to half then again to slow ahead at 7am. Shortly afterwards he ordered the mate to get out the sounding lead but before this could be done they heard breakers close by and almost immediately they sighted rocks three lengths ahead of their ship. The engines were reversed and the helm put hard over but it was too late. The *Blythville* ran aground striking the Frenchman's Rocks near her port bilge and within minutes the engines and pumps stopped as water poured into the engine room. The vessel had a heavy list to starboard and, as it was clear that she was about to sink, the crew took to the boats and reached the shore safely. When the captain returned later with some locals the ship had slipped off the rocks and vanished. At the subsequent inquiry his certificate was suspended for three months. The court held that he had not navigated his vessel in a seamanlike manner as he had failed to use the sounding lead to verify his situation.

The wreck of the *Blythville* lies in position 55°41.597'N, 006°32.019'W (GPS), on the southwest corner of Frenchman's Rocks. The remains are fused into deep and narrow gullies and between rocks; it took us a number of dives to find the wreckage as it was so well hidden and covered with a crown of thick kelp in the

shallows. There is a deep gully to the south of the most westerly rock in 15 metres, debris has fallen into this cleft which you can enter from the east end. Apart from localised areas of wreckage little remains of this large vessel. The tide can push you through the site at quite a rate. This coupled with wreckage and seals that dart past in total control can all make for an interesting dive, but one for the experienced diver.

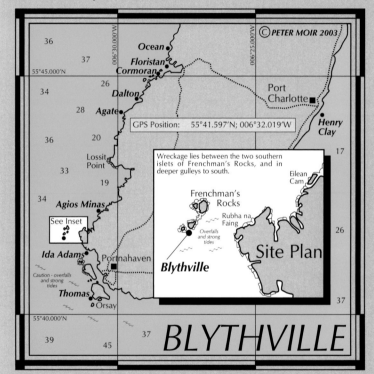

GPS Position: 55°41.597'N; 006°32.019'W

Wreckage lies between the two southern islets of Frenchman's Rocks, and in deeper gulleys to south.

A word of caution, this is a very exposed and potentially dangerous site. The tides around the rocks at certain states of the tide can be ferocious, so great care must be taken when diving this site. It is advisable to take a walk out to the headland and watch the tide in full flow around Frenchman's Rocks before navigating this stretch of water. Alternatively make sure you travel through the sound at near slack water on your first visit.

CEREALIA

115nt. Steel steam trawler.
Built by Cochrane and Son, Selby.
Launched 1905.
(ex Gudrun, ex Calabria)

Dimensions 122.0' x 21.7' x 11.3'

The Sound of Islay with its strong tides and unpredicatble eddies has caught many an unsuspecting or unwary skippper over the centuries. For some reason trawlers seem to be particularly suseptible to mishap in this strech of water with around twelve casualties, of which four remain today. The most northerly of these is the Grimsby trawler *Cerealia* which was lost on the 25th November 1920, en route to Fleetwood with a full cargo of fish. The *Cerealia* was lost when she ran aground on Sgeir Traigh, at the north entrance to the Sound of Islay in poor weather conditions and reduced visibility.

Steam trawler **Cerealia**.

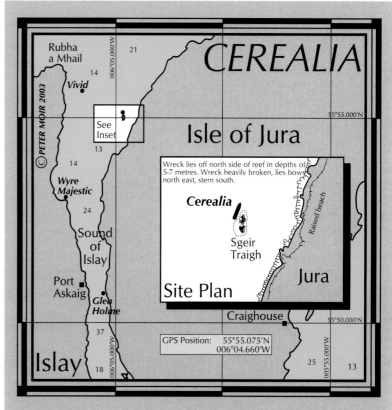

The wreck lies at the north end of the Sound of Islay, off the Jura shore in position 55°55.075'N, 006°04.660'W (GPS). The remains of the *Cerealia*, which can only be termed as wreckage, lie on the north side of a reef called Sgeir Traigh in depths ranging from 4.5-10 metres. There are a few items which are still recognisable and these include the boiler, engine and main winches, but much of the hull is flattened due to the exposure to northerly winds. Tides are negligible around the reef as you are well out of the main tidal flow through the Sound of Islay, but due to the exposed location care should be taken not to stray too far from the cover boat.

CORMORAN

74nt. Steel steam trawler.
Built by Mackie and Thomson, Glasgow.
Launched February 1909.

Dimensions 120.8' x 21.5' x 11.6'

The trawler *Cormoran* was returning from the west coast fishing grounds to her homeport of Fleetwood. Around 5:45 am on the morning of Monday 18th January, 1926 they reached Kilchiaran Bay on the west coast of Islay intending to try a few more casts before finally setting off for home. The weather was very dark with a slight haze and there was a heavy swell when, without warning, there was a sudden bump followed at short intervals by a series of other bumps before the vessel came to an abrupt stop. The crew knew instantly that they had run aground and a quick inspection showed that they were making water fast. It was decided to abandon ship immediately. Five of the crew and the captain started to get out the ship's boat but, before they could assemble the whole crew, the trawler took a lurch to port followed by a larger, alarming lurch to starboard almost turning turtle in the process. This second lurch threw the lifeboat and the men working at it, except the captain, into the sea. The remaining five crewmen had to jump from their swaying ship onto a rock and scramble to the shore. They spent the night, cold and injured, huddled beneath two blankets they had been able to salvage from the wreck, before morning broke and they spotted smoke rising from a nearby house. As they walked towards it they met the local postman. He took them to a farmhouse where they were given hot drinks and food to revive them.

The men ashore thought they had lost their shipmates who had been thrown overboard but thankfully, later in the week, news came through from Tiree that they had landed safely there after three days adrift in the ship's boat. They later learned that the five men had been thrown into the sea but had managed to clamber aboard the lifeboat which had also been thrown clear and luckily was afloat upright beside them. Unfortunately the captain had not escaped from the ship and was apparently killed when the boiler blew up. The plight of the men in the boat had been grim as there was no plug in the boat and it had continually filled with water. They had to use their boots to bail the water out and to improvise rowlocks to make the oars useable. They had no food, no water, no shelter, no dry clothing and the strong offshore currents were sweeping them further out to sea. They managed to rig up a makeshift sail from an oar and a piece of tarpaulin but had little control over their craft as they drifted north. Luckily, three days later, they were washed ashore, completely exhausted, frost-bitten and hungry but alive, on the island of Tiree.

The Wreck Today

The wreck site of the *Cormoran* lies among the rocks on the south side of the entrance to Kilchiaran Bay in position 55°44.983'N, 006°28.616'W (GPS). At low tide, there is wreckage visible above water high and dry among the rocks. The remains of the boiler are also visible protruding from the water close to the shore. This visible wreckage fixes the approximate position but the main concentration lies slightly further south west as shown on the chart.

Steam trawler **Cormoran** ashore at Kilchiaran.

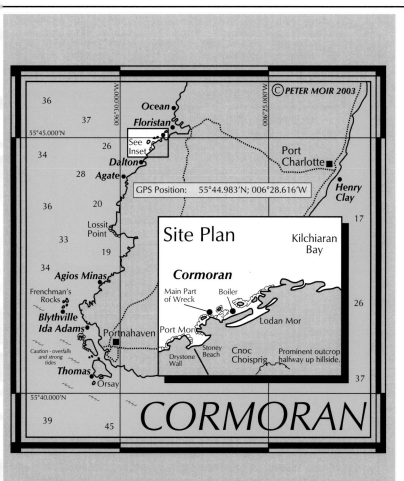

She has been well salvaged and little recognisable remains but there are still fairly substantial amounts of wreckage lying in 4 to 6 metres among the rocks. Due to the shallow nature of the site the wreckage is heavily overgrown with seaweed. Only potential hazard on this site is swell which, if encountered, would probably make the wreck undiveable.

CRISCILLA

350gt. Steel steam trawler.
Built by Cochrane and Son, Selby.
Launched 1929.

Dimensions 135' x 25' x 14.5'

The life of a fisherman on board a trawler is a hard one particularly in winter. October/November of 1931 was no exception and so it was with some relief that the crew of the Fleetwood trawler *Criscilla* headed south from the fishing grounds after a week of bad weather with constant wind and rain. Skipper Charlie Walters navigated through the channels between various islands off the west coast sheltering where possible from the worst of the weather giving the crew some welcome respite from the continuous rolling and buffeting of their ship. The *Criscilla* was a fairly new vessel and they were making a steady 14 knots despite the sea conditions when they entered the north end of the Sound of Islay in the early evening of November 2nd.

The night was misty and visibility was very poor so, as they approached the area of Black Rock towards the south end of the sound, the skipper slowed engines and everyone on board, except the men in the engine room, were posted on deck to keep a lookout for the light on the rocks or the lighthouse at McArthur's Head, the red sector of the light would indicate that they were too near the rocks. They did not know it but their luck was out. The light on the Black Rock was not working. At 10:40pm the ship ran onto the end of the reef at Black Rock and quickly became badly holed as she bumped up and down on the jagged rocks which soon could be seen protruding through the hull into the engine room.

For two and a half days the crew fought vainly with the rising water in an attempt to save their ship but, at 6am on the 6th, the skipper decided that she was in danger of sinking and decided to abandon ship. Another Fleetwood trawler, the *Flydea*, was standing by and the crew made it safely to her in the *Criscilla's* boat. They returned the following day and took off many of the removable items from the ship before abandoning her and heading home.

In early December salvage operations were started on the wreck using a new compressed air system and there were high hopes of saving the *Criscilla*. In fact she was successfully refloated but, just as the salvors felt that they had succeeded and the ship floated off the reef, her stern caught again on the rocks and she stuck fast once more. This time she was doomed. The falling tide caused her to keel over, the compressed air that had been keeping her afloat escaped and she sank beneath the surface. Her masts were visible above the surface for many years before they too finally succumbed to the rushing tides of the sound and all signs of her above water were gone.

The Wreck Today

The wreck is charted and lies in a strong tidal area in position 55°47.647'N, 006°03.909'W (GPS). It lies to the southwest side of a small reef that almost breaks the surface some fifty metres from Black Rock. The wreck faces north with the bow the deepest section of the wreckage lying in 12 metres. The wreck itself, which is completely covered in colourful encrusting sealife, lies with a heavy list to starboard and is well broken but large sections remain intact. The bow rises 5 metres from the seabed with the remainder of the ship spread across a rocky seabed which rises gently past the huge boiler and engine amidships to the stern, with propeller still in place, in around 8 metres. Spread

Steam trawler *Criscilla* ashore Black Rocks, Sound of Islay.

across the seabed at the stern are piles of slates which probably formed the cargo of another ship which came to grief on the Black Rock. It is not certain, but the authors believe this to be the remains of the cargo of the Welsh schooner, *Mary Ellen*, which was lost in the Sound of Islay in the vicinity of

Black Rock on 21st September, 1879. Close by, between the small reef and Black Rock itself, the authors found another small modern wreck, the *Nancy B*, a local inshore fishing boat, also lying in just over 10 metres. As previously stated the tides in the vicinity are fierce, reaching 7 knots at peak of springs, making a dive on slack water, which is often only a few minutes long, essential.

DALTON

1255nt. Iron steamship.
Built by A. Leslie & Co, Newcastle.
Launched 1881.

Dimensions 315.4' 34.7' x 24.7'

The *Dalton* was en route from New York to Glasgow with a cargo of wheat, oil and wood when, around midnight on 27th September, 1895 she ran aground in dense fog at Tormisdale on the west coast of Islay. The sea was calm at the time and, as she was aground not far from the shore, Captain Arthur Barton and his crew of twenty eight easily managed to get ashore safely.

She was inspected by the local Lloyd's agent the following day who reported water in the engine room and holds with the vessel lying facing the shore, heading ESE with a list to starboard. On the 30th the sea got rough and although a diver from the Liverpool Salvage Association stood by to inspect the damage he could not enter the water safely. Within a week she had broken in two astern of the engine room and had become a total wreck.

The Wreck Today

The wreck of the *Dalton* lies in Tormisdale Bay in position 55°44.414'N, 006°29.348'W (GPS). The wreckage lies in an area from the middle to the north side of the bay and is scattered along a series of rocky gullies running out to sea in 6 to 9 metres. Much of the wreck is concreted into the seabed, the wreckage is often covered with a heavy growth of weed and kelp during summer months, there is little of substance remaining.

Once again the only significant hazard to the diver is the potential of a heavy swell due to the exposed nature of the site.

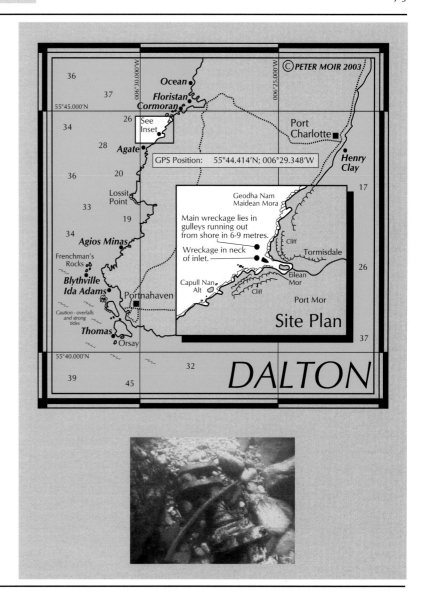

MV *Eileen M.*

EILEEN M

134nt. Steel motor vessel.
Built by Waterhuizen Shipbuilders,
Waterhuizen.
Launched 1939.

Dimensions 136.5' x 25.3' x 10.2'

The graphic accounts in the newspapers of the day of the plight of the seven crewmen aboard the tanker *Eileen M*, which ran aground on the Mull of Oa in the early hours of the morning of the 12th January, 1966, focused on the many different ways that they could have lost their lives. Fortunately they survived but they were faced with an extremely dangerous situation with the ship aground on a treacherous shore,

Mull of Oa

Laggan Bay
Kintra

Port Ellen

High cliffs

Alt a Chleibh

Rubha Dubh na h-Otha / *Eileen M*

Limelight *Islay III*

Site Plan

Broken wreckage in 10-13 metres. Wreck lies NE/SW stern to shore.

Milewater
Pattersonian
Barle *Harald*
See Inset

Caution - overfalls and strong tides

GPS Position: 55°34.766'N 006°17.616'W

© PETER MOIR 2003

EILEEN M

The ship, skippered by Irishman Frank McGuichian, had been en route from Ardrossan to Port Ellen and Lochboisdale, when she ran aground on the Mull of Oa as she tried to negotiate the entrance to Port Ellen harbour. The crew eventually were forced to attempt to get ashore as the ship was in danger of slipping back into deeper water or perhaps exploding, they were worried that the grounding of the ship on the rocks might create a spark which would ignite their deadly cargo. They managed to launch their boat safely and everyone clambered aboard but, as they could not find anywhere on the shoreline where they could safely disembark, they were forced to return to their precarious position aboard the *Eileen M*. Thankfully their distress calls had been picked up and, less than an hour later, the Port Askaig lifeboat pulled alongside and took them off safely.

The ship was left, with her bow ashore, lying with a forty five degree list to port and awash from the poop deck aft. Although salvage experts were called for, three days after her grounding she was abandoned as a total wreck. She was later heavily salvaged for scrap.

The Wreck Today

The remaining wreckage of the *Eileen M* lies in 10-13 metres in position 55°34.766'N, 006°17.616'W (GPS), which is at Rubha Dubh na h-Otha. The wreck lies on the east side of a reef with the shallowest section of wreckage at around 8 metres. The only substantial remaining portion appears to be a large section of the hull lying on a rocky seabed among deep kelp. When the authors explored the site the most interesting aspect of the dive was the underwater company of razorbills and guillemots "flying" past in the clear Islay water. The site, which is subject to a gentle tidal flow, is completely exposed to swell from the south and west.

pounded by a huge swell making launching their rubber lifeboat extremely difficult, and sitting aboard a ship with a lethal cargo of highly inflammable oil and diesel fuel which they expected to explode at any time. Even if they could have made it to the shore they could not have climbed the vertical cliffs of the Mull leaving them at the mercy of the biting January winds with death from exposure another possible danger.

ELLIDA

267nt. Wooden brig.
Launched 1859.

It is a strange coincidence that two Norwegian vessels called *Ellida* should go ashore and wreck in two different places on the Scottish west coast within twenty four hours of each other. The story of the loss of the *Elida* on Arran on 10th December, 1890 and the story of the loss of the *Ellida* twenty four hours later on Islay have other similarities as they were both lost in the same dense fog that shrouded the whole west coast of Scotland that December.

The *Ellida*, under the command of Captain Hansen, was en route for Drammen from Belfast in ballast when she went ashore on Islay. The crew managed to scramble onto the rocks safely and started to climb the steep cliffs, which they encountered ashore. As they moved higher in the darkness with no signs of the top they decided to stop and wait for daylight before proceeding. When dawn broke they found themselves perched precariously on a narrow rocky ledge above a forty foot sheer drop to the sea.

They clambered up the remaining cliff to the top and wandered around until they came to a farmhouse occupied by a local farmer, Mr McCrae. They made a makeshift tent from the sails of their wrecked ship and stayed there for three days while salvaging what they could from their ship before making their way to Port Ellen and then to Tarbert where they boarded the steamship *Grenadier* for Greenock. As they boarded the ship to leave Islay they were amazed to find that they were joined by the crew of another Norwegian barque, the *Vesterbotten* which had been wrecked nearby on the same night as they had gone aground. No doubt the two crews spent the voyage sharing their experiences of shipwreck on Islay.

WYLIE&LOCHHEAD L^{TD}
GLASGOW.

ENA

632nt. Steel steamship.
Built by Fredrikstad Machine Works.
Launched 1908.

Dimensions 228.6' x 36.2' x 14.4'

The Mull of Oa is not a pleasant place to be when caught in a dense fog. The strong currents and rugged shore have made it the graveyard for many vessels. Unluckily for Captain Bonds and his crew on the steamship *Ena* that is exactly the predicament they found themselves in on the night of 20th October, 1911. Their grounding was almost inevitable and shortly before midnight the *Ena* ran ashore on the south side of the Mull near Stremnish. At first the weather was calm and a number of the crew chose to stay aboard while the remainder scrambled ashore. Later the weather began to deteriorate and the remainder of the crew and the single lady passenger aboard were also forced to abandon ship in two of the ship's boats. One boat quickly managed to reach the shore two hundred yards from the stranded ship but the occupants of the second boat spent an unpleasant night at sea fearing that they would be smashed on the rocks if they tried to land in darkness. They reached Port Ellen early the next morning, cold and exhausted but otherwise unharmed.

The *Ena* was lying in a very exposed position. For more than two weeks divers and salvage team worked to repair her but, just before they were ready to refloat her, the weather turned and, on 3rd November, she broke in two and the stern sank into deep water. She was abandoned as a total wreck.

The author's have dived wreckage lying in shallow water in position 55°34.766'N, 006°17.616'W (GPS), The wreckage is heavily broken and lies in very shallow water no deeper than 4 metres. Note pieces of metal plate and a shaft can be found onshore from the wreck site lying among large rocks and boulders.

Steam trawler **Exmouth** ashore near Saligo.

EXMOUTH CASTLE

322t. Wooden sailing ship.
Built Newcastle. Launched 1818.

The loss of the emigrant ship *Exmouth Castle* on 28th April, 1847 is one of the most tragic peacetime incidents of all of the Islay shipwrecks. The ship was owned by Mr John Eden of South Shields and had departed from Londonderry bound for Quebec on Sunday 25th April with two hundred and forty emigrants plus an additional three women passengers and eleven crew aboard. The conditions aboard can only be imagined as the ship was only registered for one hundred and sixty five but, by counting two children as one adult, they were able to stay within the very easy going regulations of the time.

On Monday, the calm weather and seas they had set out in turned into a violent storm. For two days Captain Booth battled with the terrible conditions but eventually decided to run for shelter. For most of this time his unfortunate human cargo was battened below decks.

On the evening of the 28th they saw a light which they mistakenly took to be Tory Island - it was in fact the light at the Rhinns of Islay. By the time the captain realised his mistake it was too late. They were swept nearer and nearer the Islay coast and finally they were driven ashore near Coul Point. The mast toppled over as they hit the shore and three lucky crewmen managed to scramble to safety before it was washed away. No one else escaped as most of the people aboard were still secured below decks. The *Exmouth Castle* was quickly smashed to pieces and two hundred and fifty one men, women and children lost their lives. Over the next few days one hundred and eight bodies were washed up along the west coast of the island.

The wreck was reported ashore on a reef off Eilean Geodha Mhoir just south of Coul Point. This section of coast is particularly rugged, with many deep inlets in the rocky coastline; it is highly likely that some metal remains from the *Exmouth Castle* will lie in the base of one of these. A memorial to the tragic loss has been erected at Sanaigmore, some miles to the north of the wreck site.

EXMOUTH

236gt. Steel steam trawler.
Built by Cochrane and Son, Selby.
Launched 1912.

Dimensions 120.0' x 21.1' x 11.7'

The coast of Islay is scattered with wrecks of the Fleetwood trawler fleet. In the early hours of the morning of 9th March, 1938 the *Exmouth* was to join them. The ship was homeward bound when it ran into dense fog off the Islay west coast and onto rocks off Smaull Point. The area is completely exposed to the Atlantic swell and as soon as they went aground huge waves began to break over the ship. Three of the crew of eleven were washed away as they tried to get into the ship's boat and were drowned. As the remaining eight crewmen rowed safely ashore their ship was already being smashed to pieces and quickly became a total wreck.

FLORISTAN

3483nt. Steel steamship.
Built by J Readhead, South Shields.
Launched August 1928.

Dimensions 415.3' x 54.2' x 27.6'

The Strick Line steamship *Floristan* had been loaded at Manchester with a varied cargo including locomotive parts and military stores. She set sail on 15th January, 1942 for Freetown and the Persian Gulf and reached Islay where she was to await the assembly of a convoy. The exact reason for her wrecking is not known but at 9:30pm on the 19th January she ran aground at the entrance to Kilchiaran Bay. The Port Askaig lifeboat was launched at 11:35pm but by the time she reached the stranded vessel the crew had already reached the shore safely in the ship's boats.

The first report of the fate of the *Floristan* was made to her owners and to the insurers at Lloyds the following day and stated that there was little prospect of salvage as her back had broken. On the 21st the weather had subsided enough for the master to get aboard his ship and make a full investigation of the situation. He reported the ship lying across the entrance to the bay with her bow close to the north shore, sitting on an even keel aground fore and aft with her back broken immediately behind the bridge. She had water in all her holds and in the engine room but he expected to be able to salvage most of the cargo. Once again the Islay weather was to take a hand as during the next week the sea pounded the ship and by 27th she had broken in two and been driven further inshore. The bow was almost submerged and listing heavily towards the shore and, although salvage of stern section cargo was still felt to be possible the position of the wreck made approach by coaster to offload any cargo impossible.

The wreck of the *Floristan* lies in position 55°45.129'N, 006°28.234'W (GPS) which is at the north entrance to Kilchiaran Bay. The wreckage is spread over a wide area with the contents of cargo holds being some of the more recognisable items. The seabed in the area is around 10-12 metres, but the wreckage is piled high and in some areas reaches to within 5-6 metres of the surface. The huge

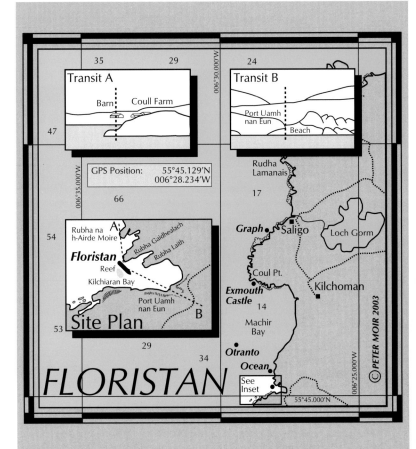

chassis of railway vehicles lie upside down and surrounded by jeeps, tyres, batteries and many other items of military supplies. The boiler is the only large visible item of the ship remaining. The only hazard at this site is the exposure to the west and the prevailing wind and swell. Even in good weather conditions the site may be subject to a ground swell, and beware the reef to the southwest of the wreck which almost breaks surface at low tide.

SS *Floristan*.

GLEN HOLME

532nt. Iron steamship.
Built by Denton & Gray & Co, West Hartlepool.
Launched July 1870.
(ex MARGARET BANKS)

Dimensions 213.6' x 29.2' x 16.2'

The *Glen Holme*, registered in Maryport and owned by Hine Bros, was bound for Ardrossan with a cargo of pit props in May of 1893 under the command of Captain Wilson. As she sailed south through the Minch her engines failed and, around 8:40pm on Friday 26th, she was towed into Stornoway. The engines could not be repaired and so, the following morning, she set off, under tow by the tug *Commodore* which was also heading for Ardrossan, for the long slow trip to the Clyde. On the same Saturday morning, as the *Glen Holme* and the *Commodore* left Stornoway, the steamer *GPA Koch* left Greenock bound for Copenhagen. As midnight on the 27th approached, the three vessels reached the opposite ends of the Sound of Islay. Around 2am, close to Port Askaig, they collided, with the *GPA Koch* hitting the *Glen Holme* on her port side amidships inflicting serious damage and smashing her own bow. The *GPA Koch*, while also badly damaged, was able to turn round and return to Greenock for repairs but the *Glen Holme* was forced to beach on the shore opposite Port Askaig. Her crew barely had time to scramble ashore before she heeled over and sank in six fathoms.

The Wreck Today

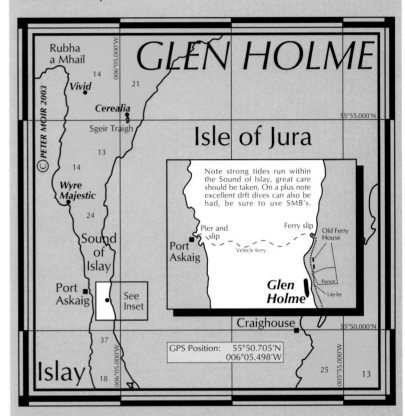

The wreck of the *Glen Holme* can be found on the Jura shore of the Sound of Islay, approximately 400 metres south of the Feolin Ferry. The wreck lies parallel to the pebble beach in depths up to 10.5 metres with bows pointing south. The wreck appears to have been heavily salvaged at some stage since her loss but still retains some ship like features. The wreck lies in position 55° 50.705'N, 006°05.498'W (GPS) and during the summer is heavily over grown with kelp. The wreck is also subject to the strong tidal streams that run up and down the Sound of Islay. We recommend slack water for this dive.

HMS *GRAPH*

760dt. Steel submarine.
Built by Blohm and Voss, Hamburg.
Launched 1941.
(ex U-570)

Dimensions 213' x 20' x 16'

The story of HMS *Graph* began on 27th August, 1941 when she was captured from the Germans after an air attack. She had been on her first patrol from her base at Loh fjord in Norway and was under the command of Kapitanleutnant Hans Rahmlow. Off Iceland she was sighted on the surface by the air crew of a Lockheed Hudson Mk3 of 269 Squadron under the command of Squadron Leader James Herbert Thompson. Before they could attack the submarine dived but, because of an error in setting the hydrophones, she resurfaced almost immediately. This time the British were not to be denied and, in an attack which later earned the squadron leader and one of his crew the DFC, they executed a perfect straddle with their four depth charges which caused Rahmlow, in fear of being sunk, to surrender. Adolf Hitler, infuriated at loosing one of his new submarines in an act he regarded as cowardice ordered Rahmlow's court martial and execution. Luckily for Rahmlow he was imprisoned in the UK and the order was never carried out. Meanwhile the submarine was towed first to Iceland, then ultimately to Vickers yard in Barrow in Furness where she was refitted and emerged as HMS *Graph*.

She was based at Holy Loch and made a number of patrols in the Bay of Biscay and the North Sea even managing to sink one of her sister U-boats in October of 1942. In early 1944 she was taken to Chatham Dockyard for a planned refit but as she was entering the dockyard she hit the harbour wall and was badly damaged. It was then decided that she should be towed to the Clyde and used for depth charge tests. She was stripped of all of her internal fittings and left Chatham, under tow by the tug *Empire John*, in early March.

On the morning of March 18th, they were in the North Channel when the weather deteriorated with 50 mph winds forcing them almost to a standstill. At 4:10am the 16" manilla tow line parted and the *Graph* drifted off into the night. Despite the efforts of the crew of the *Empire John* and HMS *Bullen* they could not get a second line aboard. The *Graph* was pitching and rolling in mountainous seas and at one point she even collided with the *Empire John* damaging the tug's steering. The tug was forced to leave the scene and to run for Campbeltown for repairs. The *Bullen* was joined by another tug, *Allegiance*, but still they could do nothing to stop the submarine drifting north towards Islay. She finally came ashore near Coul Point around dawn on the 20th. During the next four weeks the wreck was smashed to pieces in a series of violent storms.

The *Graph* was heavily salvaged and as a result there is only a small amount of wreckage remaining. Some of the salvage equipment is still visible ashore, which helps to mark the site of the wreck. The remains are in position 55°48.216'N, 006°28.484'W (GPS), which is about three quarters of a mile north of Coul Point. The wreckage lies in a gully close to the rocks running at

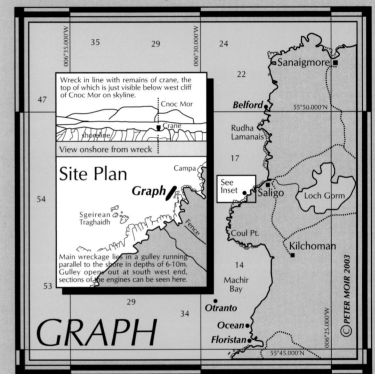

an angle of forty five degrees to the shore. The gully is about 10 metres deep at the seaward end and slopes gradually to around 6 metres. Along the length of the gully the wreckage has been pounded into the seabed by the swell that almost continually affects the coastline here. There are a few larger pieces of wreckage and, like most of the wrecks along this coastline, the remaining brass items have been polished to a shine by the abrasive effect of swell and sand.

GUETHARY

1930nt. Steel barque.
Built by Nantais de Construction, Nantes.
Launched 1901.

Dimensions 277.0' x 40.4' x 22.5

At 1:48pm on 22nd October, 1914 the French barque *Guethary* ran aground below the light on Eilean a'Chuirn off south east Islay. The cause of the loss is not known but it is difficult to see how the ship could have failed to see the light from the island therefore it must be assumed that she was disabled in some way, probably by bad weather. In any case, her voyage from New Caledonia to Glasgow with a cargo of mineral nickel was to be her last because, despite hopes to the contrary, she became a total wreck. Her crew of twenty-two made it safely ashore. She was reported by the local Lloyds agent to be hung amidships and no doubt broke up quickly in bad weather.

The barque *Guethary*.

The Wreck Today

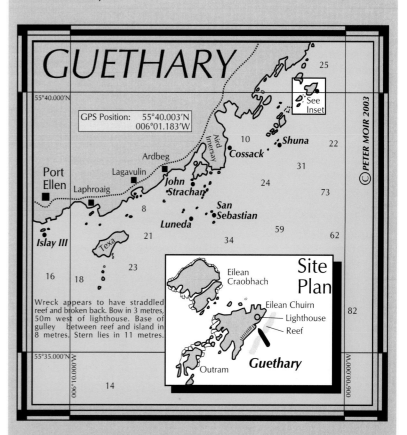

The remains of the *Guethary* lie on a sloping rocky seabed within 50 metres of the light on Eilean a'Chuirn in approximate position 55°40.003'N, 006°01.183'W (GPS). She lies on a north south axis with the bow pointing almost directly towards the shore lying in less than 5 metres while the stern lies in over 10 metres. There are still substantial amounts of wreckage although she has clearly been heavily salvaged at some point.

HARALD

1435nt. Iron sailing ship.
Built by T Royden and Son, Liverpool.
Launched November 1877.
(ex HORNBY CASTLE ex DUNCAN COUPLAND).

Dimensions 233.7' x 37.9' x 22.9'

The graceful sailing ship *Harald* was en route from Cardiff to Sandefjord in ballast, under the command of Captain Aas with a crew of twenty plus the captain's wife and child, when she ran aground on the Mull of Oa in fog at 6pm on August 16th, 1909. She ran onto the rocks two hundred yards west of Rubha nan Leacan and stuck fast with a heavy list to port exposing her hatches to the open sea. The crew made it safely the hundred yards or so to the shore and the following morning reached Port Ellen to report the fate of their ship. At first it was hoped that she might be refloated but her position was very exposed and it was clear that, if the weather deteriorated she was doomed. After two weeks work, the worst happened and the weather turned, she was abandoned as a total loss on August 30th. The hulk was later sold where she lay and heavily salvaged.

The Wreck Today

The extensive remains of the *Harald* lie in position 55°34.702'N, 006°16.388'W (GPS) which is 150 metres west of Rubha nan Leacan. The site is easily located as her sunken bow lies a few metres south east of a prominent shark fin shaped rock which is visible at all states of the tide. The wreck lies on

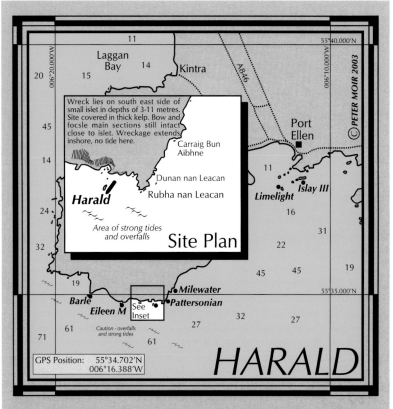

The iron ship *Harald,* ashore Rubha nan Leacan.

a north east, south west orientation with her bow section rising some six metres from the seabed at ten metres and the rest of the wreck spread over a wide area in depths from 3 to 11 metres. There is no tide on the wreck itself but the site is very exposed to the prevailing wind and swell and would be completely undiveable in anything other than calm weather. The tide rip off Rubha nan Leacan has to be seen to be believed and requires very careful boat handling to negotiate, as short steep waves rear up unexpectedly in front of the boat and could easily overturn even the most robust small craft. If approaching the site from Port Ellen keep close in shore as you pass the headland and you will miss the worst of it.

HENRY CLAY

1250t. Wooden sailing ship.

The *Henry Clay* was a large American sailing ship which sailed regularly across the North Atlantic from New York, her port of registry, to Europe. In September of 1861 she left Liverpool bound for home but after hitting a sunken rock in the North Channel she was forced into Loch Indaal to make repairs.

They dropped anchor and waited for the weather to calm down before attempting to repair her damaged hull. On the 28th the weather deteriorated and soon the moored ship was being lashed by huge waves which eventually became too much for the ship's anchor ropes. The huge ropes snapped under the strain and the *Henry Clay* was left to the mercy of the elements. She was driven across the loch and came ashore at the southwest end of the village of Port Charlotte on the north shore of the loch. The passengers and crew scrambled safely ashore but, despite attempts to pull her off by the *Lady Franklin*, she was to become a total loss.

The Wreck Today

The wreck lies in position 55°44.206'N, 006°22.685'W (GPS), in depths of 3 to 4 metres close to shore, off the last house on the shore at the west end of Port Charlotte. Little remains except parts of a winch and a few small sections of mast and hull timber among the kelp and rock patches. A number of artefacts have been recovered from the site, and these can be seen in the museum in Port Charlotte. Today most of the wreckage that exists is well buried in the sand or carpeted with thick kelp, especially during summer months.

HOHELUFT

83nt. Steel trawler.
Built by Deutsche Werke AG, Rustringen
Launched 1921.
(ex OSTPREUSSEN)

Dimensions 125.3' x 22.6' x 9.2'

Christmas Day 1925 should have been a day of quiet celebration for the crew of the German trawler *Hoheluft* as they made their way home from a long trip to Scotland. They had spent the days prior to Christmas at Tarbert, Loch Fyne, buying herring from the local fishing boats for sale on the German market by her owners, the Hamburg Wholesale Fishery Company. Having filled her holds, Captain Geiss set off on the homeward journey, intending to pass down the west coast of Ireland before heading east along the English Channel to the port of Altona in Germany. As they passed the Mull of Kintyre the sea became rough and they battled on through the waves pounding against the port bow of the trawler. They did not know but they were gradually going badly off course and heading towards the rocks beneath the towering cliffs of the Mull of Oa on Islay.

Friedrich Geiger, a member of the crew, was in his bunk when, around 11pm there was a shuddering crash as the ship ran aground on rocks some thirty yards from the Islay shore. He rushed on deck to find his shipmates hanging to the rigging as waves lashed the ship. They did not try to launch the ship's boat as, although they were only a short way from the shore, there were too many rocks between them and the shore for a boat to have any chance of making it. In a very short time the *Hoheluft* was completely overwhelmed and the crew lost, except for Friedrich Geiger who was fortuitously washed off the deck of the doomed vessel onto a nearby rock. He managed to cling on to it all night before making his way ashore to safety. The *Hoheluft* became a total wreck. She was heavily salvaged in subsequent years although a few small bits of wreckage still exist where she went aground. The remains of a large boiler on the beach in position 55°34.885'N, 006°14.749'W (GPS) are almost certainly from the *Hoheluft*, although this position is very close to the wreck of the steamtrawler *Barle*.

IDA ADAMS

104nt. Steel steam trawler.
Built by Cochrane and Sons, Selby.
Launched 1907.
(ex RUBY)

Dimensions 125.0' x 22.5' x 11.9'

The *Ida Adams* had already had one bit of bad luck on her trip to the fishing grounds from her home port of Fleetwood. She had fractured her rudder and sternpost on September 18th, 1930 while nine miles south east of Barra Head and had to put into Oban for temporary repairs. Her twelve crew were beginning to think of home as they headed south some eight weeks later.

It was 5:15am on 21st November and they were steaming south along the west coast of Islay. Most of the crew were still in their bunks but the cook was busy in the galley cooking breakfast. The weather was bad with thick fog and drizzly rain. Suddenly there was a horrendous crash as the ship ran aground on the north side of Frenchman's Rock. In the galley the crash threw some cooking fat onto the fire but thankfully the cook managed to quickly extinguish it before rushing on deck to join his colleagues.

The ship was safe, at least for a while, and they went back below to collect their belongings but were alarmed to find that she was quickly filling with water. For an hour the crew valiantly tried to stem the inflow of water but skipper William Atkinson was forced to give up and he gave the order to abandon ship. His twelve man crew managed, with some difficulty, to launch their boat. As they pulled clear with the ship's dog Bruce safely aboard, they watched as their ship was lifted again and again by the huge swell. It was obvious she could not stand up to the punishment for long and, as they pulled away to the shore, they watched her stern sink beneath the waves, her bow rise into the air and then the *Ida Adams* disappeared beneath the surface with a loud sucking sound. The crew made it safely to Portnahaven where they were given every hospitality by the locals before they were transported to Port Askaig and back to the mainland.

INNISKEA

59nt. Steel steamship.
Built by J. Cran & Co, Leith.
Launched 1912.

Dimensions 93.0' x 18.7' x 9.5'

The *Inniskea* was on her maiden voyage when she broke down off Tory Island, North Ireland in October 1912. She was taken in tow by a tug to return to her native Glasgow for repairs but, as they negotiated the troubled waters off the Mull of Kintyre on the night of October 8th, the cable parted and the disabled ship drifted off into the darkness before another line could be attached. The *Inniskea* was driven north by the wind and was not relocated until the following morning when she was spotted close to the towering cliffs at Stremnish near the Mull of Oa. The SS *Pioneer* steamed to the scene but, by the time she arrived, the *Inniskea* was too close to the shore to be approached safely. They could only stand by and watch as the new ship was driven onto the rocks. The crew of the *Inniskea* managed to jump safely ashore but the vessel was left jammed among the rocks close to the foot of the cliffs.

When a salvage team finally managed to board the ship on the 12th they found her with a sixty-degree list to starboard with rocks sticking through the hull at various places and all compartments flooded and tidal. The next day a gale from the south broke the ship apart and she was abandoned.

ISLAY III

187nt. Iron paddlesteamer.
Built by Tod & McGregor, Meadowside, Glasgow.
Launched May 1872.
(ex PRINCESS LOUISE)

Dimensions 211.4' x 24.1' x 12.4'

The MacBrayne's paddlesteamer *Islay III* ran aground on Sheep Island, Islay at two o'clock in the morning of 15th July, 1902. She had been at the end of her regular, twice weekly journey from Glasgow to Port Ellen and was newly under the command of Captain Cameron. She had encountered dense fog as she approached Islay and ran aground near this low lying island less than half a mile from Port Ellen harbour. Interestingly this was the second time in five months that the ship had run aground. Although she was lying with a severe list to starboard she remained firm on the rock allowing all the passengers to be transferred safely, by boat, to the shore on the Ard. The cargo was also quickly removed but the ship became a total wreck.

PS *Islay III*.

The wreck lies in position 55°37.183'N, 006°11.066'W (GPS) on the south side of Sheep Island (or Eilean nan Caorach to give it the Gaelic name shown on most charts of the area). The actual site is close to a reef that only just breaks the surface at low tide lying 200 metres from the shore of Sheep Island. The main items of wreckage remaining visible are her two massive boilers lying in 12 metres at the base of the reef. The seabed around the

Paddlesteamer *Islay III* ashore near Port Ellen.

Site Plan

The Ard

Ceann nan
Sgeirean

Coalas Eilean nan Caorach

Sgeir
Phlocach

Eilean nan
Caorach

Sgeir
Thraghaidh

Islay III

Forward section lies on top of reef and in gullies running down to the base of the reef, shallowest parts around 3 metres. Mid section and stern lie at base of reef on a level sandy seabed in 14 metres.

Laggan
Bay 14

Kintra

A846

Port
Ellen

Limelight

See
Inset

© PETER MOIR 2003

Milewater

Barle *Pattersonian*

Eileen M Harald

Caution - overfalls
and strong tides

GPS Position: 55°37.183'N
006°11.066'W

ISLAY III

boilers is strewn with metal ribs and plates and the remains of one of the paddle wheels but clearly the wreck has been heavily salvaged. The wreckage of the bow lies on the top of the reef in less than 3 metres and the deepest parts of the remains are around 14 metres. The site is exposed from the south but, apart from the possibility of some swell close to the reef when the wind is from this direction, is fairly sheltered and is free from tidal movement.

JOHN STRACHAN

42nt. Iron steamlighter.
Built by Swan & Co., Glasgow.
Launched 1885.

Dimensions 66.0' x 17.9' x 8.1'

The details of the loss of the Glasgow steamlighter *John Strachan* on 8th December, 1917 while on a voyage from Port Ellen to Loch Etive, are not known. Some clues can be gleaned from the wreck which lies off Eilean Imersay in position 55°38.212N, 006°05.533'W (GPS). The site is close to Ardbeg Distillery and among a series of treacherous reefs that stretch along the whole

JOHN STRACHAN

GPS Position: 55°38.212'N
006°05.533'W

Guethary

Shuna

Cossack

Ardbeg

Lagavulin

John
Strachan

Port
Ellen

Laphroaig

Islay III

Texa

Luneda

See
Inset

© PETER MOIR 2003

Wreck lies south of rocks off south
west tip of Eilean Imersay. Seabed
depths range from 6 metres at the
stern to 9 metres at the bow
which points south east.

55°35.000'N

Site Plan

Ardbeg

Eilean
Imersay

John
Strachan

Carmichaels
Rock

Cam
Sgeir

Luneda

San
Sebastian

The wreck today lies upright in 8 metres facing southeast. She is intact, lying with a slight list to port, with her stern resting on the edge of the reef and the bow slightly deeper on a sandy seabed. The hull, which is covered in colourful sponges and other encrusting sealife, is falling away around the stern accommodation allowing light to flood into this part of the wreck. Otherwise all that remains is the void of the empty hold and a small-locker room at the bow.

LIMELIGHT

143gt. Motor vessel.
Built by Rennie Forresit SB Co, Wivenhoe.
Launched 1916.

Dimensions 89.0' x 19.1'

length of this part of the Islay coast. The hull of the ship is completely intact and undamaged making loss in a severe storm unlikely. The only other observation about the wreck itself is that the single hold is completely empty.

With this detective work and some imagination it seems that the ship must have run aground on the reef, either due to poor visibility or perhaps she became unmanageable due to her lack of cargo. At some point she must have slipped off the reef into her current position.

The entrance into Port Ellen from the sea is not an easy one and a number of vessel have come to grief on the many rocky shoals lurking just beneath the surface close to the harbour itself. The MV Limelight, inward bound to Port Ellen with a cargo of 126 tons of bricks and 50 tons of bagged lime, was one of these casualties. In the early hours of the morning of 10th October, 1966 she went aground on Sgeir Thraghaidh which lies about a quarter of a mile south west of the harbour. With the Limelight stuck fast on the rock her captain sent out a distress message that was picked up by Oban Radio at 4:24am that morning. Within an hour the Islay lifeboat had been launched and was speeding to the scene.

Motor vessel **Limelight**.

Site Plan

Ceann nan Sgeirear

Sgeir Fhada

Wreck lies in two sections on north side of rock, and parallel to reef edge. Depths range for 3-9 metres. Bow lies to south of main wreckage and is inverted. Main section upright and intact, heading NE.

Limelight

Sgeir Thraghaidh

Sgeir Phlocach

Laggan Bay

Kintra

Port Ellen

See Inset

Islay III

Milewater

Barle

Pattersonian

Eileen M Harald

Caution - overfalls and strong tides

© PETER MOIR 2003

GPS Position: 55°37.116'N 006°11.699'W

LIMELIGHT

When she reached the grounded coaster the lifeboat stood by as the crew hoped that their ship might float off the rock at high tide. As the tide rose water began filling the hold and the crew were taken off as a precaution but she held fast. An inspection later in the day showed that, apart from the water in the hold, the ship was dry and hopes were high that she could be saved. With a salvage attempt planned for the next day the crew returned to their ship to make the necessary preparations. However, the weather was to take a hand and during the night of the 11th the crew had to be taken off again as the wind increased and a swell began to work the ship on the rock. The next day there was four feet of water in the engine room and it was too rough to get pumps aboard to keep the incoming water at bay. During the day the weather got worse and the watching crew and salvage team could see that, if the weather continued, the ship would be lost. Two days later, after removal of all moveable gear and fittings, the *Limelight* was abandoned. On the 21st she finally broke in two and slipped off the rock. She was later extensively salvaged for scrap.

The remains of the *Limelight* in 3-9 metres on the north west side of Sgeir Thraghaidh in position 55°37.116'N, 006°11.699'W (GPS). The wreck is in two major sections with the bow section nearest the rock and the stern section a few metres further out. The bow section, which lies upside down and rises to within a few metres of the surface, faces towards the stern section which strangely is facing in the opposite direction leaving the bow and stern of the wreck facing directly towards each other. The site is sheltered except for winds directly from the south and is therefore not subject to strong tidal streams or swell except in severe weather conditions.

Steam trawler *Luneda* ashore off Ardbeg, Islay.

badly damaged fourteen month earlier in the Faroes and you woul think that they were bound to run int trouble again.

Possibly none of this amazin history was in the crew's minds as the left Fleetwood on Monday 8th February, 1937 bound for the Faro fishing grounds. In the early hours o the following day they were caught ir a heavy snow storm which reduced the visibility to almost nil. The skipper Richard Snape, was on deck with two of his twelve man crew and had jus sent deck hand Charles Emery below to call the next watch when the suddenly ran hard aground on rock near Ardbeg. The ship shuddered to a halt and despite all their efforts to get her off using the ship's engines she remained fast.

LUNEDA

116nt. Steam trawler.
Built by Cochrane and Sons, Selby.
Launched November 1912.

Dimensions 130.0' x 23.0' x 12.7'

Eventually she listed alarmingly causing the skipper to order the ship's boat to be launched. The noise of the hull grinding and tearing on the sharp rock rang in the crew's ears as they quickly got into the boat and drifted away from their doomed ship. By now the snow was falling so heavily that they had no choice but to drift until daylight to try to get some idea of where they were They were to spend four cold, uncomfortable hours in the open boat before help arrived. Even when the snow abated and they could see that they were of Ardbeg they were afraid to try to make for the shore due to the many hidden dangerous reefs that lie of this part of the coast.

If the crew of the Fleetwood trawler *Luneda* had been a superstitious group they would probably have chosen not to sail together. Between them they had experienced an incredible sixteen shipwrecks. The chief engineer James Wilson had himself been wrecked nine times previously, the bosun had been on five other wrecked ships while two other members of the crew had each been wrecked once. Add to this the fact that the *Luneda* herself had been ashore and

As dawn broke the skipper of the steam lighter *Pibroch* noticed the wreck lying jammed on the rocks and steamed to the rescue. When he reached the *Luneda* and found that it was deserted he immediately began a search for the crew and luckily spotted the frozen crew in their boat some distance out to se shortly afterwards. They were landed safely at Port Ellen but their ship became a total wreck.

The wreck of the *Luneda* lies on a small reef called Sgeir Bratach which is marked but not named on the chart of the area. The position is 55°37.488'N, 006°05.644'W (GPS). The wreckage lies in a narrow gully between two rocky outcrops which almost break the surface two hundred yards west of the reef called Iomallach which is charted and is visible at all states of the tide.

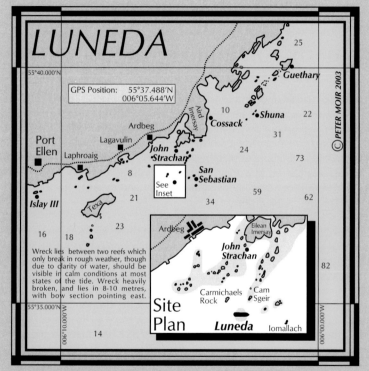

The wreck is well broken but is an interesting dive. As is common with wrecks in the area the most recognisable feature is the large boiler that lies half way along the gully. The bow of the ship faces east and is located at around 10 metres with the rest of the wreckage strewn along the rocky gully to the stern, with propeller in place, at 8 metres at the other end. The site is not subject to any tidal flow but can be very exposed to a heavy swell when the wind is from the south or east.

MARY ANN

250bn. Wooden brig.
Launched 1828.

Dimensions 84.0' x 22.0'x9.0'

Many island communities regarded the spoils of shipwrecks as fair game to help relieve the tedium and poverty of their existence and it was always particularly exciting when the cargo contained liquor. The story of the wreck of the Greenock brig *Mary Ann* was to become one of the most infamous in the history of Islay.

The voyage in May 1859 from Glasgow to New Brunswick with a cargo of 300 tons of pig iron, a large quantity of spirits and other general cargo had gone badly from the start. Shortly after setting off, Captain Pryce found that his ship was leaking badly and he had to put into Dublin for repairs. After repairs were completed they set off again but only got as far as Islay when she sprang a leak again. The captain, with his ship in danger of sinking beneath him, had no choice but to abandon her. The drifting hulk was taken in tow by a local fisherman who pulled her to Kilchoman Bay where she settled in shallow water.

The ship quickly began to break up in the surf spilling her valuable cargo into the sea to be washed ashore along the beach in the bay. News of the island's good fortune spread like wildfire and hundreds of islanders arrived for a gigantic party. Soon there were dozens of inebriated fisherfolk lying unconscious among the rocks along the seashore. Sergeant Kennedy and Constable Chisolm of the local police attempted to stop the pilfering but it was an impossible task. They managed to keep some kind of order during the day but, as night fell, the scenes got even more rowdy with fights breaking out between the gallant policemen and crowds of drunken islanders. The two men were forced to beat a hasty retreat taking refuge in Coul Farm from a group of thirty or forty who were now screaming like savages.

The next morning the beach looked like a battlefield with unconscious bodies strewn everywhere. One man, Donald McPhayden, had drunk so much that he had died from alcohol poisoning and later during the day two more died. Others were being carried away to be revived from their drunken stupors. There were still even some men fighting amongst themselves and a few drinking, singing and dancing. The *Mary Ann* herself was quickly reduced to a pile of smashed and broken timber and forgotten, but the escapades of the wreckers became infamous as one of the most unsavory incidents in the island's long history of shipwrecks.

MAYTHORN

593nt. Wooden barque.
Built in Quebec.
Launched 1864.

Dimensions 154.6' x 30.6' x 19.4'

The *Maythorn* left Liverpool with a cargo of pig iron and other general cargo bound for New York on Thursday 24th September, 1869 and sailed south into the Irish Sea. Shortly after leaving port they encountered a strong southerly wind and turned north to take the alternative route through the North Channel and then west into the Atlantic. Captain Anderson was to regret his decision to change course. As they reached the North Channel the captain retired to his bunk and was not to return on deck until it was too late and his ship was close to running aground. In the early hours of the morning of the 27th a light was seen to starboard and the coast of Islay appeared out of the darkness. The duty officer called for the captain but the 25 minutes it took him to arrive sealed his ship's fate and she ran aground on a reef near Port Ellen and became a total wreck. Captain Anderson was severely criticised at the subsequent enquiry both for being below deck for seven hours and for taking so long to come on deck when called for by his junior officer.

MILEWATER

112nt. Steel steam tug.
Built by R Duncan & Co, Port Glasgow.
Launched 1898.
(ex SUSAN McCAUSLAND ex FLYING CORMORANT)

Dimensions 135.2' x 24.0' x 12.0'

At one o'clock in the morning of 10th May, 1931 the inhabitants of the village of Port Ellen were awakened by the loud discharge of distress rockets fired from yet another ship ashore on the treacherous Mull of Oa. It was particularly dark and cold that night as the town and the nearby coastline was shrouded in a thick damp blanket of fog but the members of the local rocket brigade jumped from their beds, clambered into their clothes and rushed out into the cold night. They quickly got out their lifesaving equipment and raced to the assistance of the crew of the disabled ship.

Meanwhile the seven man crew of the Belfast steam tug *Milewater* which had indeed run aground in the fog on the east side of the Mull of Oa below Stremnish Farm struggled to get the ship's boat lowered into the water. Thankfully the night was fairly calm and they were able to get ashore safely with the help of the farmer from Stremnish and his four sons before the rocket crew or the Campbeltown lifeboat, which had also received the distress call, reached the scene. Interestingly the *Milewater* had been en route to Tiree from Larne to assist in the discharge of cargo from the wreck of SS *Malve* that had gone ashore at Tiree earlier in the year but instead was to become a wreck herself. By the following day reports from the local Lloyds agent indicated that the ship was settling back into the water and was already submerged from midships aft.

The Wreck Today

The wreck of the *Milewater* has been located in position 55°35.003'N, 006°15.711'W (GPS). She is well broken and lies in 5 to 11 metres of water close to the shore off Mullach Mor.

Steam tug *Milewater* ashore at Stremnish.

OCEAN

1300nt. Iron barque.
Built by Reid & Co, Port Glasgow.
Launched August 1873.
(ex AMYONE)

Dimensions 231.1' x 37.1' x 23.4'

The *Ocean* left Dublin on 1st November, 1911 bound for Norway in ballast with a crew of fifteen under the command of Captain A. Christopher. She sailed north and into a violent storm and on the 3rd, while off the west coast of Islay, her sails were blown away and she drifted, unmanageable, towards the rocky shore.

Early in the morning of the 4th, as dawn broke, two local men, Andrew Stevenson and Donald Ferguson, spotted the stricken vessel drifting off Machrie and followed her as she was swept north, ever closer to the shore. The crew huddled helplessly in the bow waiting for their ship to strike and hoping for a chance to save themselves.

She eventually came ashore, bow first, on a promontory just north of Kilchiaran Bay but, before the crew could jump ashore, the huge seas canted her round forcing the stern towards the rocks. Within a few minutes of striking the second time she broke in two leaving the crew in an even more perilous situation as they expected her to disintegrate at any minute. The brave captain took a rope and swam the short distance to the shore but was sadly killed as the swell smashed him against the rocks. As the wet, freezing crew members considered their situation the stern mast crashed down forming a tenuous link with the shore as it fell onto the nearby rocks. They began to scramble along it pulling themselves towards safety. Two men were swept off the mast and drowned but twelve others made it safely to the shore, five of them helped by the two brave men from Machrie who, by this time, had arrived on the scene and, with the security of a rope to the shore, plunged into the sea to help the remaining crew members. The last crewman, an old man, sat for four hours on the stern hatchway with the waves crashing over him but would not move to save himself. Eventually he disappeared below and was never seen again. By 2pm that day the ship had been smashed to pieces. The floating debris, which filled the many rocky gullies where she went ashore, was left as the only indication that a ship had wrecked there.

The Wreck Today

The wreck of the *Ocean* lies 900 metres north of Kilchiaran Bay in position 55°45.610'N, 006°28.112'W (GPS). Due to its exposed location, few parts of the vessel remain recognisable, key elements remaining include sections of steel mast, winches, anchor and chain and sections of keel and hull. The wreck has been compressed against the face of the rock shelf and barely extends further than 5 metres out to sea. There are a few gullies that run inshore and more wreckage can be found here. The bulk of the wreck lies in 3-5 metres of water, note the seabed shallows offshore from the wreck to around 1.5 metres, so take care when navigating in the area.

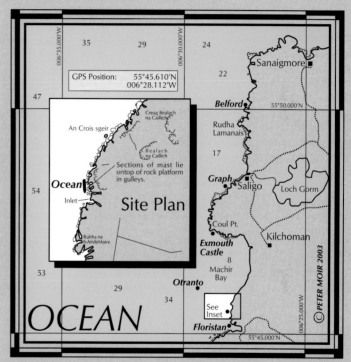

Sections of the masts can be found above waterline lying in rock pools on top of the rocks, these are not visible from sea level, but clearly broke off as the vessel was dashed against the rocks after her loss. This is not really a dive, as at low water springs you can stand on wreckage at the bow which is located to the south of the debris field. Kelp is also an extreme nuisance, catching on regulator, knife and fin straps. Due to the depth, this site can only be dived in extremely calm condition, and perhaps best over winter months when the kelp may have died back a bit.

OTRANTO

12,124gt. Steel steamship.
Built by Workman Clark & Co, Belfast.
Launched March 1909.

Dimensions 535.3' x 64.0' x 38.6'

The *Otranto* only managed five years service for her owners the Orient Steam Navigation Co., before the outbreak of the First World War. She was requisitioned by the government, converted into an armed merchant cruiser and served throughout the war. On 24th September, 1918, as the war neared its climax, she set sail on her final voyage from New York bound for Glasgow and Liverpool. She sailed in convoy HX50 escorted by the US cruisers *Louisiana* and *St. Louis* and the destroyer USS *Dorsey*. Captain Ernest W G Davidson and his 362 crew had 665 American troops aboard. On October 1st this compliment was supplemented by the unlucky crew of the French sailing ship *Croisine*, run down by the *Otranto* as the convoy, with lights out, sailed straight through a fleet of French fishing vessels. The convoy of thirteen ships, with a total of almost 20,000 troops aboard bound for the battlefields of Flanders, sailed in six columns, each column 3 cables from the next. The *Otranto* was the leading ship in column 3. Column 4 to the north was led by the SS *Kashmir*, an 8,985 ton liner of the P & O Line.

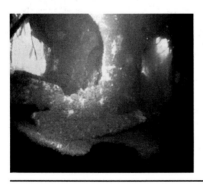

The voyage across the North Atlantic went well until, as they approached the North Channel, they encountered a violent gale which built up enormous waves and whipped the sea into streaks of white foam and spray. The convoy had been navigating for some days by dead reckoning as the visibility had not allowed any sightings to be taken. On the morning of 6th October, through the murk, the officers aboard both vessels spotted land. The master of the *Kashmir* rightly identified the land and the breakers that were less than two miles off his port bow, as the coast of Islay. The Officer of the Watch aboard the *Otranto* thought that the land he could see, little over a mile from his starboard bow, was Inishtrahull. Both ships' helms were put hard over and their inside screws stopped to steer away from the danger seen, the *Kashmir* to starboard, the *Otranto* to port, tragically turning them towards each other. The *Kashmir* turned quickly but the *Otranto* laboured in the huge seas. At 8:45am the two ships collided, the *Kashmir* striking the *Otranto* amidships on her port side almost at right angles despite the attempts by both crews to avoid the collision by reversing rudders and engines. The two ships, both badly damaged, quickly drifted apart and lost each other in the haze. The *Kashmir* survived but the *Otranto* was doomed. Water poured through a huge hole in her side soon extinguishing her fires and, despite letting go her huge anchors, she drifted helplessly in the direction of the rocky Islay coast.

HMS *Mounsey*, commanded by Lieutenant F W Craven, was the first ship to answer the SOS calls from the *Otranto* and by ten o'clock she was in sight of the stricken ship. It is difficult to imagine the scene during the rescue which followed. The massive liner dwarfing the destroyer with both rearing and plunging in the enormous swell and the disciplined lines of US troops waiting for their chance to jump onto the heaving deck of the *Mounsey*. The ships came together four times, the *Mounsey* smashing against the *Otranto's* sides. Each time wave after wave of men jumped for their lives. Many fell between the ships' sides and were crushed or drowned while many others were killed or badly injured as they crashed onto the destroyer's deck. The *Mounsey* then sailed for Belfast with 596 men aboard and in grave danger of sinking herself due to the overcrowding. This left around 400 still aboard the now rapidly sinking *Otranto*. She had hit bottom less than a half a mile from the shore and, as she was in danger of breaking up, Captain Davidson gave the order to abandon ship, only 16 were to survive the swim to the shore. The next day the bodies of the victims, including Captain Davidson, were washed ashore along the west coast of the island. They were buried in a special burial ground above Machir Bay overlooking the site of the loss of their ship.

It was the worst convoy disaster in the whole of the war. At the subsequent inquiry both ships were found equally to blame for the incident.

SS *Otranto*.

GPS Position: 55°45.796'N
006°28.611'W

Transit A

Centre end gable of large barn at Coull Farm inline with fence running down to shoreline.

Barn | Fence   Coull Farm

Machir Bay

Transit B

Cnoc nam Muc-chlach   Mast

Aline mast on hilltop between two prominent formations in cliff face below.

OTRANTO

24

Sanaigmore

22

Belford   55°50.000'N

Rudha Lamanais

32

17

Graph

Saligo   Loch Gorm

A

Coul Pt.

Exmouth Castle   Kilchoman

28   8 Machir Bay

Otranto

Ocean Floristan

B

55°45.000'N

© PETER MOIR 2003

The wreck of the *Otranto* is charted and lies in position 55°45.796'N, 006°28.611'W (GPS) which is at the south end of Machir Bay. The position quoted will put you in the middle of the engine room area, close to the propshafts. The wreck has been very heavily salvaged over the years but a huge amount of scattered wreckage still exists. Most impressive are her six huge boilers that sit in two parallel lines rising 5 metres from the seabed, although when visited in 2002 some of these were beginning to break up. The depth around the wreck is between 7 and 16 metres with the remains spread over a wide area on both sides of the reef on which she ran aground. Her deck guns lie to the shore side of the main wreckage, one is still prominent

at the north end of the wreckage. The site is subject to minimal tidal streams but is very exposed to the inevitable Atlantic swell, which can make diving difficult in other than ideal weather conditions.

Inside the shell of one of the boilers.

PATTERSONIAN

119nt. Steel steamship.
Built by J. P. Rennoldson & Son, South Shields.
Launched 1915.
(ex BLAYDONIAN)

    Dimensions 135.3' x 23.6' x 9.1'

The *Pattersonian*, which was owned by J A Gardner & Co, was en route from Ayr to Port Ellen and Tiree with stores for the RAF bases on the islands in the last days of World War II when she stranded on the Mull of Oa on 11th September, 1945. She had been caught in the vicious tides off Rubha nan Leacan in dense fog and had been swept ashore among the rocks on the headland. The crew managed to get ashore safely but the ship was doomed. Salvage crews boarded the ship on the 13th but found her tidal throughout and, as she was exposed to the continual buffeting of the Atlantic swells and was working on the rocks in a reported four knot tide, she was immediately abandoned as a total wreck.

The wreckage of the *Pattersonian* is scattered in shallow water among the rocks north east of Rubha nan Leacan in position 55°38.810'N, 006°15.917'W (GPS). The tidal rips off the point here are extremely fierce and great care must be taken by both diver and boathandler in the vicinity of the wreck.

ROTHESAY CASTLE

7016gt. Iron steamship.
Built by Harland & Wolff, Belfast.
Launched 1935.

  Dimensions 443.5' x 61.3' x 32.0'

The *Rothesay Castle* was owned by the Union Castle Line and left New York on her final voyage on 27th December, 1939 bound for Glasgow with a cargo of food. As they approached the Scottish coast and the notorious killing ground in the North Channel, Captain Ernest William Hyde Furlong ran his ship at its full speed of 16 knots and steered a zig zag course in an effort to avoid the attentions of the German U-boat commanders. Unfortunately in his zeal to avoid the German submarines he ran his ship ashore on the north west corner of Islay near Nave Island. At a later enquiry the cause of the loss of the ship was found to be the captain's incorrect sailing procedure and his failure to take depth soundings. His certificate of competency was suspended for a year.

The *Rothesay Castle's* SOS message was heard by the coastguard in the early hours of the morning of the 5th of January and quickly the Port Askaig lifeboat was manned and on its way to the reported position, 5 miles north of Coul Point. On reaching the area the crew of the lifeboat could not immediately find the grounded ship and it was not until dawn, some hours later, that she was finally located. She had run onto a reef stretching to the south west of Nave Island, close to Eilean Beag and was lying on an uneven, rocky bottom with water in holds 1,2 and 3. By the following morning the sea and the swell had done their worst and her back was broken rendering her a total wreck. An inspection a day later by a Lloyds agent confirmed this and fourteen of the crew were taken off by the lifeboat, which had been at the scene for over thirty hours. They were taken back to Port Ellen and sailed for Glasgow. The next day the rest of the crew were taken off and she was abandoned. It was not long before the massive swell smashed the ship to pieces and she disappeared beneath the surface.

The Wreck Today

The swell that so quickly destroyed the *Rothesay Castle* makes this wreck an exciting dive that should only be tackled by experienced divers or in perfect weather conditions. The wreckage lies in around 8 metres to the south west of Eilean Beag in position 55°53.216'N, 006°21.733'W (GPS). Although the ship has been heavily salvaged, there is still a substantial amount of wreckage, with her prop shaft providing the most spectacular aspect of the dive. The shaft is raised from the seabed, probably as a result of the stern area being upside down, and points into the distance like a huge gun, reaching to within two

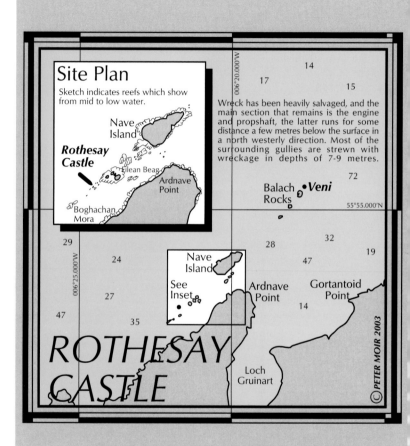

metres of the surface. Around it large pieces of hull, keel and the engines are still visible. The site is very exposed and very susceptible to swell which, combined with the often jagged metal of the wreck, make the dive only for a calm day and for the most experienced diver although, probably because of this fact, there is more wreckage remaining than on many of the other Islay wrecks.

SAN SEBASTIAN

123nt. Steel steam trawler.
Built by Collingwood Shipbuilding Co.
Launched 1918.

Dimensions 125.7' x 23.5' x 12.7'

The Boston Deep Sea & Ice Company's trawler *San Sebastian* ran aground on rocks off Ardbeg in poor visibility in the early hours of the morning of 16th January, 1937 as she steamed north towards the fishing grounds from her home port of Fleetwood. As she struck a reef about two miles offshore she rolled over onto her side and sank almost immediately. She went down so quickly that her crew had no time to prepare or to fire distress signals and they were plunged into the icy water to fight for their lives. Of the crew of thirteen, nine made it to various nearby rocks but four were lost.

Small groups of men huddled together on the exposed rocks until dawn when the coaster *Pibroch*, on the last stage of her voyage from the Clyde to Lagavulin Distillery, passed by and noticed the frozen men waving from the rocks. Eight of the crewmen were taken aboard and ferried to Ardbeg but the

last man, Captain Richard Pook, was missed as he had reached a rock a little further from the wreck. His crew thought that he had been lost with their other colleagues. As the day wore on the captain began to think that he would have to spend another lonely, cold night on his rock and, thinking that he might not survive, decided to try to reach the shore swimming from rock to rock. He had covered about a mile towards the shore when, at around

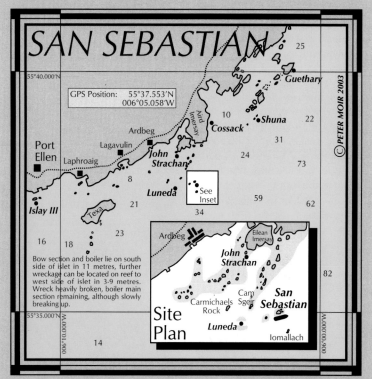

2pm, some eleven hours after his ship went down, his movements were noticed from the shore by a local fisherman called McAllister who put out in his boat and brought the exhausted skipper to safety. At the subsequent enquiry held in Liverpool Captain Pook was found totally to blame for the loss of his ship in not verifying his position, not being on deck when he should have been, setting a wrong course and making no allowance for the tide. His

San Sebastian.

certificate was suspended for 12 months and they even refused to grant him a mate's certificate in the meantime.

The Wreck Today

The wreck of the *San Sebastian* lies on the south east side of a reef called Garrisgeirs which is shown but not named on charts of the area. It lies north west of the reef called Iomallach, which is named on the charts, and close by the wreck of the *Luneda*. The approximate position of the *San Sebastian* is 55°37.553'N, 006°05.058'W (GPS). The larger parts of the wreck, including her huge boiler, lie at the foot of the reef in 11 metres on a sand and shingle seabed. There are also substantial portions of wreckage spread across the top of the reef in 3 or 4 metres. The site is not subject to tidal flows but can be exposed to a heavy swell when the wind is from the south or east.

SS **Shuna** ashore near Eilean a Chuirn, Islay

SHUNA

912nt. Steel steamship.
Built by J. Crown and Sons, Sunderland.
Launched September 1915.

Dimensions 250.0' x 37.3' x 17.2'

October 1936, like many other winter months in the Western Isles, brought a series of gales that created havoc with the lives of many islanders and brought communications to a halt. The steamship *Shuna* became the victim of one of these gales when she went aground near Eilean a'Chuirn on October 17th. As she clung to the rocks her distress calls went unheard in the chaos on the island. Her luck was to change as a Northern and Scottish Airways flight heading for Islay flew over her and she was spotted by the plane's pilot, Captain J.A. Harkins. At first Captain Harkins thought nothing much about it but, on landing, he was astonished to hear that no one on the island knew about the wreck and that, as a result, nothing was being done to mount a rescue. The telephone lines on the island were down due to the storm and it was only once he was airborne again that a radio message could be relayed via Renfrew to Port Askaig lifeboat which immediately launched and headed for the grounded ship.

When the lifeboat reached the site they could see that there was little they could do for the ship but, as the weather had calmed somewhat, the crew were in no immediate danger. They took off and landed six of the twenty crewmen and returned to the wreck to stand by. An inspection by a salvage crew on the 20th revealed the *Shuna* had driven right over a shallow reef and was now aground amidships with her forward end awash and, although the remainder of the ship was undamaged, the buckled hull plating under the bridge made it clear that successful salvage was impossible. The remaining crew were taken off and the *Shuna* was left to her fate as the weather closed in once again. On the 28th it was reported that she had parted amidships and both ends had sunk on either side of the rock.

The Wreck Today

The wreck of the *Shuna* lies where she sank in position 55°39.142'N, 006°02.431'W (GPS) which is on a small reef lying south of Ceann nan Sgeirean. The major portion of the wreckage lies in 12 - 15 metres on the seaward side of the reef but there is also wreckage in shallower water including her boiler, which sits on top of the reef in around 4 metres. Although well broken due

to the attentions of various salvage teams there is still a lot of wreckage to be explored. The site is somewhat exposed to winds from the south and east but, like all of the sites on this part of the Islay coast, is sheltered from the worst of the swell and tides affecting the rest of the island.

THOMAS

765nt. Wooden barque.
Built in Nova Scotia.

The *Thomas* left Greenock for Halifax, Nova Scotia at 7am on 14th August, 1857 under the command of Captain Bell with a cargo of railway machinery valued at £16,000, a considerable sum in 1857. She was towed by steam tug as far as the Cumbrae's then sailed off on her long voyage west across the Atlantic. By midnight she had passed the Mull of Kintyre making good time in a steady moderate breeze. Early the following day the wind died and she wallowed helplessly unable to make headway for all that day and most of the next. In the early evening of the 16th she was enveloped in thick fog and started drifting northwards towards Islay. The captain ordered continual soundings but, unaware of the drift north, found nothing to disturb him until, at 10:40pm, the crew heard breakers close to their starboard bow. The helm was put hard over but it was too late. Caught in the fierce tide off the Rhinns of Islay she swept ashore under the lighthouse. Distress guns were fired but the local fishermen at Portnahaven could not find the wreck in the poor visibility. The crew made it safely ashore and later returned to salvage the sails and other loose fittings. A week later she was reported to be breaking up and all hope of salving the machinery aboard was abandoned.

The Wreck Today

The wreck of the *Thomas* is Islay's most unusual wreck. She lies at 55°40.249'N, 006°30.933'W (GPS) in a deep gully directly under Orsay Lighthouse making a dramatic dive in the right conditions. In bad conditions the site would be horrific. The gully is 17 metres deep at the outer end sloping gently to about 12 metres at the inner end and is 4 metres

wide narrowing at points to less than 2 metres. Incredibly, the wreckage has been absorbed into the rock sides of the gully and metal items including parts of the machinery cargo can be seen shining in the rock. The seabed too includes tangled metal among the boulders. The power of the sea in a storm in this narrow inlet can only be imagined but the absorption of the wreckage in the rock itself gives testament to its awesome power. Definitely a site to be avoided in rough weather or heavy swell. 100 metres offshore the

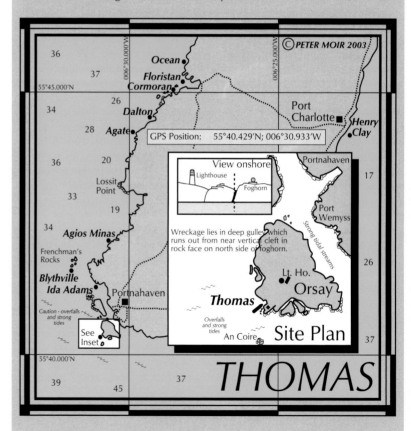

© PETER MOIR 2003

GPS Position: 55°40.429'N; 006°30.933'W

View onshore

Lighthouse

Foghorn

Wreckage lies in deep gulley which runs out from near vertical cleft in rock face on north side of foghorn.

Thomas

Lt. Ho.

Orsay

Overfalls and strong tides

An Coire

Site Plan

THOMAS

boisterous tide rip, reaching 6-8 knots at mid tide, is another potentially dangerous aspect of this site. However in good weather, good underwater visibility and with the exercise of due care the dive is very good. The wreck, the underwater rock formation and the sealife, particularly in the deep rock bowl at the head of the gully, make a memorable combination.

Concreted rail track shoes in base of gully.

TOBAGO

430nt. Steel steamship.
Built by Lindholmens VA, Gothenburg
Launched 1900.
(ex LATAVA ex SUNDMAR ex ERICA VINGA

Dimensions 191.0' x 30.6' x 12.3'

The Latvian steamship Tobago's last voyage began as it was to end - badly. On July 26th, 1940 she was involved in a collision with a hired trawler in Reykjavik harbour and had to delay her departure for repairs before setting off for Ardrossan on the 8th of August. It is not clear if the damage from the collision contributed to her loss as records are vague due to wartime reporting restrictions but the next report of her whereabouts, from the SS Highwood on the 13th, states that the Tobago was ashore near the Rhinns of Islay with the Highwood standing by to take off her crew. A more accurate report the next day placed her one mile south of Lossit Bay with foredeck submerged six feet at high water and likely to become a total wreck. Local reports indicate that she was heavily salvaged at a later date and the authors could find no trace of her at the reported site.

TUSCANIA

8714nt. Steel steamship.
Built by A Stephens & Sons, Glasgow.
Launched September 1914.

Dimensions 549.3' x 66.0' x 41.7'

The Cunard-Anchor liner Tuscania never sailed for her owners on a peacetime voyage. Her maiden voyage from Glasgow and Liverpool to New York was in February 1915. In September of the same year she was involved in a dramatic mid Atlantic rescue of 339 passengers and 70 crew of the burning Greek liner Athinai. In 1917 she was requisitioned as a troop carrier under the Liner Requisition Scheme and it was on this service, in early 1918, as the First World War reached its climax, that she left New York on her final voyage as part of convoy HX20 bound for Liverpool. The convoy consisted of eight troop and provision ships escorted by a small fleet of torpedo destroyers. She had 2500 US troops aboard plus her own officers and crew numbering close to 200 under the command of Captain Peter McLean.

The nervous chatter of the troops aboard increased as they neared the British coast but many of them would not live to face the Germans in the trenches. As they sailed towards the North Channel they were heading straight for the German submarine UB77 commanded by Captain Wilhelm Meyer lying in wait to pounce on the approaching ships. Captain Meyer first sighted the convoy in the late afternoon of 5th February and set a parallel course to pick out his target and choose the right moment for his attack. They were about seven miles north of Rathlin when he fired three torpedoes from 4,000 yards at the Tuscania. Two of the torpedoes raced harmlessly behind the ship but the third hit her amidships.

It was immediately obvious that the blow was fatal. She listed heavily to starboard severely hampering the launching of her lifeboats. Some of the boats fell into the sea as they were being lowered tipping their occupants into the icy water and, at other parts of the ship where lowering was impossible, some of the men jumped into the sea in an attempt to save themselves. Meanwhile the SOS radio message was answered by three of the escort destroyers, Grasshopper,

Mosquito and *Pigeon*, who raced to the scene and clustered round the sinking ship to take off more survivors. Some four hours after the initial impact of the German torpedo the *Tuscania* slowly slipped beneath the surface. It was some days before the final death toll of 166 was established as the survivors were taken to various ports by the different ships that had helped in the rescue.

SS *Tuscania*.

The wreck of the *Tuscania* is reported to lie in approximate position 55°29.382'N, 006°20.113'W some 6 miles due south of the Mull Of Oa where a monument stands to commemorate the loss of both the *Tuscania* and the *Otranto*. Seabed depths around the wreck are around 105 metres and the wreck rises some 14-16 metres in places. The wreck, along with other deep water wrecks in the North Channel such as the *Calgarian, Empire Heritage* and HMS *Audacious* have been dived by a number of teams suitably trained and experienced to dive on what must be some of the most challenging dives around the coast of the United Kingdom. The conditions on the wreck are variously reported from dark, low visibility with strong tide to not requiring a torch and a spectacular site. What is clear, this is probably one of the most extreme wreck sites available to divers and should only be visited by those suitably trained and experienced to dive to these depths.

VENI

1781nt. Steamship.
Built by W. Pickersgill, Sunderland.
Launched July 1901.

Dimensions 324.1' x 47.1' x 21.8'

As the crew of the Air Ministry meteorological ship *Weather Recorder* set off for their lonely vigil at their station in the North Atlantic they could have no idea of the part they were about to play in a dramatic sea rescue off the coast of Islay. As they steamed through the North Channel, with the lights of Londonderry off their port bow, a mayday message crackled from the ship's radio. The Norwegian steamship *Veni*, en route from Leith to Sfax, North Africa, in ballast, had run aground and was sinking fast. She gave her position as off Colonsay. It was the early hours of Sunday January 11th, 1948 and a 50mph gale had pushed the ship east of her intended course. She was in fact on the Balach Rocks, a treacherous, unlit reef lying two miles off Ardnave Point. Captain Ford on the *Weather Recorder* sent a message to the *Veni* telling them that he would be at the scene about 4:30am.

Members of the Veni crew safe in Greenock last night.

MET. SH

ISLAND OF ISLAY

DANGEROUS REEFS

RAIL DRIVERS' CALL-UP IS DEFERRED

CALL-UP to the Services of railway drivers and firemen has been deferred. Recruits to the footplate and for the workshops and maintenance yards are now being given top priority.

Aerial view of the wrecked Norwegian steamer Veni.

U.S. Jews Buy Super-H.E.

SUPER-EXPLOSIVES discovered in two secret dumps in the New York area were bought by the Jewish Agency to arm Jews in Palestine against threatened Arab

Aboard the *Veni* Captain Pederson and his twenty seven crew were relieved to hear that help was on its way as their ship, which was badly holed and bumping heavily on the seabed, was gradually slipping off the reef and sinking as she filled with water. As the *Weather Recorder* approached the area her searchlight was illuminated and directed into the stormy night sky to attract the attention of the *Veni's* crew. This signal was answered by a series of red flares from the *Veni*. The crew of the *Veni* had manned the pumps hoping to stay afloat until the *Weather Recorder* arrived but, as 4am approached, Captain Pederson decided that he had to get the crew off the ship and into the lifeboats as he believed that his ship was about to go down.

By now the *Weather Recorder* was only half a mile from the grounded ship and standing by to pick up the shipwrecked crew at daybreak when they could more safely approach the wreck. Thankfully the storm abated somewhat and the crew of the *Veni* managed to launch the boats without too much difficulty. As the crew scrambled over the side of the ship the bosun and another member of the crew plunged into the water as the ship lurched in the huge swell. The bosun was injured as he crashed against the side of the lifeboat but he and the other seaman were quickly pulled into the waiting lifeboats. When they were all safely in the boats they fired white flares to let Captain Ford know that they were off the ship. The *Weather Recorder* steamed carefully to within two lengths of the *Veni* and picked up the crew who, apart from the two injured seamen who had fallen in the water, were none the worse for their adventure.

Later in the day the salvage tug *Salveda* arrived on the scene but when they inspected the wreck on the following day they quickly concluded that salvage was impossible and she was abandoned.

The Wreck Today

The wreck of the *Veni* is located in position 55° 55.465'N, 006° 17.452'W (GPS), in 18 - 20 metres of water north of the outer most reef of the Balach Rocks. The stern section is fairly in tact and other pieces of wreckage are strewn around on the sandy seabed. This is an extremely exposed site, subject to huge swell even on calm days, only suitable for experienced divers and requiring good boat cover. In anything other than calm weather the site should be avoided.

The *Wyre Majectic* aground off Bunnahabhainn - 1992.

WYRE MAJESTIC

338t. Steel motor vessel.
Built by Cochrane and Sons, Selby.
Launched 1956.

Dimensions 127.5' x 27.0' x 13.5'

The crews of the two Fleetwood trawlers *Wyre Majestic* and her sister ship *Wyre Defence* had planned to spend a last night in Oban before heading south for home. They landed their catch at Oban around lunchtime on the 18th October, 1974 but, as the harbour was particularly busy, they could not get a berth for the night. The two skippers agreed to continue their voyage home directly, planning to head down the Firth of Lorne, west of Scarba and Jura then through the Sound of Islay.

All went well until they reached the entrance to the Sound of Islay around 7pm that evening. By this time the sun had set and in the growing darkness the *Wyre Defence* was a couple of miles ahead of her sister ship. The narrow confines of the Sound of Islay, with fiercesome currents which reach 5 knots at times, is not the best passage in the dark but, as high tide was around 8pm, the skippers were unconcerned. It is not clear exactly why the *Wyre Majestic* went aground but, shortly after entering the Sound and with the bosun at the helm, she ran full speed ahead onto the rocks at Rubha a Mhail.

Her distress call was picked up ashore and the Islay lifeboat was launched from Port Askaig and was quickly on the scene. The *Wyre Defence* turned back and was also standing by her sister ship. First the lifeboat then the *Wyre Defence* tried to pull her off but neither could manage it. The *Wyre Majestic* had a large gash in her and had quickly filled with water and settled heavily on the rocks. Five of her crew were taken off by the lifeboat but the skipper and two others stayed aboard hoping that the salvage tug that had been called out would be able to get her off. The tug arrived the next day but attempts to pull her off the rocks failed. She was abandoned and became a total wreck. The wreck was salvaged to some degree but still sits where she ran aground in position 55°52.989'N, 006°07.218'W (GPS). It is possible to board her although her

structural condition looks extremely unsafe. In recent years the *Wyre Majestic* has begun to break up, no doubt hastened by the strong tides which constantly race around her hull. The photographs below were taken in 2002, and clearly show that all of the wreck forward of the wheelhouse is now below water level.

The wreck of the *Wyre Majestic* - 2002.

ISLAY

Listed below are a selection of 65 smaller vessels wrecked within this area. This list is included as a basis for further research. Names suffixed by (S) denote extensive salvage work or total removal subsequent to date of loss.

NAME	BUILT	TONNAGE	HULL	TYPE	LOST	CAUSE	LOCATION
Amity	1863		W	Bg	16.01.1875	S	Bowmore
Alma Dawson	1917	3985t	S	SS	24.11.1940	M	West of Islay
Assyria	1872	729nt	W	Bk	20.03.1884	S	Texa Island
Bonito	1867	157nt	W	Bn	21.11.1881	S	Loch Indaal
Brittany	1898	2926gt	S	SS	05.02.1918	S	15 miles West of Islay
Bulldog	1859	64gt	W	PS	14.09.1869	S	Black Rock, Sound of Islay
Bussorah	1862	625gt	I	SS	09.02.1863	F	5m West of Islay
Calgarian	1914	17515t	-	SS	01.03.1918	T	10 miles South of Islay
Carl Angell	1866	500bn	W	Bk	26.05.1886	F	Off west coast of Islay
Chevalier	1853	820nt	W	Bk	20.01.1883	S	Coul Point
Cleopatra	1793	140bn	W	Bgn	02.02.1832	S	Gartbreck, Loch Indaal
Constance	1868	93nt	W	Sk	01.05.1902	S	Sound of Islay
Cossack	1908	92gt	S	SS	13.06.1923	S	Eilean Chuirn, Ardmore Islands
Daylight	1879	34nt	I	SS	07.02.1881	S	Carnstack
Dunrobin Castle	1872	71nt	W	Sr	12.03.1879	S	Ardmore Island
Earl Lennox	1914	226t	S	Atr	23.10.1917	M	S. entrance to Sound of Islay
Edith Morgan	1866	129nt	W	Sr	16.01.1881	S	Black Rock, Sound of Islay
Edmiston	-	-	W	Bgn	06.03.1863	S	Black Rock, Sound of Islay
Eliza	-	-	W	Bk	05.04.1855	S	Laggan Bay
Eliza Charlotte	1857	37nt	W	K	06.11.1900	S	Oversay
Ella	1867	440nt	W	Bg	23.06.1893	S	Glennastle
Empire Adventure	1921	5142t	S	SS	20.09.1940	T	Off west Islay
Erwentia	1856	464bn	W	Bk	21.11.1864	S	Conisby, Loch Indaal
Fern	1891	84nt	I	SS	15.07.1907	S	Sanaig Bay
Flying Falcon(S)	1904	184gt	S	Stg	27.09.1917	S	Machir Bay
Forest Chief	1864	1054nt	W	S	06.11.1872	S	Machir Bay
Gannet	1890	112nt	I	SS	26.11.1896	S	Port Ellen
Islay I	1849	325gt	I	PS	00.01.1866	S	Port Ellen
Jacksonville	1944	6301nt	S	T	30.08.1944	T	West of Islay

NAME	BUILT	TONNAGE	HULL	TYPE	LOST	CAUSE	LOCATION
Jean	-	-	W	S	09.09.1870	S	Loch Indaal
John Laverock	1841	90nt	W	Sr	25.09.1853	S	Nave Island
John Swan	1873	508nt	W	Bg	04.01.1889	S	Sound of Texa
La Plata	1866	596nt	W	Bk	16.11.1888	S	Machir Bay
Lexington	-	344bn	W	Bk	25.12.1865	F	4 miles West of Coul Point
Lillie M	1865	377nt	W	Bk	05.08.1871	F	10mls SW Islay
Louise Felice	1867	114nt	W	S	02.12.1876	S	Port Charlotte
Maggie Cross	1869	179nt	W	Bn	14.12.1880	S	Port Charlotte
Margaret McGowan		58nt	I	Sr	11.12.1883	S	Bowmore
Mary Ellen	1862	97nt	W	Sr	21.09.1879	S	Sound of Islay
Minerva	1816	135bn	W	Bgn	15.12.1827	S	Ardbeg
Mountpark	1885	302nt	I	SS	13.06.1887	S	Sound of Islay
Nanny Lathan	1867	66nt	W	Sr	22.11.1881	S	Port an Troan
Narwhal	1893	42nt	S	SS	18.01.1897	S	Loch Indaal
Nations	1854	48nt	W	Sr	25.02.1880	S	Port Ellen
Neptune	1892	38nt	I	SS	29.09.2898	F	Off McArthurs Head
Nils Gorthen	-	1809gt	S	SS	13.08.1940		Off west Islay
Norman	1891	1041gt	S	SS	25.05.1900	F	5 miles W of Oversay Lt. Ho
Royal Recovery	1789	82bn	W	Bg	04.10.1798	C	Sound of Islay
St Tudwal	1895	207gt	S	SS	12.08.1934	F	4mls SWbyW Texa
Scotland(S)	1870	-	I	SS	14.10.1870	S	Black Rock, Sound of Islay
Sealby	1839	85nt	W	Sr	25.01.1868	S	Coul Point
Seavar	-	-	S	Str	18.05.1950	F	Off W Islay
Serb	1916	95gt	S	SS	05.12.1925	S	Goill Rock, Ardbeg
Sir Colin	1858	106nt	W	Bn	09.09.1870	S	Lossit Pt
Stockholm			W	Bg	01.12.1818	S	Saligo
Surprise	1864	79nt	I	SS	21.12.1906	S	Off Ardmore
Sutherness	1915	269gt	S	Str	10.06.1961	F	15 miles SW Islay
Swift	1838	62nt	W	Sr	22.04.1884	S	Port Charlotte
T W Stuart	1896	252gt	S	SS	20.11.1928	S	Port Ellen
Thistle	1836	264bn	W	Bk	27.01.1845	S	Laggan Point, Loch Indaal
Toward	1861	58nt	W	Sr	11.12.1883	S	The Ard, Port Ellen
Vesterbotten	1850	376nt	W	Bk	11.12.1890	S	Mull of Oa
Vivid	1883	134nt	I	Syt	08.07.1913	S	Sound of Islay
Waverley	1894	39nt	W	Str	05.05.1896	C	4mls off Oversay
Wobena	-	-	W	Bk	01.10.1873	S	Off The Ard, Port Ellen

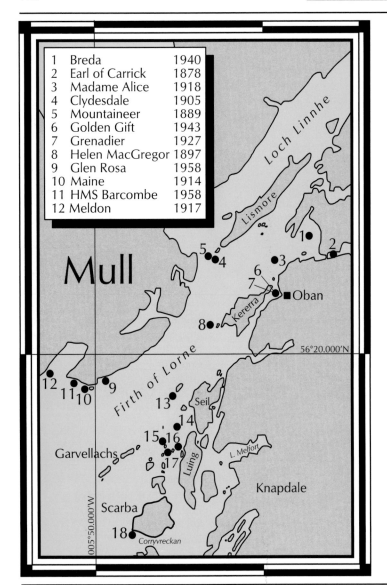

1	Breda	1940
2	Earl of Carrick	1878
3	Madame Alice	1918
4	Clydesdale	1905
5	Mountaineer	1889
6	Golden Gift	1943
7	Grenadier	1927
8	Helen MacGregor	1897
9	Glen Rosa	1958
10	Maine	1914
11	HMS Barcombe	1958
12	Meldon	1917

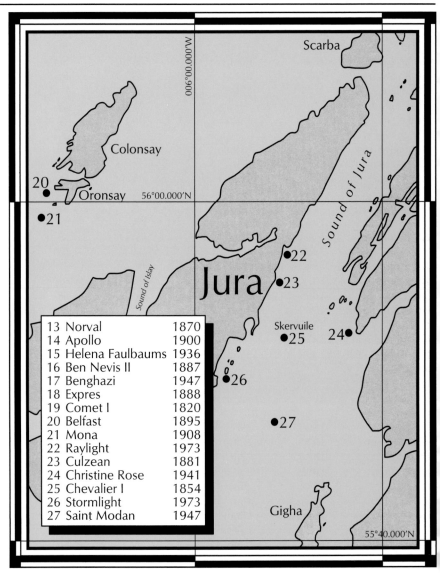

13	Norval	1870
14	Apollo	1900
15	Helena Faulbaums	1936
16	Ben Nevis II	1887
17	Benghazi	1947
18	Expres	1888
19	Comet I	1820
20	Belfast	1895
21	Mona	1908
22	Raylight	1973
23	Culzean	1881
24	Christine Rose	1941
25	Chevalier I	1854
26	Stormlight	1973
27	Saint Modan	1947

JURA, LORNE AND OBAN

Chapter 3

WEST LOCH TARBERT TO LOCH LINNHE

This stretch of water is one of the most interesting around the Scottish coastline. The imposing island of Jura, with its towering Paps, sweeps north from the Sound of Islay and forms the western shore of the Sound of Jura, a three mile wide channel which is well over 100 metres deep for much of its length. At the north end of Jura, in the narrow channel between Jura and Scarba, lies the Gulf of Corryvreckan - 209 metres deep at one point - and its famous whirlpool - the third largest in the world. Indeed, this entire area has more whirlpools, overfalls and tidal races than any other area in Scotland. The Dorus Mor at the entrance to Loch Craignish regularly has tidal streams of more than six knots. The Sound of Luing, Cuan Sound and Little Corryvreckan, between Scarba and Lunga, provide some of the most exciting drift dives anywhere.

North into the Firth of Lorne the towering cliffs of the south coast of Mull come into view. If you're lucky you could catch sight of a golden eagle here or perhaps a porpoise or two. The firth was a major staging point for convoys en route to America during World War Two. The little island of Kerrera guards the entrance to the main town in the region - Oban. The bustling coastal town with its busy harbour is the departure point for ferries to most of the Western Isles. It is also the diving capital of the west coast. North of Oban, past the raging Falls of Lora - another natural wonder as the falls reverse as the tide changes - the Firth of Lorne narrows, with Lismore and its lighthouse showing the entrance to the Sound of Mull, to the west and enters the southern reaches of Loch Linnhe which stretches to the foot of Ben Nevis, Scotland's highest mountain.

This section of coastline is less densely populated with shipwrecks than its predecessors. This is mainly because the area is less exposed to the open Atlantic and because of its narrow channels and fast flowing tidal streams, it is therefore less heavily used by larger vessels. The southern section of this area is populated with smaller vessels and it is not until you reach Belnahua and the wreck of the *Helena Faulbaums* that larger more intact wrecks can be found. Another larger and intact shipwreck in the area is that of the *Breda*, probably Scotland's most dived shipwreck, which lies in reasonably sheltered waters north of Oban. Sites south of the Island of Kerrera tend to be clear in terms of visibility with strong tidal streams clearing away any silty deposits. Once you move up into lower Loch Linnhe and around Oban while visibility is generally good, care must be taken when diving shipwrecks as they tend to be covered with silt which will reduce visibility locally when disturbed.

As noted above, Oban is the main centre for sport diving on the west coast, and attracts divers from all over the world. There are a number of dive operators working out of this port who offer trips to most areas covered by this book.

APOLLO

308nt. Iron steamship.
Built by Barrow Shipbuilding Co Ltd.
Launched April 1874.

Dimensions 182.0' x 24.1' x 12.4'

The Bono Rock at the north entrance to the Sound of Luing is well situated to catch unwary ships as they navigate through the treacherous tides of this part of the coast. The rock, which lies in the middle of the channel, doesn't break surface, even at the lowest tides, but reaches to within one metre of it. Even the kelp, which can be seen at low tide, disappears below water at high tide. It is probably therefore surprising that its only significant victim is the SS *Apollo*.

The *Apollo* was owned by J M Lennard and Sons of Middlesborough. She was en route from Aberdeen to Newport with a cargo of granite sets under the command of Captain G Guthrie when she ran aground on the rock in dense fog on 15th August, 1900. The captain blamed his misfortune on the combination of the fog, which he said had come down very quickly, and the strong tides that were running at the time. In any event, he was still steaming at more or less full speed when they hit as, when his ship ran straight onto the rock from the north, she was carried right over it leaving the stern high on the rock above water and the foredeck under water. The damage sustained during the impact was severe leaving the hull badly twisted and the boiler raised nearly a foot out of position. The crew made it to Easdale in the ship's boats but it was obvious that the ship would not be saved. The swell that continually washes over the rock made inspection by divers or removal of the cargo onto smaller vessels extremely difficult and, although the exact details are not recorded, she eventually became a total wreck.

The Wreck Today

The Bono Rock is not one rock but three reefs lying north west of the red can buoy which guides passing shipping away from it. The wreck lies between the northerly and westerly reef in position 56°16.283'N, 005°41.083'W (GPS). The

wreck itself has obviously been well salvaged over the years but a considerable amount of material still remains lying in depths of 5-11 metres. The cargo of granite sets is lying in huge piles across the site with tangled wreckage in between. The remains of the boiler and the stern section, now lying at the west side of the wreck, with rudderpost and propeller are the most recognisable items. The position of the stern section would suggest that, at some point, the wreck was swept off the rock from the north settling on the seabed facing towards the north east. The site is exposed and subject to heavy swell and is also in an area where strong tides could also be a hazard. Good boat cover is essential.

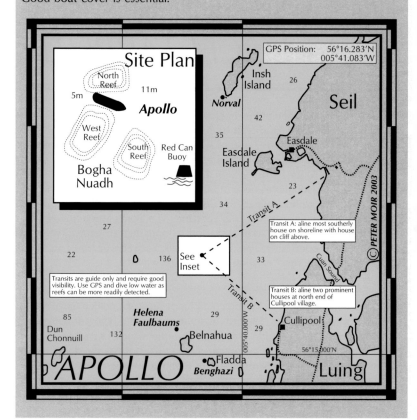

HMS *BARCOMBE*

730dt. Boom defence vessel.
Built by Goole Shipbuilding & Repair Co.
Launched 1938.

Dimensions 173.7' x 32.3' 9.5'

If it had not been for a stroke of good luck, some of the thirty four crew of the wrecked boom defence vessel *Barcombe* may not have survived. They had endured twenty two hours exposed to the cold and rain of a wintry January night and day when their distress flares were finally spotted by the crew of the fishing boat *Rosebud*. The *Rosebud* had been fishing off Tiree and would normally have taken the longer, safer route back to Oban via the Sound of Mull but skipper Tim Ross had decided to take the more dangerous route via the Sound of Iona and the south west of Mull to get his crew back home as quickly as possible. As they passed the entrance to Loch Buie, on Mull's south coast, they found the *Barcombe* ashore east of the Loch with her cold, wet and exhausted crew aboard their half submerged ship.

The *Barcombe*, under the command of Lieutenant Commander Derek Charles Godfrey, had herself been involved in the rescue of H M Submarine *Taciturn* aground in Campbeltown Loch only a week earlier, and was on her way from her home port of Greenock to Rosyth when she ran aground on 13th January, 1958 in fog. It was clear that they had made a serious navigation error because, as they hit the shore, they sent out a radio signal indicating that they were ashore on Oronsay. A huge rescue effort immediately got under way with her sister ship, the *Barrington*, and the submarine rescue ship *Kingfisher*, setting out from Greenock, the Islay lifeboat from Port Askaig, the Naval tug *Saucy* which had been in the area and the island coastguards on Oronsay, all joining the search for the grounded ship. Plans were also being made to put up search aircraft but these were abandoned, as the cloud base at Oronsay was too low for safety. After eighteen hours of fruitless searching and a worrying silence from the radio of the *Barcombe*, another radio message was received and the search area was changed to the Garvellachs. Shortly after this, some twenty one hours after the *Barcombe* had gone aground; she was spotted by the crew of the *Rosebud* on the Mull coast.

Meanwhile the crew of the *Barcombe* had spent a very uncomfortable night and day aboard their ship and ashore on the barren rocky coast of south Mull. When the ship first went aground they were plunged into darkness as the generators failed and, with no clear idea of where they were or what their situation was, decided to abandon ship and go ashore. One seaman, named Norman Lovell, volunteered to swim ashore with a line and the rest of the crew followed to find themselves on a small rocky beach at the foot of a three hundred foot cliff. The only possible route to safety was up and so they tied themselves together into teams and started the dangerous night time climb to the top. A few of them made it but most of the crew spent the night clinging to the cliff before returning, exhausted, to the beach the next morning. Their only option now was to return to their ship, which, when daylight arrived, they could see was in no immediate danger, and wait for rescue to arrive. They were very relieved when the *Rosebud* arrived on the scene. Over the next few hours the other rescue ships also arrived to take the injured to Oban and the rest of the crew back to the Clyde.

The following day divers were standing by to examine the ship but couldn't do so because of the heavy swell that pounded the ship and the coastline. The swell was grinding the half submerged vessel heavily on the rocks causing further damage to her already battered hull. She became a total wreck. She was sold for scrap to Northern Shipbreaking on 12th January, 1959 and subsequently heavily salvaged.

The Wreck Today

Due to the attentions of the salvage teams only twisted scraps of metal and a few hull plates among the rocks remain in approximate position 56°18.868'N, 005°52.392'W (GPS). The wreckage lies parallel to the shore in around 5 metres with some interesting bits and pieces still to be found under the rocks. There are reports of larger pieces of wreckage in 18-20 metres but the authors could not locate any wreckage in deeper water.

BELFAST

1293nt. Iron steamship.
Built by Palmers Shipbuilding & Iron Co, Jarrow.
Launched October 1884.

Dimensions 265.6' x 34.2' x 24.3'

The *Belfast* left Sapelo, Georgia, USA on 4th March, 1895 bound for Moville, Lough Foyle with a cargo of 1,900 tons of pitch pine, under the command of Captain John Brown with a crew of twenty one. The voyage went well until the 16th, when the weather closed in. The captain had to guide his ship for the next six days without the benefit of sustained clear weather to take navigational readings although a few glimpses of sun and stars did give some idea as to their location. On the 22nd they ran through a strong SW storm which further confused their position.

By this time they were nearing the British coast and the captain began to get concerned. He ordered sounding to begin and slowed his vessel. Each short sighting and depth sounding confirmed the ship's position until, at around 5pm on the 22nd, the weather briefly cleared once again. This apparent good fortune was to result in the loss of the ship. The captain caught a glimpse of what he believed to be the headlands at the entrance to Lough Swilly. This put them well away from the position calculated by previous sightings and dead reckoning but Captain Brown was convinced. It is likely that what he actually saw was a bank of fog. Shortly after this the weather closed in again and the *Belfast's* fate was sealed. They steamed on at dead slow pace until they spotted a light which they believed to be Inishtrahull Lighthouse and they steered towards it but it turned out to be a light on another passing ship. The captain returned to his original course and crept nervously eastwards.

By 9pm he began to think that he should turn his ship westward and hold his position until daylight but, before he took this action which would have saved his ship, they ran aground and the ship immediately began to settle in the water. Captain Brown gave the order to abandon ship and, by the time the crew launched the boats and pulled away 20 minutes after running aground, the

Belfast had already almost vanished with only her stern still visible above water. On landing the next morning they were told that they were ashore on Colonsay and that their ship had run aground on a reef, later reported as Oagdale Rock, two cables west of Oronsay Island. At a subsequent enquiry Captain Brown was admonished and not held to blame for the loss of his ship as he had taken all reasonable precautions but had made a severe misjudgement when he ignored all his calculations and relied on the one short sighting of land.

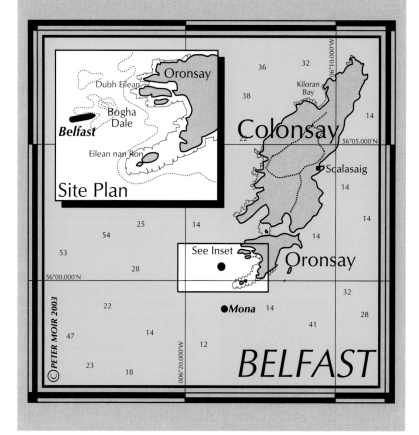

The Wreck Today

The wreck of the *Belfast* lies on the south west side of a reef called Bogha Dell off the west coast of Oronsay in position 55°00.766'N, 006°17.766'W (GPS). The remains are located in a large gulley between two reefs, depths range from 8 metres at the bow to the east down to 17 metres in the stern hold area; we were unable to locate the prop, rudder and stern section.

Substantial parts of the wreck remain including the main engine, boiler and hull although the later has broken up and large sections cover extensive areas of the white sand seabed. The site is also heavily overgrown with kelp in the shallows; this reduces considerably the deeper you go. The most impressive part of the wreck is the engine which sits up 3.5 metres off the seabed, its form and construction clearly visible. The wreck has clearly been salvaged, as all recognisable parts of the wreck have been removed with the exception of the engine, the boiler is in pieces and lies to the side of the engine.

This is a very scenic wreck site, with plenty to see. Large wrasse live in the remains of the boiler, and shoals of bib and pollock swim leisurely around the site. Visibility is normally very good, due to the coarse sand and rock seabed, the view of the engine standing sentinel, is particularly memorable.

BEN NEVIS II

44nt. Iron steamlighter.
Built in Glasgow.
Launched 1876.

The strong tides racing through the Sound of Luing make it a dangerous place for a small vessel in distress. Unfortunately for the *Ben Nevis* and her four crew this is exactly where she got into trouble and it was to prove disastrous for the vessel and the men aboard. She had sailed from Greenock and was bound for the Caledonian Canal with a cargo of coal for her owner, J Campbell, with Captain Archibald McNeil in command. When she reached the Sound of Luing, around 10am on 5th April, 1887 and was passing Fladda Lighthouse, she had developed a bad list to port, probably due to her cargo shifting. This slowed the little vessel and as she entered the tide race off the lighthouse, the combination of the list and the lack of speed made her unmanageable. One of the villagers at Cullipool later reported that he had seen the men aboard trying to pull in their small boat but it was full of water that made it impossible. A few minutes after she entered the tide race he saw her founder with the loss of all of the men on board. She sank in the middle of the fairway with the beam of her derrick visible at low tide. It is therefore probable that she was removed or broken up.

The authors have undertaken a number of memorable and perhaps speedy dives through this narrow sound, but without any sightings of wreckage, although the topography of the seabed could easily hide the hull of a small coaster.

BENGHAZI

106nt. Steam trawler.
Built by C Rennoldson, South Shields.
Launched 1917.
(ex FLYING ADMIRAL ex FILIEP COENEN
ex JOHN BULLOCK)

Dimensions 125.3' x 23.2' x 12.6'

Shipwrecks are often surrounded by stories of great heroism and selflessness. The wreck of the Fleetwood trawler *Benghazi* on the small island of Fladda in the Sound of Luing is a tale of heroism in the true sense. The efforts of second engineer Charles Bevin saved twelve of his shipmates but, in the end, cost him his life.

The *Benghazi* had been fishing near Iceland and was homeward bound for Fleetwood when she was caught in a strong northwesterly gale in the Firth of Lorne. She had called at Oban for coal and provisions after a gruelling seven day trip from Iceland and left on the last leg of her trip just after midnight on 23rd April, 1947. Ten miles south of Oban a gale struck and, in blinding rain the trawler ran onto a rock called Bogha Nuadh and heeled over until the sea was rushing in through the wheelhouse windows. The panic stricken crew quickly launched the ship's boat and were about to push off when they found that the boat's bung was missing and that it was rapidly filling with water. Charles Bevin stuck his hand in the hole and succeeded in stemming the flow of the freezing water into their craft and called to his colleagues to jump in before the trawler sank. Twelve of the crew joined him in the boat with four men, including the skipper John Anderton, the bosun and the mate staying aboard the grounded trawler. The men in the boat drifted at the mercy of the tide for two hours before they finally were washed ashore on Luing. Most of them were only half dressed and by the time they reached the shore they were freezing. They had no idea where they were and huddling together for warmth they waited for daylight but for unfortunate hero, Charles Bevin, this was too much and he died of exposure before morning, despite the desperate efforts of his shipmates to keep him alive.

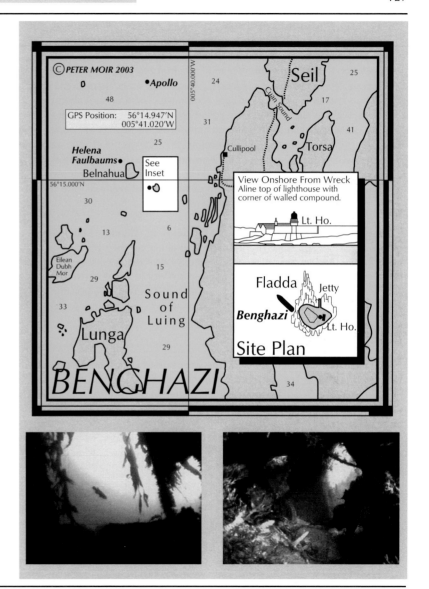

Meanwhile aboard the *Benghazi* the four remaining men were alarmed to feel their damaged ship floating off the rock and drifting off into the night, now at the mercy of the fierce tides in the Sound of Luing. They sent out a radio SOS, which was answered by the Campbeltown and Tobermory lifeboats, but, as help sped to the scene, she ran aground again on Fladda, a small rocky island in the middle of the Sound of Luing, just beneath the lighthouse. The four men aboard spent a terrifying night as she bumped and rolled on the rocks fearing that she was in danger of sinking at any moment. Some time during the night Frank Duncan, the remaining ordinary seaman aboard, disappeared and was never seen again. In the early morning the three remaining crewmen succeeded in getting onto the island and waited for rescue. When the lifeboat finally arrived, it was too rough for her to get close enough to take the three men off but eventually the weather improved and she managed to complete her rescue.

At first they were very confident that the *Benghazi* would be refloated and a salvage tug was dispatched to the scene to pull her off the rocks. Before this was accomplished, on the 26th April three days after the wrecking, she slipped off the reef and sank. Her starboard side was still visible above water at low tide and it was still hoped that she might be raised but she eventually became a total wreck.

The Wreck Today

The wreck of the *Benghazi* lies on the west side of Fladda below the wall of the lighthouse. She lies 20 metres from the shore in position 56°14.947'N, 005°41.005'W (GPS) on a sloping shingle seabed in 6-12 metres of water. The highest part of the wreck reaches to within a few metres of the surface making the wreckage still fairly substantial. The central area around the engine room appears to have been salvaged but there are still large pieces of wreckage to be seen, including the boiler and the bow section which is intact, lying on its port side, facing west away from the lighthouse.

BREDA

4387nt. Steel steamship.
Built by New Waterway Shipbuilding Co,
Schiedam.
Launched 1921.

   Dimensions 402.6' x 58.3' x 34.7'

The *Breda* like many of her contemporaries, was requisitioned for war duties in the early days of World War Two from her owners, the Royal Netherlands Steamship Company. On the 12th December, 1940 she left London, with a crew of forty-two aboard, bound for Mombassa, Bombay and Karachi and steamed north for the Lynn of Lorne. En route, on the 14th, she joined up a with number of other merchantmen in a convoy assembled at Southend. On board she had a valuable cargo including 3 Hawker Biplanes, 30 De Havilland Moths, military vehicles, cement and a huge range of other general cargo plus 10 horses thought to belong to the Aga Khan. She reached Oban eight days later and anchored to await the departure of the convoy which, to avoid the U Boats lying in wait in the eastern Atlantic, was planned to sail west almost across the ocean before turning south for the Cape of Good Hope.

In the early evening of the 23rd the crew heard the dreaded noise of two German Heinkel 111 bombers overhead and, before they could man the anti-aircraft guns, one of the German planes dropped a stick of bombs which, although they were perfectly aimed, straddled the *Breda* without a direct hit. The effect was almost as bad as a direct hit. The bombs exploded on either side of the ship and the shock of the explosion caused serious damage to a water inlet pipe. Soon she was taking water heavily which quickly killed the engines and ship's electrics. The Heinkels turned for home but, for the *Breda*, the damage was done.

Captain Fooy lowered the ship's boat and put off the twelve passengers aboard before he began a brave attempt to save his ship by running her ashore on the shallow shelf on the east shore of Ardmucknish Bay. An Admiralty tug came alongside and took on a line to begin the slow pull towards the shore and

SS *Breda.*

safety. Each inch of the way the *Breda* was gradually sinking deeper into the water but two hours later, they made it, just! She settled on the seabed at the edge of the shelving bottom some 600 hundred yards from the shore with her bow safely in the shallows. Her stern was completely submerged and her decks were awash forward to the forecastle. Finally, at about 8:30 pm, nearly three hours after the bomber attack the last crewmen aboard abandoned ship, having let the horses swim for their own lives to the shore.

The salvage of her cargo began immediately the next day but the unpredictable Scottish winter weather was to have the last word. Later on that same day she slipped of the shelving seabed and sank. Surprisingly almost no salvage was attempted and up till 1961 she lay undisturbed with her mast still showing above the surface. That year the Royal Navy swept her with a wire to a depth of 28 feet. Only a few years later she was introduced to her new friends - the sub aqua diver - she was to become one of the best known wrecks in the United Kingdom. There are few British divers' logbooks that don't contain the name of the SS *Breda*.

The Wreck Today

The *Breda* was heavily salvaged during the 1960s and '70s but still remains an impressive wreck. She sits upright on the gently sloping seabed of Ardmucknish Bay in position 56°28.558'N, 005°25.093'W (GPS). Her bow lies in 24 metres with her stern somewhat deeper in around 30 metres but her deck is some 6-8 metres shallower than the seabed making her one of the shallowest intact wrecks in Scottish waters.

The efforts of the salvage divers have caused havoc around the engineroom area and the superstructure has long since disappeared but otherwise she is complete. The main attraction of the *Breda* are her 5 cavernous cargo holds still brimming with interesting artifacts and objects including the remains of her cargo of aircraft in holds 2 and 3. The aircraft are often missed, as only the metal frames remain, lying on the starboard side of hold 2 and forward and to the starboard of hold 3. Another interesting recent find has been huge piles of Indian paper rupees in the rear starboard section of hold 4. The stern section is the most complete and is beautifully covered in dead men's fingers and coloured anemonae.

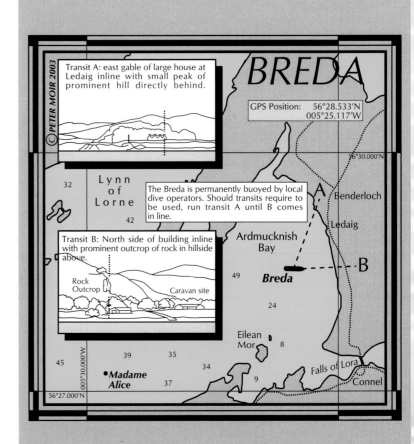

Diving on the *Breda* is easy and as safe as any wreck dive could be. She is almost always buoyed so finding her should be simple. Ardmucknish Bay is sheltered from the worst of the weather and is not subject to strong tides. Only potential problem is overcrowding! She is a very popular wreck.

CHEVALIER I

250nt. Iron steamship.
Built by J & G Thomson.
Launched 1853.

Dimensions 170.0' x 22.5' x 11.5'

The loss of the Hutchison's steamer *Chevalier* in the Sound of Jura on a calm clear night on the 24th November, 1854 started a storm of protest and indignation in the newspapers of the day. Only months earlier the paddlesteamers *Myrtle* and *Eclipse* had been lost in similarly good weather. The newspapers called for severe penalties for the men in charge of the vessels. In the case of the *Chevalier* the authorities seemed to agree as the mate Simpson, who had been in charge of the ship when she went aground, was taken into custody at Inveraray jail.

The *Chevalier* had been en route from Greenock for Portree, Lochinver and Stornoway and had rounded the Mull of Kintyre safely before heading north up the Sound of Jura. Captain Rankine had retired below and left the mate in charge for this leg of the voyage. Around 4am on the morning of the 24th a light was sighted ahead. It would appear that the crew mistook the light for the light of another ship because they took no evasive action and shortly after ran hard aground on a rock called Skerrie Eirn or Iron Rock. The light was in fact the beacon on the rock and should have warned the lookouts aboard the *Chevalier* and the mate on the bridge to steer clear. The ship was stuck fast and immediately began to fill with water from the forward compartments.

Quickly one of the boats was lowered and, with a few passengers aboard, headed for Port Askaig to raise the alarm. The majority of the crew stayed aboard the stranded steamer hoping that she might be pulled off. The tug *Conqueror* steamed to her aid but, when the *Conqueror* was at Crinan refuelling, a storm arose and the *Chevalier* began to break apart. The situation for the men aboard could have been quite serious but luckily the steamer *Islay* came by and picked them up. The crew were indeed lucky as the *Islay* did not normally pass down the Sound of Jura but had taken the route inside Jura to avoid the

heavy weather off the west coast. The *Chevalier* became a total wreck. It is not absolutely certain where the ship went on the rocks as the name of the location involved in somewhat vague in the newspaper reports of the time. Iron Rock (or Sgeir Maoile) is listed in the old West Coast Pilot as lying 1 and 9/10ths of a mile bearing 099 degrees from Lowlandman's Bay. This would

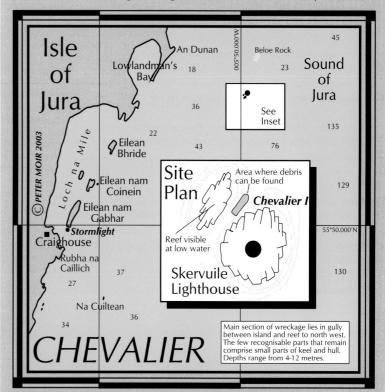

make it the rock Skervuile on modern charts. The authors are of the opinion that this is the location of the wreck of the *Chevalier*. This is supported by the discovery of scattered broken pottery and a small section of keel and hull plate in the shallow gully on the north west side of the reef. It is also known that two old portholes were found in shallow water on the north side of the rock some years ago.

CHRISTINE ROSE

91gt. Steel naval drifter.
Built in France.

During the years of the war the effects of German U-boat attacks on incoming food supplies could have been one of the deciding factors. The imposition of food rationing to reduce this possibility was one well known response by the British government. However there were many other schemes to help alleviate the problem ranging from the imaginative to the downright bizarre.

In September of 1941 the *Christine Rose* was involved in one of these projects. She had sailed with a group of scientists aboard who were studying the food chain in the sea with a view to boosting plankton levels that would have, in turn, boosted fish stocks. On this rather strange mission she had visited Loch Caolisport and was leaving the loch on the morning of 10th September when, at 9am, she ran aground on a hidden reef close to Knap Rock which lies just offshore at the north side of the entrance to the loch. The reef is only a few metres from the surface and the ship stuck fast. Tragically, just after the crew had lowered the ship's boat and they and their scientist passengers began to disembark, the *Christine Rose* slid off the rock, capsized and sank taking the small boat, still attached to the ship, down with it. The fifteen men on board were thrown into the sea - only ten made it to the shore.

The Wreck Today

The wreck of the *Christine Rose* lies where she sank in position 55°53.053'N, 005°41.473'W (GPS). The exact position is on the south east side of a reef which itself is about 100 metres east/south east of the remains of the beacon at Knap Rock. She lies in 10-12 metres on a shingle seabed at the base of the reef. The wreck lies on its port side and is well broken although many of the major features are still visible. The keel is almost totally intact with the stern section, including rudder and prop, the most recognisable. Midships she is well scattered but her engine and boiler are clearly visible. Forward the bow is broken but the single deck gun can still be seen, upside down and half buried in the sand. The

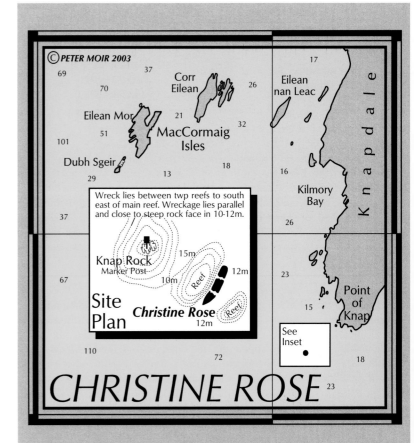

wreckage is overgrown with encrusting sealife and this, combined with the shallow depth and resultant good light make it a pleasant dive. The site is very open to the prevailing wind and therefore subject to swell and is also swept by fairly strong currents, particularly over the shallow top of the reef, at most states of the tide.

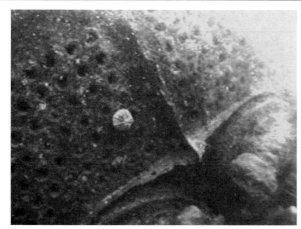

The drifter's boiler sits well above the seabed.

CLYDESDALE

232nt. Iron steamship.
Built by J & G Thomson, Glasgow.
Launched 1862.

Dimensions 196.7' x 24.1' x 13.5'

It is perhaps surprising that Lady Rock, which lies in the middle of the channel in the approaches to the Sound of Mull, has not been the site of more shipping casualties particularly considering the vicious tides that rip round the rock except for the short periods of slack water as the tides turn.

The isolated rock was to be the resting place of the West Highland steamer *Clydesdale* that ran aground there on Friday 6th January, 1905. The *Clydesdale* had sailed for Barra from Oban early that morning and the passengers were settling for a long uncomfortable voyage to the Outer Hebrides. The weather

was foul with a severe southwesterly gale lashing the ship. Around 7am, as they approached Lady Rock, they were engulfed in a blinding sleet shower. The temporary loss of visibility was enough to spell disaster for the ship which crashed onto the rock and stuck fast. It was close to high tide when she struck and, as the tide receded, she was left with her bows pointing skywards high above the water.

Around 10am the passengers were taken off by the SS *Carbinier* which was on her inward run to Oban from Tobermory and the SS *Brenda* was sent out from Oban to stand by the stranded ship. Later the SS *Fingal*, which had to abandon her run to Tiree due to the terrible weather, also reached the scene and stood by the wreck. Initially it was hoped that they could get the ship safely off the rock but the weather continued to pound her for the next week and when she was finally examined, she was found have severe damage to her hull. The *Clydesdale* later became a total wreck.

There is reported to be some wreckage on the seabed around Lady Rock but this cannot be confirmed by the authors nor can it be certain that it is from the *Clydesdale*.

SS *Clydesdale* ashore on Lady Rock.

COMET I

25t. Wooden paddlesteamship.
Built by J Wood, Port Glasgow.
Launched 1812.

Dimensions 43.5' x 11.3' x 5 8'

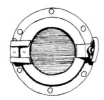

The *Comet*, a little wooden paddlesteamer, is probably one of the most famous ships in maritime history often wrongly credited with the title of the first ship to use steam power. However there is no doubt that the *Comet* can claim her own position in maritime history as the first steamer in Europe to ply regularly with passengers and to sail in open waters. Prior to her introduction trade on the upper River Clyde was by sail powered vessels, mainly by small wherry built craft designated "flyboats." Other larger ships then took over to continue the voyage from Greenock onwards resulting in a trip from Glasgow to Rothesay of three days at best.

The *Comet*, named after a meteor which was observed during her construction, was conceived by Henry Bell and with steam engines based on the invention of another famous local name, James Watt, she was launched from the Port Glasgow yard of John Wood in 1812. Her initial arrivals at the Clyde piers were greeted with huge crowds, many of whom had appeared in the certain expectation that they would see the little ship explode into a million pieces. On her initial introduction to the West Highland route in 1819 islanders fled at her approach proclaiming her as an emissary for the powers of darkness.

Her early career was very successful, so much so that she was re-engined and lengthened to provide capacity for more passengers. It was on the route between Glasgow and Fort William through the Crinan Canal that she was to end her famous career. On the homeward leg of a trip in 1820 she was caught in a storm when approaching the troubled waters of Dorus Mor off Craignish Point. Her engines were unable to cope with the vicious tides and current and the little wooden ship, with her creator Henry Bell aboard, was swept onto Craignish Point and almost immediately broke in two, splitting her hull where she had been joined when being lengthened. Luckily the passengers had congregated at one end of the ship and it was this section that remained aground when she broke up and they all managed to reach the shore safely. The *Comet* was a total loss. The famous steam engine was in fact recovered later and presented to South Kensington Museum.

PS *Comet I*

CULZEAN

1572nt. Iron sailing ship.
Built J. Reid & Co., Port Glasgow.
Launched November 1871.

Dimensions 254' x 40' x 23.9'

The tragic loss of the Greenock sailing ship *Culzean* in the Sound of Jura on the 21st November, 1881 was the end of a series of mishaps, which had started during her long voyage from Calcutta to Dundee with a cargo of jute. She had left Dundee in the summer of 1871 and was on the return trip when she was caught in a severe gale in the English Channel on October 14th. She lost her masts in the storm and sustained other serious damage. She was picked up and towed into the Tyne for temporary repairs then on to Dundee where she unloaded her cargo. Her owners, John Kerr and Co, Greenock, then arranged for her to be towed to Greenock for permanent repair.

The *Culzean* left Dundee under tow by the Clyde Shipping Company tug *Conqueror* in late November with seventeen crew aboard and a local pilot, Captain Duncan. The decision to take a large sailing ship on such a long trip, under tow, without masts or sails and therefore unable to be controlled if the tow line was lost, was to be the subject of much debate later. It was to be her final voyage.

The weather on the trip was atrocious causing them to put into port a number of times. While making the hazardous passage through the Pentland Firth they had to run to Scrabster for shelter. Later off Cape Wrath the weather was so bad that the crew feared that she might break up but they made it to Stornoway where they again took refuge from the storms. When the weather moderated they set out once more but had to put into Tobermory when it deteriorated again. Finally, when the two ships reached the Sound of Jura on the evening of the 21st, another storm swept over them and after hours of labouring in huge seas, and as they struggled past Iron Rock, the hawser broke and the *Culzean* drifted off, helpless, into the night.

It was the last that was seen of the ship; Captain Pirnie, his crew and the Dundee pilot Captain Duncan. As the storm lashed the *Conqueror* through the night Captain Morrison had to fight to save his own ship which he kept in position off the light at Iron Rock, head into the sea, until day-break. At first light they set off in search of the *Culzean* which they found and reported to be on the Jura coast, north of Lagg Bay, underwater except for a small portion of her bow section. There was no sign of her crew. Wreckage was strewn along the shoreline and was washed ashore on the mainland coast opposite and on the MacCormaig Isles at the entrance to Loch Sween. The bodies of the crew also washed ashore at various locations around the sound over the next few days.

EARL OF CARRICK

161nt. Iron steamship.
Built by Abercorn SB Co., Paisley.
Launched 1875.

Dimensions 137.1' x 21.1' x 11.0'

Contemporary reports of the wreck of the Maryport steamship *Earl of Carrick* on 23rd September, 1878 are somewhat vague. In the Greenock Telegraph of the day she is reported to have been en route from Wilmington (presumably in Devon) to Boness with a cargo of steel rails under the command of Captain Wilson Holmes. It is likely that her actual destination was Bonawe and when attempting to negotiate the treacherous waters of the Falls of Lora, the captain lost control of his ship and she stranded. The wreck is reported at the Connel Narrows, lying in two pieces with the stern section near the south shore and the forward section another eighty yards to the north.

There have been reports of wreckage underwater beneath the bridge. There are indeed metal remains near the south shore directly under the bridge but the authors could not determine whether this wreckage is simply debris from the construction of the bridge itself or remains of the wreck. Currents under the bridge are wild with eddies, downdrafts, undercurrents, whirlpools and every other kind of hazard water can create. If your intention is to look for wreckage, entry during the short slack water period is essential. Otherwise the site is best left as one of the most exciting drift dives in Scotland and only for the very experienced. Sealife underwater is fantastic owing to the inflow and outflow of water on each tide.

EXPRES

322nt. Wooden barque.
Built Risior, Norway.
Launched 1868.

Dimensions 115.1' x 27.4' x 15.1'

E Larsson, master of the Norwegian barque *Expres*, told a harrowing story after he was rescued from his wrecked ship on Scarba in November 1888. They had set sail from Archangel bound for Newport with a cargo of wooden battens but after a reasonable voyage across the North Sea they had encountered terrible conditions as they approached the Orkneys and for most of the voyage since then. They had lain in the shelter of Colonsay for some days but eventually, having lost all the ships anchors, they were forced to run before the wind. It is difficult to imagine the horror of the exhausted sailors as their ship was driven towards the maelstrom of Corryvreckan. As they approached the Gulf itself and its world famous whirlpool on the late afternoon of Wednesday 21st, the tides were against them and a successful charge through the boiling surf was impossible. Their ship was finally doomed and went ashore on the southwest side of Scarba. Luckily, despite the terrible sea conditions, the crew managed to escape to the shore. The ship went ashore heavily with severe damage to her keel and stern post and she completely lost her rudder. It is likely that she became a total wreck.

GLEN ROSA

42nt. Motor vessel, 'puffer type'.
Built Northwich.
Launched 1944.
(Ex VIC 29)

Dimensions 65.6' x 18.3' x 8.9'.

In days gone by it was often the case that during a violent storm a number of ships could be lost at the same time but it is very unusual in modern times that, with the benefits of electronic navigation equipment, there should be two shipwrecks within a few miles and within a few hours of each other. However, in January of 1958 this is precisely what happened.

On the 13th HMS *Barcombe* went ashore near the entrance of Loch Buie on the south coast of Mull. The sister ship of the *Barcombe*, the *Barrington*, was standing by the sunken boom defence vessel intending to carry out a salvage survey. On the night of Wednesday 15th, an officer on the *Barrington* heard voices hailing his ship through the fog and shortly afterwards was astonished to see a small boat pull along side with the four shipwrecked crew of the Glasgow puffer *Glen Rosa* aboard.

Captain Kaj Anderson of the *Glen Rosa* related his tale as soon as he boarded the *Barrington*. They had sailed from Troon to Bunessan with a cargo of 120 tons of coal for her owners G & G Hamilton of Bothwell Street, Glasgow. As they approached Mull the fog was very dense and, just before nine o'clock, there was a loud crunching sound as she ran ashore. The captain said that he had a problem with his compass, which had been affected by a local magnetic anomaly in the Loch Buie area. They fired all their distress rockets but to no avail and, as their little ship was grinding on the rocks in the swell and they feared she might slip off into deep water, they took to the ship's boat and decided to head for Loch Buie to raise the alarm. By the time they pulled away into the night the *Glen Rosa* had indeed sunk deeper beneath the surface and only her funnel was still showing above water. Luckily they came upon the *Barrington* a couple of hours later.

The *Glen Rosa* was to become a total wreck. She was subsequently heavily salvaged where she lay and today the main signs of the loss are scattered pieces of rusting metal on the shore. There are a few small remnants of the wreckage, including the engine block, in the shallows in approximate position 56°19.534'N, 005°47.564'W.

GOLDEN GIFT

42nt. Steam drifter.
Built by Richards, Lowestoft.
Launched 1910.

Details of the loss of the *Golden Gift* are vague due to wartime censorship although she was not lost as a direct result of war action. After surviving service during the Great War she was requisitioned once more from her owner G. Catchpole of Lowestoft in November of 1939 for Navy harbour duties and stationed at Oban. At 1:58pm on the afternoon of April 6th, 1943 she was run down by the SS *Lochinvar*. The collision swung the drifter round and onto the beach just north of the North Pier allowing the crew to jump ashore without even getting their feet wet. However the collision had smashed the side of the *Golden Gift* in the engine room area and she quickly filled, slipped off the beach and sank near the shore. The seabed here slopes steeply and she disappeared completely beneath the surface.

The Wreck Today

The remains of the *Golden Gift* lie where she sank close to the shore north of the North Pier, Oban Bay in approximate position 56°24.983'N, 005°28.557'W (GPS). The wreck, which is easily accessible from the shore, lies at the foot of a muddy slope in 12-14 metres on her side with all wooden structures gone and only the crumbling metal framework and boiler remaining. Some of the wreckage still stands proud of the seabed covered in sealife but the silty nature of the area makes the visibility reduce rapidly. We understand it is now forbidden to dive in the Oban Harbour area and, as such, the wreck is off limits, unless you can convince the Harbourmaster to give you permission for a dive.

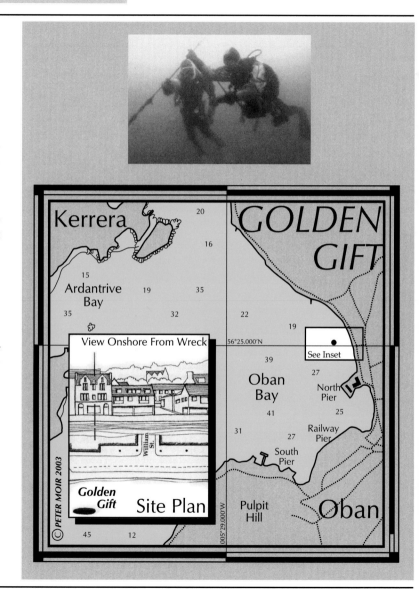

View Onshore From Wreck

Golden Gift Site Plan

© PETER MOIR 2003

GRENADIER

357gt. Steel paddlesteamer.
Built by J & G Thomson.
Launched 1885.

Dimensions 222.9' x 23.1' x 9.3'

The MacBrayne steamer *Grenadier* served for many years for the company on the Iona and Staffa run from Oban. Her graceful clipper lines made her very popular with day trippers although her insatiable appetite for coal made her less popular with her owners. It was from this regular trip that she returned to her usual berth at the North Pier, Oban on the evening of 5th September, 1927. It was to be her last trip.

Around 12:45 the sleeping town was awakened by a series of long blasts from the *Grenadier's* siren quickly followed by the discharge of a rocket from the Police station - the prearranged signal to call the Fire Brigade. As some of the townsfolk began to make their way down to the harbour, the North Pier and the surrounding streets were illuminated by huge flames leaping from the moored steamer. The fire spread rapidly and by the time the Fire Brigade arrived she was already totally engulfed in flames. The unfortunate crew had been asleep on board and had to flee for their lives. Some managed to make it to the gangway but it too was soon on fire and the rest of the crew had to scramble over the side of the ship and into small boats which had by now arrived on the scene. Three men lost their lives on the ship. The efforts of the Fire Brigade made no impression on the flames and so her stern was pulled away from the pier and allowed to sink in the harbour which finally extinguished the fire. The bodies of the three dead men were later recovered by divers. The *Grenadier* was raised but was so badly damaged that she was taken to Ardrossan and broken up.

"Grenadier" After The Disaster

HELEN MACGREGOR

44nt. Iron steamlighter.
Built by William Swan, Maryhill.
Launched 1876.

Dimensions 65.5' x 17.6' x 7.5'

The investigations at the Board of Trade inquiry in March 1898 into the loss of the *Helen Macgregor* centred on the seaworthiness of the vessel. The many witnesses called gave no consistent story as to her condition but could only report that, during the year prior to her loss, a fair sum of money had been spent on various repairs which should have made her sound. It was reported by one witness that he had seen three or four inches of water in her bilge as she passed through the Crinan Canal but, as she had been sitting for twelve hours during the previous night with no pumps working, this would not have been unusual for a vessel of the age of the *Helen Macgregor*.

As all four crew members, including Captain McDougall, were lost when the vessel sank off the west coast of Kerrera on 28th November, 1897, the cause of her sinking can only be surmised. She left Glasgow, bound for Salen in the Sound of Mull, with a cargo of coal on 23rd November and passed through the Crinan Canal on the 26th after spending the night at Ardrishaig. Her master told one of the lock keepers that he thought his vessel was too heavily laden as they steamed slowly through the canal. This could be the vital clue that points to her fate the following day. When she sailed from Crinan the following day the wind was moderate from the southwest. The last confirmed sighting of the steam lighter was as she passed through the Sound of Luing and past Fladda. By this time the wind had increased to gale force. What followed is not certain but the next sign of the *Helen Macgregor* was the bodies of three of her crew washed ashore on the south west side of Kerrera and bits of wreckage, later identified as from the *Helen Macgregor* along both the Kerrera and mainland coasts. The storm had been a violent one and perhaps, slightly overloaded, the little ship had taken on water from a large wave and foundered or had broached in the rough sea which would have been almost exactly on her stern. The only certain thing is that she was lost, with all crew, somewhere off the southwest of Kerrera.

HELENA FAULBAUMS

1188nt. Steamship.
Built by Grangemouth Dockyard Co.
Launched June 1920.

Dimensions 280.1' x 41.9' x 18.9'

Fifteen gravestones in the little cemetery of Kilchatten on Luing are a sad reminder of the loss of the Latvian steamship *Helena Faulbaums* in a wild hurricane on the night of 26th October, 1936. There were only four survivors from her crew of twenty when she sank off the small island of Belnahua at the north end of the Sound of Luing during a storm which, at the time, was regarded as the worst in living memory.

She left Liverpool early on the 26th October after unloading her cargo of timber and was bound for Blyth, Northumberland in ballast, to take on a cargo of coal for her return trip to her home port of Riga. As the day wore on and she steamed further north the wind began to increase and Captain Nikolai Zughaus decided to make for the Firth of Lorne to take shelter. By the time she was abreast of the Garvellachs the sea was boiling in a full scale hurricane and the empty ship, with her propeller half out the water thrashing the surface, was buffeted by huge waves making her almost impossible to control. Finally she became totally unmanageable to such an extent that the crew thought that the steering had in fact broken although it is likely that the combination of the violent seas and the strong currents around the Sound of Luing was in fact to blame. Captain Zughaus ordered both of her anchors let go, each with ninety fathoms of chain, but it was to no avail. The first SOS radio message was sent out at 8:48pm but, although it was answered by Portpatrick and Malin Head Radios who immediately tried to launch Port Askaig lifeboat, the storm was so bad that all communications with Islay were lost and the message had to be relayed by the BBC. The lifeboat was eventually launched but the *Helena Faulbaums* was doomed. At 10:05pm she was swept onto the north west end of Belnahua and the radio message was changed to " Now ashore." The radio operator bravely stayed at his post tapping out the distress call and went down with the ship.

SS *Helena Faulbaums*.

The ship was being pounded against the rocky shore by huge waves and, as the crew struggled on the heaving deck in driving spray to prepare themselves to try to get ashore, she slipped off the rocks and began to sink. The Captain, seeing the position of the ship which was quickly settling by the stern, immediately gave the order to abandon ship and the men scrambled over the side to attempt to cross the short distance to the shore - only four made it. It took only a few short minutes to struggle onto the rocks but when they looked back their ship had gone. Three of the four men spent the night in the ruins of an old house where they ingeniously managed to light a fire with a pack of wet matches one of them had in his pocket. The fourth man, injured as he struggled ashore, spent a cold night clinging to the rocks before he met up with his colleagues in the morning. Around 8:30am the next morning they spotted the Islay lifeboat and managed to attract the crew's attention by waving a pillowcase. The sea was still very rough making it impossible for the lifeboat to come in-shore so they had to be hauled aboard by breeches buoy before they could finally be taken to safety. They were landed at Crinan later that morning and taken by car to Glasgow. The bodies of their dead shipmates began washing ashore on Luing that same morning. The crew, except for the captain whose body was taken back to Latvia, were buried on Luing in a solemn ceremony on the 2nd November.

The Wreck Today

The wreck of the *Helena Faulbaums* lies in seabed depths of 54-65 metres off the north west corner of Belnahua in position 56°15.267'N, 005°41.689'W (GPS). She sits on an even keel with bow towards the island and is almost completely intact, with the exception of the wheelhouse and bridge area and the masts and funnel. As the ship was in ballast the holds are empty, making the central section of the wreck the most interesting. The depth on the deck is 50-54 metres depending on the tide, with the shallowest part of the bridge rising a few metres above the deck.

One of the more impressive features of the wreck is the bow area. Here the plates have fallen away from the main frames to provide a bird cage effect, shoals of bib can often be seen darting in and out of the focsle. Equally impressive is the height of the bow with port anchor chain running south and down onto the seabed, as if it were trying to stop the tide sucking the *Helena Faulbaums* into the depths.

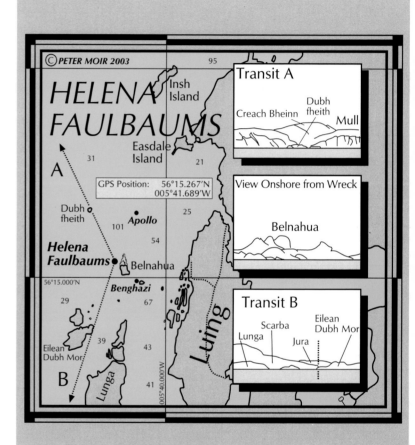

The wreck is sheltered from the worst of the tide which sweeps through the Sound of Luing, especially on the ebb, but good boat cover is essential. The dive is best undertaken at low water slack, with the precaution of delayed SMB's should the tide start to run. Clearly the major hazard for the diver is the depth and, although visibility is generally good, this is a dive for the most experienced diver only.

MADAME ALICE

194nt. Steel steamship.
Built Dublin Dockyard Co.
Launched October 1904.
(ex BAY FISHER)

Dimensions 168.7' x 25.8' x 10.4'

As with many vessels lost during the wars, there are few details of the sinking of the *Madame Alice* in the records available. She was lost on the 16th February, 1918 on a voyage from Fleetwood to Stornoway with a cargo of empty barrels and seventeen crew aboard. She was sunk in a collision near Oban with the steam yacht *Iolaire*, which was on Admiralty duty at the time. The crew of the *Madame Alice* made it safely to the shore. The *Iolaire*, whilst badly damage, survived the collision but was tragically lost less than a year later, when she ran aground on the Beasts of Holm near Stornoway with the loss of over two hundred lives.

The Wreck Today

The wreck of the *Madame Alice* lies in 40-42 metres in the Firth of Lorne approximately a mile offshore from Ganavan Sands in position 56°27.233'N, 005°29.483'W (GPS). She sits almost upright with a slight list to starboard on a muddy seabed with her bow heading southwest. The wreck is still fairly intact although the superstructure in the bridge area is beginning to fall inwards on itself and the stern is smashed and disappears into the seabed. This is presumably the result of the collision that caused the loss of the vessel as the rest of the hull appears to be intact. The stern is covered extensively by fishing nets and so great care must be taken, particularly as the muddy seabed and the silt that covers the wreckage, deposited by the tides rushing through the Falls of Lora from Loch Etive, quickly reduces visibility as the diver swims past. Forward of the bridge the large single hold is well filled with silt. Huge seapens cover the seabed around the wreck but otherwise the wreck itself is not covered with the same profusion of encrusting life that would normally be associated with such

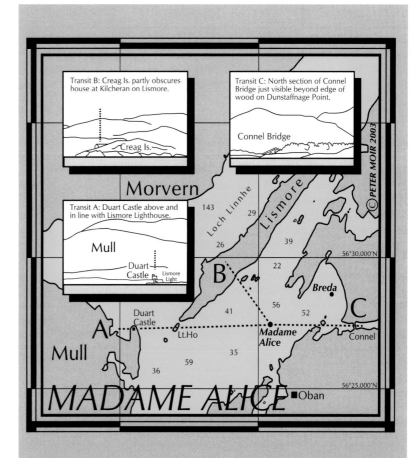

a wreck. Apart from the depth and the fishing nets their are no great hazards on this dive but clearly it is not for the inexperienced diver. She lies more or less on the route of the Lismore ferry from Oban so watch out for it but otherwise surface traffic in the area is light.

MAINE

1690nt. Steel steamship.
Built by Wm. Gray & Co., West Hartlepool.
Launched 1887.
(ex SWANSEA)

Dimensions 315.2' x 40.2' x 20.2'

The Royal Fleet Auxiliary hospital ship HMS *Maine* was stationed at Lamlash, Arran in the months before the start of the First World War. She had sailed from there, via Campbeltown, to pick up patients from the minelaying fleet engaged in manoeuvres in Loch Linnhe, in June, 1914. As she steamed into the Firth of Lorne on the 16th she was enveloped in dense fog and as a result she ran aground at around 2am the next morning on the Mull coast close to Frank Lockwood's Island. There was no panic aboard as it was obvious that she was in no immediate danger and the crew began an orderly evacuation of the patients. They were taken ashore and housed in tents that had been erected to give them shelter while they awaited rescue. As soon as the fog cleared a number of naval vessels headed for the scene and by mid afternoon six ships were standing by off shore and the evacuation of the patients for transportation to Oban, had begun.

SS *Maine*.

At first it was hoped that the *Maine* could be refloated but, after examination, it was decided that the salvage would be too costly as she was seriously damaged and would sink if she was pulled off, unless extensive repairs were carried out on site. She was then abandoned until she was broken up where she lay after the war. The remains of the *Maine* can be seen ashore on the Mull coast behind Frank Lockwood's Island. The Hydrographic Department have her charted at 56°18.633'N, 005°50.335'W. There are reports of wreckage underwater but the authors could not find any signs of this.

MELDON

1572nt. Steel steamship.
Built by R Stephen & Co, Newcastle.
Launched November 1902.

Dimensions 310.0' x 43.1' x 20.5'

There are few details of the loss of the British steamship *Meldon* on 3rd March, 1917. She was owned by the Dawson Steamship Company and registered in Newcastle. Her fate was sealed when the German submarine *U-78* laid a pattern of mines in the Firth of Lorne in the first few weeks of 1917. The *Meldon* sailed from Penarth, South Wales with a cargo of coal and was northward bound when she struck one of the mines off the Garvellachs forcing her master to run for Loch Buie to put her ashore before she sank. The crew got safely ashore but the ship became a total loss although what actually happened when she reached the shallow water on the shores of Loch Buie is not clear. She certainly went ashore but, surprisingly in the circumstances, it is actually her stern that is closest to the shoreline.

The Wreck Today

The wreck of the *Meldon* lies off the north west shore of Loch Buie in position 56°19.542'N, 005°55.597'W (GPS) which is approximately a quarter of a mile north east of Rubha Dubh. Her rudder post breaks the surface at most states of the tide making her very easy to find. If she is not visible above water, care should be taken when approaching the area of the wreck as it will be only a few feet below the surface. The wreck should still be able to be simply located as the kelp on the stern will be visible in the clear water.

The wreck lies on a gently sloping shingle seabed with the stern sitting in around 8 metres and the remains of the bow in 13 metres. The stern section is the most intact with her cast propeller and rudder still visible. Moving forward she gradually becomes more broken although engine and boiler are still recognisable. Forward she is very broken but the bow itself rises dramatically

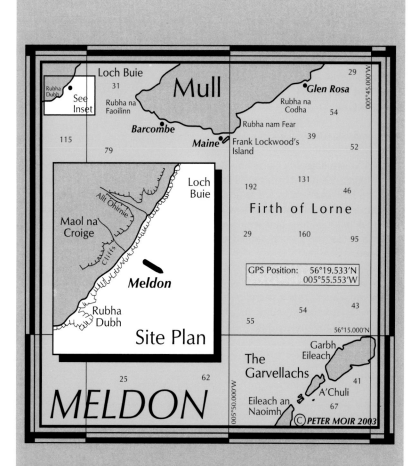

out of the seabed and reaching 5 or 6 metres towards the surface. There is no tide in the loch and the position on the north west shore leaves the wreck sheltered from the prevailing wind although it will probably be subject to some swell in heavy weather as it sweeps round the point at Rubha Dubh.

MONA

204nt. Iron steamship.
Built by Barrow Shipbuilding Co.
Launched May 1878.
(ex MARGARET)

Dimensions 160.0' x 24.2' x 14.0'

The Ayr Steam Shipping Company steamship *Mona* left Ayr at 6am on Sunday 16th August, 1908 and by nightfall that same day she had steamed to Bunessan, Mull and had taken on board around 1000 sheep and 65 bullocks for a farmer in Wigtownshire. At 8am the following morning Captain Todd crept out of Loch na Lathaich, round Iona and set a course for the Sound of Islay. His seven crew and the cattlemen aboard settled down for a leisurely return voyage to the mainland.

The peace of the summer's day was shattered some four hours later when they heard a loud grating sound beneath the ship and they shuddered to a halt. The *Mona* had run aground on an isolated rock called Bogha Chubaidth, approximately four miles south west of the Island of Oronsay. The sea was calm

SS *Mona* entering Ayr Harbour.

but the captain ordered all passengers into the boats and they were taken ashore to Oronsay and on to Colonsay where a telegram was sent calling for assistance. Meanwhile, aboard the *Mona*, Captain Todd was alarmed to see his ship filling with water and, deciding that she was in some danger of capsizing, the crew also came off the ship and stood by on a nearby rock. Some time later the *Mona* heeled over but remained jammed on the rock. Most of the animals aboard either spilled out into the sea or were drowned, trapped on the ship. Only around 80 sheep made it to the shore.

Initially it was hoped that the *Mona* could be refloated but the salvage team knew that they were working against time as her position was very exposed and the first spell of bad weather would probably see her lost. The following Saturday the wind changed to a westerly and increased in force and, as night fell and the salvors packed up for the day, the swell was beginning to build. When they returned the next morning the *Mona* had disappeared. The remains of the *Mona* lie on the east side of Bogha Chubaidth in position 55°59.361'N, 006°17.767'W in depths of 5-8 metres.

MOUNTAINEER

51nt. Iron paddlesteamer.
Built by J&G Thomson, Glasgow.
Launched May 1852.

Dimensions 195.6' x 18.2' x 8.2'

The *Mountaineer* was a fast, beautiful ship and, in her day, rated by many of her passengers as the best ship afloat on the Scottish west coast routes. After her sea trials, during which she set a new speed record for running the lights from the Cloch Lighthouse to the Cumbrae Light, she served her owners Messrs D. Hutchison on the Ardrishaig route before moving her base to Oban serving the ports on the west coast. Friday 27th September, 1889 saw her on her last run of the season, from Gairloch to Oban, when within sight of her home base and with passengers and crew preparing for their arrival, she ran aground on Lady Rock off the south tip of Lismore.

She was steaming at full speed at the time with both wind and tide in her favour and as a result the ship crashed onto the rock with such force that she almost went right over it. If she had not stuck fast on top of the rock it is certain that she would have sunk immediately and that many people would have lost their lives. As it was, the *Mountaineer* held fast on the rock, and, as the tide ebbed, she was left high and dry above sea level. Her hull was badly damaged but she sat upright on top of the rock with no other apparent damage. The forty passengers aboard were alarmed at first but quickly settled down when they could see that they were in no immediate danger.

Captain McCallum and his crew quickly started to get the passengers ashore where they were given hot tea to keep them warm. Distress rockets were fired and soon the steamlighter *Sunflower* and shortly afterwards, the steamer *Fuselier*, arrived on the scene. With some difficulty owing the heavy surf and strong current, the passengers were ferried out to the *Fuselier* and then taken to Oban. Over the next few days, with calm weather, much of her fittings and machinery were removed before the inevitable storm arrived during which she broke her back and started breaking up. She was abandoned as a total wreck.

PS *Mountaineer* living up to her name!

NORVAL

631nt. Wooden sailing ship.
Built by McMillan, Dumbarton.
Launched July 1864.

Dimensions 161.8' x 30.8' x 19.5'

The *Norval* was registered at Greenock and was inward bound from Montreal to Glasgow under the command of Captain Taylor with a cargo of deals, battens and staves when she ran aground in fog on the southerly tip of Sheep Island near Easdale in the early hours of the morning of 20th December, 1870. Almost immediately she went ashore it was obvious that she would become a total wreck although her crew safely disembarked and she did not break up until two weeks later. The rocks off Rubha Sassunaich are well formed to trap and destroy a wooden sailing ship like the *Norval*. She jammed, port side towards the shore between the small reef lying beneath the surface a few yards off shore and the jagged rocks of the island itself.

Work started immediately to offload the cargo before she broke up but the exposed position of the wreck and the continual pounding from the swell soon began to take its toll and by the end of the following week it was reported that her deck was 'strained and started' and raised three feet above normal level. Large rocks had penetrated her hull at various points, much of the copper sheathing on her hull was already torn off and all her masts were down. The salvors were in fact lucky to get a period of relatively calm weather at this time of year and had managed to remove much of her cargo when, on New Years Eve, a storm got up and by the morning she had disappeared leaving her remaining cargo to float off across the Firth where it was picked up by local smacks to be returned to the salvors.

As would be expected there is very little left of this wooden ship but scattered along the narrow rocky gully round Rubha Sasunnaich, Insh Island (Sheep Island was the traditional name for the island now called Insh) in position 56°18.452'N, 005°40.498'W (GPS) are the remains of the *Norval*. To the west the gully slopes down to 10 metres with copper pins and sheathing to be found among

the rocks with a lot of concretion on the bottom of the gully. At the far end of the gully in this direction an anchor chain stretches out to the northwest. To the east the gully runs in front of a small rocky islet and slopes steeply from 5 metres to 15 metres. In this part of the gully there are more copper pins and sheathing, piles of chains and some small cast cannon.

RAYLIGHT

73nt. Steel motor vessel.
Built by Scotts Shipbuilding Co., Greenock.
Launched September 1963.

Dimensions 97.3' x 21.1'

The first indication of a problem on the *Raylight* was a mayday message received by Oban Radio at 3:45am GMT on Christmas Day 1973. The ship was adrift in the Sound of Jura with engine out and being swept towards the Jura shore. The Islay lifeboat was launched at 4:15am and they, plus a coast rescue team, headed for the helpless ship drifting a quarter of a mile off shore at Tarbert Bay east Jura.

The *Raylight* adrift with lifeboat in attendance.

MV *Raylight*.

The *Raylight* dropped anchor in Tarbert Bay but, as it was blowing a F9 gale from the south east, it was obvious that the anchor would not hold her off shore. The lifeboat could not get alongside to pull her out so another message was sent for help of a larger vessel to tow her clear. A number of ships answered the call including the tug *Flying Spray* which set out for the scene from the Clyde, the West German MV *Alexandra S* and the MFV *Niels Risager* both of which were fairly close to the disabled ship. Unfortunately for the *Raylight* and the three crewmen aboard luck was not on their side. The *Alexandra S* got a tow wire fouled in her own propeller and the *Niels Risager* had to return to port with engine trouble leaving the *Raylight* helpless once more. Even the *Flying Spray*, still many miles away in the Firth of Clyde, had to race to Campbeltown for shelter in the increasing storm.

By 3:20pm the anchor of the *Raylight* was dragging and it was decided that the crew should leave their ship. They transferred to the lifeboat, which immediately returned to Port Askaig leaving the *Raylight* to drift ashore. The next day the *Raylight* was reported ashore in shallow water lying with a forty five degree list with propeller severely damaged and rudder missing. On the 27th salvage teams finally boarded the ship and found her flooded in all compartments to sea level. The *Raylight* was later salvaged and returned to coastal trade. Her fate was finally sealed a few years later on 4th August, 1975 when she struck the Highland Rock off the Co. Antrim coast and sank in 20 minutes.

SAINT MODAN

237gt. Steel Steamship.
Built by Scott and Son, Bowling.
Launched 1910.

Dimensions 122.2' x 21.6' x 9.4'

The crew of the Glasgow steamer *Saint Modan* only just managed to escape from their sinking ship before she sank in deep water in the Sound of Jura on the 6th November, 1947. They were en route from Glasgow to Kinlochleven with a cargo of coal when they ran into thick fog off the west coast of Gigha. Around 2:15am they ran aground on a rock near the island and although they quickly refloated the damage was done. A hasty inspection revealed that the vessel was leaking badly near the bow and they raced at full speed for the coastline of Jura hoping to beach her near Craighouse. As they steamed to the south of Iron Rock Light the pumps were struggling to cope and with water reaching danger level and the ship developing a critical list to port the crew decided to abandon ship. Three minutes later the *Saint Modan* sank. The crew rowed to Craighouse which they reached safely to be taken in by the local postmaster until they could be ferried to the mainland in a passing steamer.

SS *Saint Modan.*

STORMLIGHT

71nt. Steel motor vessel.
Built by W J Yarwood, Northwich.
Launched 1957.

Dimensions 88.3' x 21.0' x 9.2'

The *Stormlight* was en route from Campbeltown to Oban when she ran aground on Eilean nam Gabhar at the entrance to Craighouse, Jura at 7:10pm on December 15th, 1973. Despite gale force winds there was no panic and the crew were soon taken off by Islay lifeboat which arrived at the scene in answer to distress calls. The next day the wreck was clearly visible from Craighouse Pier and it was hoped that she could be saved. As the tide flooded she refloated but could be seen bumping hard on the seabed as she was trapped between the reef and the rocks of the island. She became a total wreck and at some point rolled over onto her port side and remained jammed between the island and the reef, stern towards the shore and with her starboard gunwale above sea level.

The MV **Stormlight.**

The Wreck Today

Over the years the effects of the waves and the tides, and possibly the attention of a salvage team, have gradually broken the ship apart so that today only the bow section remains reasonably intact lying in 5 metres in position 55°50.015'N, 005°56.218'W (GPS), on a rock and sand seabed. The shallowest part of the wreck still almost breaks the surface so care should be taken when approaching by boat. Otherwise the site is very sheltered and provides an interesting short dive at the end of a day of deeper diving.

JURA, FIRTH OF LORNE AND OBAN

Listed below are a selection of 65 smaller vessels wrecked within this area. This list is included as a basis for further research. Names suffixed by (S) denote extensive salvage work or total removal subsequent to date of loss.

NAME	BUILT	TONNAGE	HULL	TYPE	LOST	CAUSE	LOCATION
Accord (S)	1918	-	S	Sdr	14.04.1928	S	Loch Don
Advance	1873	41gt	I	SS	14.08.1873	F	1 mile west of Cullipool
Alice May	1866	399nt	W	Bk	25.01.1868	F	Near Oronsay
Alla	1887	20nt	S	Syt	26.11.1912	F	Ardlussa, Jura
Alnwick Castle	1841	50nt	W	Sr	09.09.1870	F	Off Ardnan Pt, Jura,
Ann Catherine	1845	23nt	W	Sk	22.11.1881	S	Ramsey Pt, Lismore
Appletree	1907	84gt	W	Dr	15.10.1940	C	South of Lismore Lt Ho.
Ariel	1844	24nt	W	Sk	04.01.1884	C	Crinan
Bella	1884	26nt	W	Sk	25.10.1893	S	Ballachullish
Britannic	1901	45gt	W	K	21.02.1925	S	Easdale
Carrigart	1912	84gt	Dr	F	11.05.1933	F	Off Ruadh Rk, Sound of Jura
Cartsdyke	1878	58nt	I	SS	01.12.1881	S	Marcus Pt, Easdale
Clementson	1804	182gt	W	Bgn	29.12.1812	S	Colonsay
Dalvey	1852	23nt	W	Sk	29.09.1892	S	Loch Etive
Delia		535t	W	Bk	27.12.1865	S	Colonsay
Effie Bella	1876	26nt	W	K	14.09.1914	S	Oban Pier
Exit	1866	84nt	W	Sr	28.06.1892	S	Falls of Lora
Flashlight	1870	493nt	I	SS	07.01.1897	S	Loch Don
Florence Graham	-	-	W	Bk	09.02.1861	S	Inch Island
Flowerdale	1878	488gt	I	TSS	00.00.1904	S	Lismore
Gael (S)	1897	-	-	SS	31.01.1927	S	Sound of Jura
General Von Thun	-	-	W	S	03.05.1847	S	Jura
George A. West	1913	85gt	W	Str	12.09.1927	S	Leathogeir Rk, Lismore
Glencoe	1863	8nt	W	Syt	08.08.1887	F	Firth of Lorne
Glenlivet	1861	145nt	W	Bn	24.05.1883	S	Loch Buie
Hafton	1910	80gt	S	SS	02.09.1933	F	Firth of Lorne
Helen Wilson	1902	44gt	W	Dr	05.02.1917	F	Ardentrive Bay, Kerrera
Hugh Crawford	1829	43gt	W	Sl	25.10.1862	F	Lismore Light, 5 m north east
J P Wheeler	-	-	I	S	01.01.1866	S	Oban

NAME	BUILT	TONNAGE	HULL	TYPE	LOST	CAUSE	LOCATION
Janet	1848	32nt	W	Sk	10.09.1877	S	Iron Rocks, Jura
Joseph Weir	-	-	W	Bk	24.11.1861	S	North end of Jura
Kingfisher	1882	76gt	W	Tr	01.04.1924	F	Oban Bay
La Naide	1835	34nt	W	Sk	02.10.1880	F	Off west Lismore
Lapwing II	1903	211gt	S	SS	1918	S	Near Oban
Lena	-	136nt	-	Bn	29.12.1879	S	Oban
Maple Valley	-	249nt	-	-	26.01.1866	S	Glengarisdale, Jura
Mary Johanna	1851	22nt	W	Sk	28.12.1879	S	North Lismore
Mary Wilson	1858	176nt	W	Bg	28.10.1887	S	Seal Is, Oronsay
Mayflower	1882	38nt	I	SS	28.10.1898	S	Goat Island, Sound of Mull
Mayfly	1867	41nt	W	Syt	05.09.1899	S	Gray Rk,Lismore
Merganser (S)	1883	39nt	I	SS	30.12.1901	S	Dog Isle, Loch Don
Mysie	1871	41gt	I	SS	04.08.1881	F	1 mile off Easdale
Norseman	-	325gt	W	Bg	24.04.1938	S	Lowlandsman Bay, Jura
Nyland	1940	1374gt	S	SS	06.12.1940	S	Torran Rocks
Ossian	-	42nt	I	SS	08.04.1897	F	4mls S Ardsheil, Loch Lihnne
Plover	1892	62nt	I	SS	11.11.1893	S	Shuna, Loch Lihnne
Regina	-	378nt	W	Bk	08.10.1872	F	Lynne of Lorne
Richard Roper	1851	79gt	W	Sr	29.09.1879	S	Cuilen Rk, Jura
Rook (S)	1878	275nt	I	SS	21.01.1881	S	Loch Don
Rosslyn	-	-	I	SS	22.12.1894	S	Loch Buie, Mull
Rover's Bride	-	53nt	W	Sr	29.01.1876	S	Oronsay
St George	-	-	W	Bg	11.01.1866	S	Colonsay
Sanda I	1865	522gt	I	SS	06.12.1887	S	Loch Spelve, Mull
Snowflight	1898	43gt	W	SS	12.02.1928	F	Sound of Luing
Stanley	1875	490gt	W	Bk	08.12.1902	F	5 miles SW of Dubh Artach
Stirling Castle	1814	-	W	PS	00.01.1828	S	Ardgour, Loch Lihnne
Swan	1887	14nt	W	SS	15.07.1901	C	Oban Bay
Telephone	1878	40nt	W	K	15.01.1908	S	West Jura
Thalia	1904	185gt	S	Syt	11.10.1942	C	Lynne of Lorne
Trout	1876	50gt	I	SS	00.00.1881	-	West end of Crinan Canal
Waterloo	1816	220bn	W	Bgn	19.02.1822	S	Oronsay
Wilhelm Arbeg	-	856nt	W	Bk	03.04.1874	S	Southwest side Scarba
William Carson	1841	245nt	W	S	03.05.1847	S	Jura
Willing Lass	-	13nt	W	Sk	28.12.1879	S	Oban Bay
Young Fisherman	1914	95gt	W	Dr	29.11.1940	S	Oban

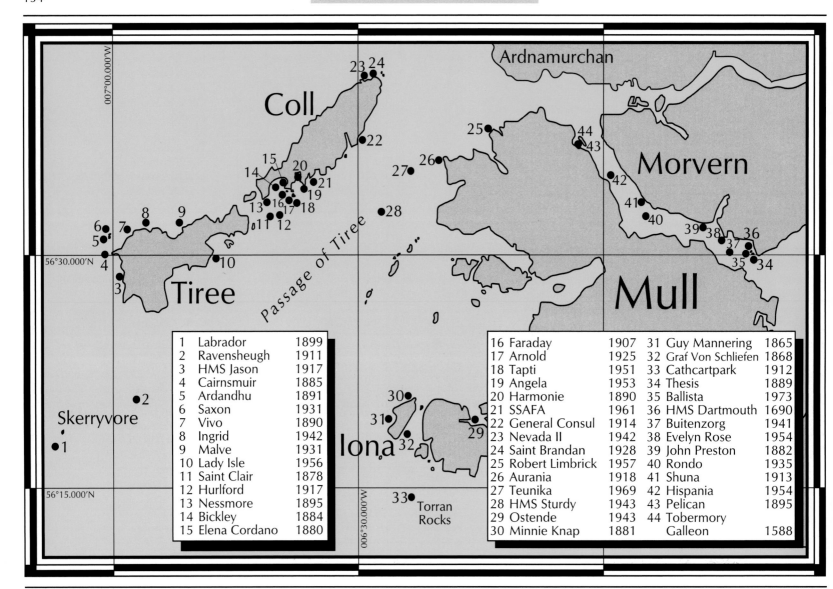

1	Labrador	1899
2	Ravensheugh	1911
3	HMS Jason	1917
4	Cairnsmuir	1885
5	Ardandhu	1891
6	Saxon	1931
7	Vivo	1890
8	Ingrid	1942
9	Malve	1931
10	Lady Isle	1956
11	Saint Clair	1878
12	Hurlford	1917
13	Nessmore	1895
14	Bickley	1884
15	Elena Cordano	1880

16	Faraday	1907	31	Guy Mannering	1865
17	Arnold	1925	32	Graf Von Schliefen	1868
18	Tapti	1951	33	Cathcartpark	1912
19	Angela	1953	34	Thesis	1889
20	Harmonie	1890	35	Ballista	1973
21	SSAFA	1961	36	HMS Dartmouth	1690
22	General Consul	1914	37	Buitenzorg	1941
23	Nevada II	1942	38	Evelyn Rose	1954
24	Saint Brandan	1928	39	John Preston	1882
25	Robert Limbrick	1957	40	Rondo	1935
26	Aurania	1918	41	Shuna	1913
27	Teunika	1969	42	Hispania	1954
28	HMS Sturdy	1943	43	Pelican	1895
29	Ostende	1943	44	Tobermory	
30	Minnie Knap	1881		Galleon	1588

MULL, COLL AND TIREE

Chapter **4**

SOUND OF MULL TO SKERRYVORE

These three neighbouring islands, with their hundreds of associated smaller islands and reefs, could not be more varied. Mull, the most southerly and largest of the three, is dominated by towering mountains with Ben More, at 996 metres, the highest point. This busy island, with its main ferry port at Craignure and its main population centre (and dive centre) at Tobermory, varies dramatically from coast to coast. To the east, the shelter of the Sound of Mull, with its racing currents and collection of intact deep shipwrecks, is overlooked by the historic castle at Duart Point. This contrasts with the wild west coast, where the famous islands of Iona, with its ancient cathedral and burial ground, and Staffa, with Fingal's Cave running deep into its dark basalt column cliffs, are worth a stopover on any trip. Although more exposed, fewer shipwrecks are recorded here than in the shelter of the Sound.

Further west the flat, barren islands of Coll and Tiree are almost deserted by comparison. Arinagour on Coll is merely a collection of a few houses and a hotel near the ferry terminal. On Tiree, Scarinish is not much bigger. The most striking feature of both these islands are the beautiful and deserted white sand beaches, particularly those on the west coast. All round both Coll and Tiree the coastline is dotted with shipwrecks from earliest to modern times.

The last area included in this chapter rates as one of Scotland's most remote places - the barren rock of Skerryvore, some 12 miles off the Tiree coast. The towering lighthouse, first lit in 1844, is normally only visited by seals and the odd person on a maintenance visit. It is a long, but worthwhile trip to reach the rock, although it should only be considered in perfect weather.

The Sound of Mull is probably one of the most popular dive destinations in the United Kingdom, the main attractions are the intact wrecks which can be found in the relative shelter of the Sound, as well as the dramatic scenery which surrounds the area. Strong tides run through the Sound of Mull and dictate the dive routine for the day, this tidal flow also encourages the dense and colourful sealife which covers most of the wrecks, making them popular for underwater photography. To the west of Mull wrecks sites are more exposed and tend to be more broken up either by salvage works or by the elements. There are a number of deep water wrecks between Mull and Coll which must be worthy of exploration by those suitably trained and experienced. The islands of Coll and Tiree have also claimed their fare share of ships over the centuries, and like the west coast of Mull, most of the sites have received the attentions of salvage contractors as well as the regular pounding of winter storms.

ANGELA

211nt. Steel motor vessel.
Built by Van Der Werf Scheepsboun, Westerbroek.
Launched 1948.
(ex ZEPHYR)

Dimensions 167.3' x 27.1' x 8.8'

The Finnish motor coaster *Angela*, under the command of Captain Niska, was en route to Goole from Larne in ballast on 9th April, 1953 when she was caught in a storm off the south east coast of Coll. The empty ship was riding high in the water making her very difficult to steer in the heavy seas. The strong winds pushed her closer and closer to the coast of Coll and she eventually went aground between Friesland Rock and Crossipoll Bay around 3:50am on the morning of the 10th.

The crew immediately launched the ship's boat but found that they were too close to shore to use it as it plunged and heaved in the surging swell. The ship's first mate, a man named Von Gertden, volunteered to try for the shore. He jumped from the ship with a rope tied round his waist and managed to scramble ashore through the heavy surf as his anxious crewmates looked on. Then, one by one, the crew members pulled themselves to the shore arriving exhausted, but alive, to thank the brave Von Gertden.

At first there was some hope that the *Angela* could survive as the storm passed leaving her lying with a 43 degree list and with forward hold and engine room awash, but otherwise intact. The captain, second mate and the engineer returned to their ship to await the arrival of the Metal Industries salvage tug *Salveda*, securing their ship to the shore with six metal hawsers. When she reached Coll the *Salveda* stood by waiting for many days for a chance to get her off. It is not known if any such attempt was made but the next report in Lloyds is dated April 30th and states that she was breaking up and had been abandoned as a total wreck.

The wreck of the *Angela* lies scattered among the rocks and gullies and in shallow water near the shore on the headland just east of Loch Gorten in position 56°34.966'N, 006°35.935'W (GPS). She is easy to locate as large pieces of wreckage are scattered, high and dry, among the rocks and are clearly visible from the sea. The underwater wreckage is concentrated in one

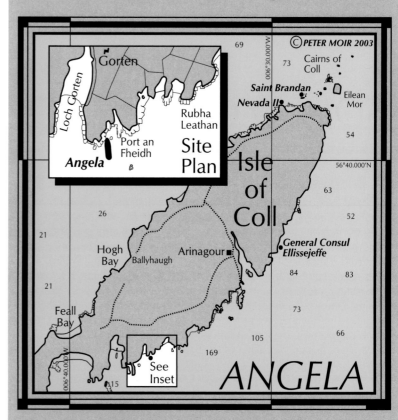

gully, amid boulders and kelp in depths of 2-8 metres. There is nothing significant of interest as only girders and some rusted plating have survived the efforts of the salvors. The site is sheltered, except from the east, and is not subject to any tidal flow.

ARDANDHU

757nt. Iron steamship.
Built by Henry Murray, Port Glasgow.
Launched 1879.

Dimensions 235.9' x 31.1' x 17.0'

The Ardan Steamship Company's *Ardandhu* had her first brush with disaster in January of 1881 when she was holed in a collision with the State Line steamship *State of Indiana* in fog while lying anchored near Bowling on the River Clyde. She sank almost immediately on the south side of the narrow channel but was to survive this mishap as she was successfully raised a few days later. She was not to be so lucky the second time!

On 9th September, 1891 nearly ten years after her first misadventure she sailed from the port of Riga, bound for Fleetwood, with a cargo of railway sleepers. Captain James Smith and his eighteen crew sailed her uneventfully across the North Sea, round the north of Scotland and by the 16th took her south through the Minch, passing Ushinish Light, South Uist shortly after midnight. The weather became stormy and the visibility very poor in the heavy drizzling rain as she pounded through a west south westerly gale. Despite her engines pushing her at full power her headway was reduced from her normal top speed of eight knots to nearer six as she rolled and crashed through heavy seas. However there was no concern among her crew as the various watches steered her on her south west by south course towards Tiree.

Around 5:15am on the 17th, with the storm abating, the mate called the captain to the bridge as the visibility had closed in and by then was very poor indeed. The captain did not take charge of his ship but returned below and, while the lead line was made ready, the *Ardandhu* continued at full speed. He returned to the bridge around 7:30am and, shortly after, rocks were sighted half a mile from the port bow. The captain ordered the helm to port and his vessel, responding immediately, turned to starboard away from the danger. No sooner was this manoeuvre completed than another group of rocks were spotted off the starboard bow and, although another order to put the helm to port was

given, she ran aground, at full speed, with a shuddering crash.

Captain Smith ordered engines full astern but she was stuck fast. The deck cargo was jettisoned to lighten the ship but, in the meantime, an inspection below decks revealed holes on the port side of the engine room with water in both fore and aft holds. The ship had run aground on the Hough Skerries which lie off the west side of Tiree. Islanders from Tiree came out to the stranded ship and took off the crew leaving their ship settling into the water on the exposed reef. She became a total wreck. At a subsequent enquiry, Captain Smith was found to be responsible for the loss of his vessel due to careless navigation. His certificate was suspended for six months.

ARNOLD

704nt. Iron steamship.
Built by J Blumer & Co, Sunderland.
Launched 1881.
(ex TYRI ex CAPRI)

Dimensions 231.0' x 35.0' x 14.7'

The Swedish steamship *Arnold* left Belfast for the Hamble on the 17th January, 1925 but was never to reach her destination. Contemporary reports of her loss are surprisingly brief only stating that on the following day she ran aground on rocks off Soa, Coll. Although the crew managed to escape safely the ship was reported aground with the forepart full of water and stern on the rocks. Within hours of going aground she broke in two and became a total wreck.

There is a large wreck lying to the west of the northernmost of three rocks which are charted and break the surface a low tide to the south west of Eilean Iomallach. The authors are of the opinion that this is the *Arnold* although no conclusive evidence could be traced. We have no records of any other large steamship lost in this vicinity.

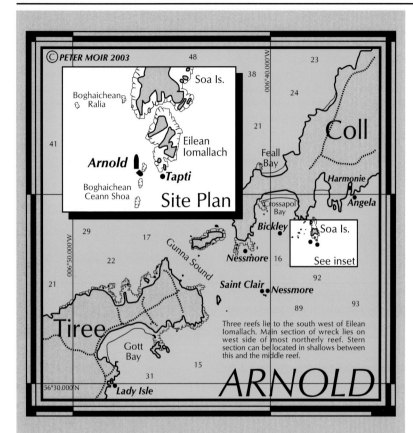

AURANIA

8499nt. Steel steamship.
Built by Swan Hunter, Newcastle.
Launched 1917.

Dimensions 520.5' x 64.8' x 42.6'

In a short period of ten fateful days from the 27th January to the 5th February, 1918, within a few square miles off the north coast of Ireland, the British war effort suffered three heavy blows with the loss of the SS *Andania* on the 27th of January, then SS *Aurania* on the 4th February followed by the SS *Tuscania* the next day. All three were liners built for the Transatlantic trade, had been requisitioned by the Government to be used as troop carriers and were employed in this service bringing US troops from the States to the battlefields of Europe and all were sunk by torpedoes from German U-Boats in the western approaches to the North Channel.

SS *Aurania.*

In any case there is definitely a wreck here in position 56°33.843'N, 006°39.063'W (GPS). The wreck, which is pointing north, lies along the side of the reef in depths of 8-12 metres. She has clearly been subject to heavy salvage but otherwise is probably not often dived despite her proximity to the popular wreck of the *Tapti*. Many of the major structures of the ship are still visible including boilers, engine, and propeller shaft with broken cast propeller still attached and stern steering gear. Her holds and some of the deck structures are also still apparent. The site is exposed to the south and east and could be subject to some tidal flow at some states of the tide.

The *Aurania* had just completed her seventh war time Atlantic crossing and, after unloading her complement of soldiers, had departed again from Liverpool, bound for New York, to pick up yet another consignment of young American troops. She was unescorted, relying on her speed to avoid any enemy submarines she might encounter. Meanwhile, Ober Leutenant Erhard Schulz, commander of the German submarine UB-67, had been ordered to take his ship and join his fellow countrymen lying in wait for the approaching troop carriers off the north coast of Ireland. German High Command in Berlin knew that if they did not stem the flow of troops from across the Atlantic the war would be lost.

Schulz could not believe his luck when, soon after arriving at his station, the *Aurania* steamed into view. He fired three torpedoes at her and saw and heard at least one hit her on her port side before diving to escape from the vicinity and the attentions of any escort ships. On board the *Aurania* all hell had broken loose. The torpedo had made a direct hit in the engine room area, instantly killing eight crewmen and flooding the boiler room. Her fires were soon extinguished by the rising water and she was dead in the water but at least she was still afloat. The steadily increasing wind was blowing from the west and was slowly but surely pushing the stricken ship towards the Irish coast. The crew had no choice but to abandon her. She drifted ashore in County Donegal but was quickly refloated and taken in tow, bound for the Clyde to be repaired. The fate of the Cunarder was to have one final twist, because as she was being towed towards the Clyde, the tow lines snapped and she drifted north along the Scottish coast before finally coming ashore for a second and last time on the north west corner of Mull at Caliach Point. The huge ship was quickly smashed to pieces by the surging swell pounding against the rugged cliffs.

The Wreck Today

After the end of the war the *Aurania* was heavily salvaged by James Gush of Greenock but still remains a fascinating wreck. She lies about 100 metres off shore just south of Caliach Point in position 56°36.142'N, 006°19.505'W (GPS) in depths from 15-20 metres although there is also a lot of small pieces of wreckage nearer the shore in shallower water. The most impressive items of wreckage are her massive boilers which sit 6 or 7 metres proud of the seabed but there is a mass of other tangled wreckage spread across a wide area. Visibility in the area is generally very good making this a terrific wreck site. The site is very exposed to the prevailing wind and swell and is also subject to current at some states of the tide. Care must be taken not to wander into the overfalls which form just north of the wreck site off Caliach Point itself.

BALLISTA

200t. Iron steamship.
Built by WJ Yarwood & Sons, Northwich.
Launched 1939.

The unusual story of the wreck of the *Ballista* saw the would-be salvage vessel herself become the victim of a shipwreck. The *Ballista* was owned by Elliot Diving Co., and was engaged in the salvage of coal from a ship, reputedly called the *River Tay* although the authors have not been able to trace any wreck of this name in the area, sunk on Eilean Rubha an Ridire in the Sound of Mull in the late 1940s.

The *Ballista* was anchored near this small island, which lies at the east end of the Sound of Mull, on the night of 5/6th February, 1973. During the night a severe gale with 70 mph winds swept across Scotland causing the stern mooring of the *Ballista* to snap and, despite the efforts of her crew to keep her off using the ship's engines, she came ashore right on top of the wreck the divers had been salvaging the day before. The three men aboard only managed to make a mad dive for the ship's boat and escape before she hit the rocks and sank. They drifted ashore and had to spend an uncomfortable night on the barren island sheltering beneath their dinghy. They signalled with a torch to a number of passing ships during the night but it was morning before their luck changed. In the early light of dawn they spotted some distress flares washed ashore from their ship and using these easily attracted the attention of the passing car ferry *Bute*, whose officers raised the alarm. The men were picked up shortly after by the Burghead fishing boat *Eminent* and taken to Oban.

The Wreck Today

The mast on the wreck of the *Ballista* was visible above water for many years on the westerly point of Eilean Rubha an Ridire but in the last couple of years this too has disappeared beneath the surface. Some parts of her superstructure do still appear above the surface at low water on spring tides.

The wreck lies in position 56°30.171'N, 005°42.039'W, and makes a pleasant shallow dive as a diversion from the deeper, more challenging wrecks of the Sound. She lies upright in depths of 3-10 metres. Beneath her keel the remains of the previous wreck that attracted her owners to the site are also still visible. The hull of the *Ballista* is still intact but otherwise she is merely a shell, patrolled by curious wrasse and pollock and shrouded in heavy kelp. The site is sheltered from the usual strong currents of the Sound of Mull but venture a few metres from her stern and the current can catch the unwary and sweep them out into the main channel. Otherwise the site is fairly benign.

BICKLEY

401nt. Iron steamship.
Built by A Simey & Co., Sunderland.
Launched April 1877.

Dimensions 176.0' x 28.0' x 14.6'

The Belfast steamship *Bickley* had been en route from Liverpool to Copenhagen under the command of Captain Mahood when she ran aground on a reef off Crossipoll, Coll at 5am on 6th October, 1884. Salvage crews were quickly on the scene to begin removing her general cargo and it was expected that the ship herself, which was lying down by the head with her forehold full of water, would also be saved. Contemporary records don't reveal whether attempts to refloat her were actually made or indeed if she was finally removed. The authors believe that she was substantially salvaged but that the large boiler, which lies in 10 metres of water on the east side of the reef charted in the centre of Crossipoll Bay approximately half a mile east of Runan Faochag, could be from the *Bickley*.

SS **Buitenzorg.**

BUITENZORG

4520nt. Steel steamship.
Built by Kon. Maats de Schelde, Flushing.
Launched 1916.

Dimensions 445.7' x 54.0' x 37.0'

At 3:05pm on January 14th, 1941 a wireless message reached the Lloyds' office in London - "SOS - aground sinking fast!" It was from the Rotterdamsche Lloyd Dutch steamship *Buitenzorg* on a voyage between Dundee and Calcutta with a general cargo. The message was received from the ship as she sailed through the Sound of Mull. The next message, received later that day, said that the ship had struck rocks 49 degrees one cable from Gray Island - this probably would mean that she had run aground on Eilean Rubha an Ridire - and that she had gone down within 15 minutes. Luckily the crew had managed to escape before she went down. The wreck was located two days later in a position 155 degrees 9.25 cables from Ardtornish point in 48 fathoms.

The loss of a ship is often surrounded by rumour and speculation which grows over time as stories are exaggerated or enhanced by the narrator. The details of the loss of the *Buitenzorg* are vague - there are even conflicting reports on her route. Lloyds records indicate that she was en route to Calcutta from Dundee while the records in the Dutch Maritime Museum in Amsterdam indicate the reverse. Her cargo which apparently included tea and latex, would make an inward voyage to Dundee more likely although why the ship would then be in the Sound of Mull is unclear. Possibly she was island dodging in an attempt to evade the German U-Boats lurking off the west coast. Alternatively the Lynn of Lorne was used extensively as a convoy assembly area and a ship outward bound from the UK would very likely be in this vicinity. There are local rumours on Mull that an explosion was seen at the stern of the ship just before she sank and that perhaps she had been sabotaged. This seems unlikely given the wireless message received at Lloyds. The final mystery revolves round her cargo - there have been strong rumours in the Western Isles since the war that her cargo included 300 tons of tin which would be worth a small fortune at today's prices. Two missing pages in the cargo manifest in Amsterdam further add to this mystery. The wreck has been the subject of a sophisticated salvage attempt using remote controlled underwater cameras but if the tin is actually there it remains hidden in the ship's deep holds buried in 50 years of silt.

The wreck is charted in 56°30.237'N, 005°44.541'W with the bow in 103 metres and the stern in 90 metres. The least depth is shown as 72 metres.

CAIRNSMUIR

1123nt. Iron steamship.
Built by London & Glasgow SB Co., Govan.
Launched August 1876.

Dimensions 290.3' x 33.7' x 23.9'

The *Cairnsmuir*, which was owned by a Leith syndicate and managed for them by Mr Francis Reid, left the port of Hamburg on 2nd July, 1885 at the start of a long ocean voyage to China. Their route would take them via Glasgow, where the last of her cargo for the Orient was to be loaded, before the real voyage began. The captain for what was to be her last trip was Mr John Georgie and she had a crew of twenty five aboard.

The voyage proceeded normally, passing through the Pentland Firth on July 4th, rounding Cape Wrath between 5 and 6pm that evening and then south into the Minch. Here the weather became hazy but this was normal for the area and, as the captain set his course from Eilean Glas towards Ushenish Light, there was certainly no cause for any alarm. By 9:30pm the weather cleared again and Ushenish Light was clearly seen off the starboard bow. Once again the captain ordered a slight course change to south west by south magnetic which would take them close to Skerryvore Lighthouse. The captain estimated the distance to Ushenish light by sight - it was probably this action that was to result in the loss of his ship. By the afternoon of the 5th, the weather had closed in again, but still the ship continued on its course unaware of the danger lurking ahead. At midnight the captain went below handing over the watch to his chief officer.

Despite two calls to the bridge from the chief officer, who clearly was becoming uneasy about the ship's position, the captain maintained his course until, at 2:45am on the 6th, the ship ran aground on a shallow reef called Bo Mor off the west coast of Tiree.

Captain Georgie rushed on deck and immediately took charge, ordering the ship's boats lowered before trying to pull her off the rocks by reversing the engines. This was to no avail and after a quick inspection below revealed that there was already eight feet of water in the engine room, he ordered the crew into the boats. They stood by the ship for two hours but, as the weather was still deteriorating, they eventually rowed ashore and landed safely on Tiree.

On the island of Tiree the wreck attracted a lot of interest as news spread quickly that her cargo included large quantities of wine, beer and spirits. This was to be another "Whisky Galore" story in the Western Isles. The local Customs officer did his best to round up the crates that washed ashore on the island as the ship began to break up over the next few days, but for some reason most of the cases he found washed ashore were empty! We can only guess what happened to the contents although at least one of the islanders, a large man by the name of Kennedy, was reported to have stripped and dived into the breakers to bring ashore a case he had spotted in the surf and, despite a direct challenge by the Customs Officer, he made off with his prize - no doubt he faced criminal charges for his efforts at some later date. At first it was hoped that the ship itself might be salvaged and a tug was dispatched from the Clyde to assist. However a report by the Salvage Association five days after she ran aground stated that she had capsized with her decks now awash and she was declared a total loss. She was later heavily salvaged by James Gush from Greenock.

At the subsequent enquiry the master was found guilty of careless navigation by failing to verify his position when off Ushenish Light and his certificate was suspended for three months.

The Wreck Today

The *Cairnsmuir* has clearly been heavily salvaged as only scattered metal plates and girders remain in the narrow gullies among Bo Mor reef in position 56°29.841'N, 007°01.548'W (GPS). The reef lies about half a mile off Rubha Chraiginis and is best located by echo sounder just before low tide when the surface will be disturbed by the tide running over the shallow reef and the deep kelp will be visible from the surface. The wreckage lies in the centre of the reef in around 8 metres of water. The site itself is very exposed to wind and swell from all directions and is also subject to strong currents at certain states of the tide. Low tide and calm weather are strongly recommended for a visit to the *Cairnsmuir*.

Steamship *Cathcartpark.*

Wreckage lies among gulleys in middle of reef, little remains of any size. Strong tides run across reef, which can assist with its location in calm conditions. Good boat cover essential.

CATHCARTPARK

453nt. Steel steamship.
Built by Carmichael & McLean, Greenock.
Launched August 1897.

Dimensions 208.2' x 29.7' x 13.6'

The *Cathcartpark* was owned by the Denholm Line and was en route from Runcorn to Wick with a cargo of salt when she ran aground on Sheep Island, one of the Torran Rocks, near Iona on the 15th April, 1912. Despite the vessel lying with a forty five degree list, the crew, under the command of Captain Thomas Blair, managed to lower two of the ship's boats and rowed safely ashore, one landing at Iona and the other on the mainland of Mull. Over the next week the ship was gradually broken apart by the incessant hammering of the waves. By the 18th salvage experts reported the keel up and her hull plates parting. By the 22nd the deck was awash even at low tide and the *Cathcartpark* was abandoned.

DARTMOUTH

266t burden. Wooden 5th rate warship.
Built by John Tippets.
Launched 1655.

Dimensions 80' x 25' x 12'

The warship *Dartmouth* served in many different parts of the world and had proved an excellent, highly manoeuvrable sailing ship. She underwent a major refit in 1678, including the fitting of a new keel, then returned to service to continue her successful career. However in the spring of 1690 she began a campaign which was to prove to be her last. King William and his queen, Mary, the new monarchs of Great Britain, sent the ship, under the command of Captain Edward Pottinger, to assert their authority over the people of Scotland, many of whom felt greater allegiance to the Jacobite cause. The *Dartmouth* was based at Greenock in March of 1690 and over the next six months raced around the Scottish coastline providing assistance as required to William's land based troops.

In October of 1690 the *Dartmouth* and two other smaller ships were sent to Mull to force McLean of Duart, an ardent Jacobite, to sign Articles of Allegiance to William and Mary. As the ships sailed into the Sound of Mull a violent storm arose and the crews aboard the vessels were relieved when they reached the shelter of Scallcastle Bay, an emergency anchorage to this day, and dropped anchor to wait out the storm. For three days they rode at anchor but, around 6pm on the 9th October, the anchor cable parted and the *Dartmouth* was driven before the wind across the Sound of Mull. Records of what actually happened are of course vague but local folklore and subsequent archeological evidence suggest that she heeled over dramatically first to port then to starboard, almost capsizing a number of times, as she swept across the Sound finally to be driven ashore, stern first, on Eilean Rubha an Ridire. It is not known exactly how many died but of the estimated 130 men aboard only 6 survived as she was quickly smashed to pieces on the rocks.

The Wreck Today

This historic wreck site was the subject of a lengthy archeological exploration in the 1970s under the direction of Colin Martin of the University of St Andrews. The wreck was discovered in 1973 and was given protected status in April of 1974. In 1979 this protection was in fact removed but was reinstated in 1992, meaning that you must have permission to dive the site.

Much of the wreckage, which included a substantial portion of the starboard side of the hull, 19 iron guns, the ship's bell and a significant quantity of other artefacts, were removed for preservation during subsequent exploration.

However the site, which lies on the north west side of the island near the modern wreck of the *Ballista* in position 56°30.197'N, 005°41.991'W (GPS), still makes an interesting shallow dive with at least three of the guns still remaining under water. The wreck site lies in shallow water from 3-6 metres and is overgrown with kelp. In addition the shallow nature of the site means that the sand of the seabed moves around somewhat, alternately covering and uncovering areas of interest.

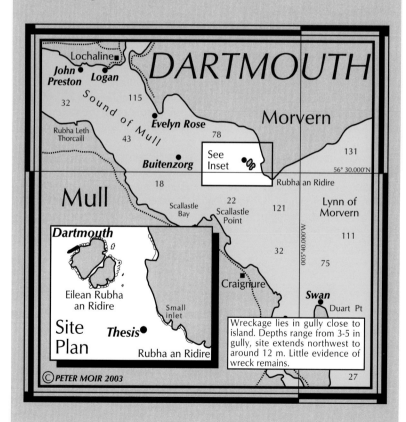

Wreckage lies in gully close to island. Depths range from 3-5 in gully, site extends northwest to around 12 m. Little evidence of wreck remains.

© PETER MOIR 2003

ELENA CORDANO

511nt. Wooden barque.
Built by Brignole Lavagna, Italy.
Launched 1870.

Dimensions 133.8' x 31.4' x 20.3'

The Italian barque *Elena Cordano* left Ardrossan on Thursday 25th November, 1880 bound for Demerara with a cargo of 850 tons of coal and twelve crew aboard. The initial stage of her voyage was routine as she sailed out of the Firth of Clyde and west through the North Channel but, off the north coast of Ireland, she encountered a fierce storm. She became unmanageable in the violent winds leaving Captain Ravassion no choice but to run north before the storm. As she swept north huge waves were continually breaking over her deck and two of her crewmen were lost overboard. Another wave badly injured the captain's legs as a heavy wooden spar was thrown across the deck like a match stick. Finally the disabled ship was driven into the shallows at Crossipoll Bay on the south east corner of Coll grounding about a quarter of a mile from the shore. The surviving crew members manage to struggle ashore through the surf but their ship was doomed. The huge Atlantic swell quickly smashed her to pieces as she settled into the seabed of the sandy bay. She became a total wreck.

EVELYN ROSE

130nt. Steam trawler.
Built by Cochrane and Son, Selby.
Launched March 1918.
 (ex LORD BYNG ex WILLIAM JACKSON)

Dimensions 138.5' x 23.8' x 12.8'

The Grimsby trawler *Evelyn Rose* had an adventurous career before her fatal encounter with the rocks at Ardtornish Point, Sound of Mull on the last day of 1954. In December 1948 she sprang a leak off Iceland but managed to limp safely home. A year later, she tore a huge hole in her bows when she ran aground in the Western Isles. Only a few months prior to her loss she was ashore again, this time on the west coast of Kerrera.

The night of the 30th December was calm and clear as skipper Dawson steered his ship into the Sound of Mull past the sweeping beam of Lismore Lighthouse. Most of his 13 crew were below decks asleep as they steamed north west towards Tobermory, leaving only the skipper and two deckhands on watch. Just after midnight the trawler ran hard aground on Ardtornish Point within 50 yards of the light there. The crew scrambled from their bunks and rushed on deck to see their ship ashore, with her bows aiming skywards at a crazy angle. They quickly started to get the ship's boat ready but, disastrously, before they could get it into the water, the ship slipped off the rocks and sank beneath their feet. Only two of the crew, who happened to be at the bow at the time, managed to struggle free and reach the shore. The rest of the crew were either pulled down with the ship or were swept away in the strong tidal streams that run past Ardtornish Point. The two surviving crew members could hear their shouts as they disappeared into the darkness. The survivors walked almost five miles to the nearest habitation to raise the alarm but, by then, it was too late. The rest of the crew were lost and the *Evelyn Rose* sank in deep water near the shore. The seabed here drops almost vertically to over 70 metres and as far as the authors can ascertain the wreck has not been located.

FARADAY

60nt. Iron steam trawler.
Built by Cook Welton & Gemmell, Hull.
Launched 1897.

Dimensions 108.2' x 21.0' x 11.3'

The flashing lights of the many lighthouses off the west coast of Scotland provide a coded message to boats plying their trade among the islands that keeps them safe from rocks hidden in the night or in conditions of poor visibility. Knowledge, or at least careful observation, of these coded flashing signals is essential to keep a ship from running ashore in the area. Lack of this knowledge or care in observing the signals turned out to be disastrous for the Hull trawler *Faraday* and her crew.

Steam trawler **Faraday.**

The *Faraday* left her home port on 4th October, 1907 bound for the fishing grounds on the Scottish west coast with a crew of eleven. Her skipper, Albert Rogers, had never been to the area and so took on William James Berry as a pilot to assist. However, although Berry was somewhat familiar with some parts of the Scottish coastline, he had never visited the area between Barra and Tiree which was where they were bound. They steamed north, then through the Pentland Firth, round Cape Wrath and south through the Minch before reaching their objective safely on the 6th October. It was here that an extraordinary series of blunders began as they incorrectly identified the light they saw that night as Barra Head Light. This, and an ongoing catalogue of carelessness, ultimately resulted in the loss of their vessel.

They proceeded south and started fishing. The fishing was good and from the 7th to the 13th they swept back and forth catching over 20 tons of fish in the rich waters of the area. Each night they could see the light flashing and, although they took a few lead soundings to supposedly verify their position, in their minds they had no doubt where they were. At one point they spotted land to the south which they identified as Tory Island but this too was almost certainly wrong as, in all likelihood, it was Malin Head. The light they had initially identified as Barra Head Light was in fact Skerryvore which lies many miles south of Tiree. The coded flashes of the two lighthouses are completely different but through all this time neither skipper nor pilot checked it.

In the early hours of the morning of the 14th the skipper decided it was time to head for home. Still believing the light to be Barra Head they set a course for the Minch. The errors continued. At 3am they spotted another light to the south - this they identified as Skerryvore despite the fact that it would have been impossible to see Skerryvore from their identified position. It was in fact Dubh Artach. Later, yet another light was spotted at 3:45am - this time they identified it as Liath Light, Castlebay. It was in fact Scarnish on Tiree. Their fate was inevitable. At around 5:45 they crashed ashore, at full speed, on Tumbla Island, Coll. The skipper reversed engines to try to pull her off but to no avail. The crew escaped safely but the vessel, lying awash in shallow water in an exposed position with a heavy list to starboard, was to become a total wreck. The *Faraday* was heavily salvaged by James Gush of Greenock in August of 1908.

GAUL

94nt. Steel steam trawler.
Built by Cook Welton & Gemmell, Hull.
Launched 1905.

Dimensions 130.0' x 22.3' x 12.1'

The Hull registered trawler *Gaul* was wrecked on the north coast of Tiree on 30th March, 1926 during a storm with the loss of 7 of her 9 crew, fortunately a lamp trimmer, Edward Thompson and a deckhand, George Pratt managed to survive the tragedy. The *Gaul* was owned by the New Docks Steam Trawling Company of Fleetwood and had been chartered to carry a consignment of fish from Iceland to Grimsby.

By the 2nd April her position was not good, lying 600yards offshore and parallel to the beach at the north end of Traigh Bail-a-mhuilinn. This location was extremely exposed and did not provide a good proposition for salavge due to the lack of depth near the wreck. The *Gaul* eventually broke up and became a total wreck later that month.

GENERAL CONSUL ELISSEJEFFE

886nt. Steamship.
Built by J Crown, Sunderland.
Launched January 1902.
(ex SVENBORG ex ADA)

Dimensions 250.5' x 35.8' x 16.1'

The *General Consul* is one of the many wartime wrecks around the coast of Coll and Tiree. As such exact details of her loss are not known but reports from the captain of the SS *Dirk*, passing Coll on the 21st February, 1914; describe her ashore, with her forepart ablaze, one mile from Arinagour. He also reported men ashore near the wreck. She was a Danish steamship, registered in Copenhagen and owned by Dansk DM Pselsk. Her owner's distinctive colours, with black funnel, white band and a red Maltese cross featured in the reports of the captain of the *Dirk*. She had been en route from Liverpool for Stettin with a general cargo including farm machinery when she went aground. Her cargo and non ferrous fittings were extensively salvaged in the years after the 2nd World War.

The Wreck Today

The wreck of the *General Consul* lies on the east coast of Coll a quarter of a mile north of Eilean Nam Muc in position 56°37.768'N, 006°29.524'W (GPS) which is approximately a mile north of the entrance to Arinagour. The wreck, which is about 50 metres from the rocky shore, is scattered down a steep boulder slope and is well broken although substantial portions of hull are still visible indicating that she lies parallel to the shore with bow facing north. Her two huge boilers and the condenser have tumbled out of the wreck, probably

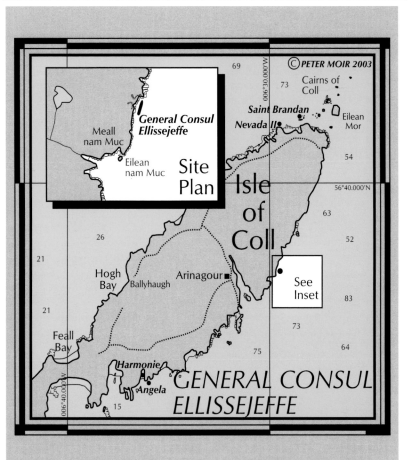

Site Plan

Isle of Coll

GENERAL CONSUL ELLISSEJEFFE

© PETER MOIR 2003

GRAF VON SCHLIEFEN

270t. Wooden barque.
Built in Rostok.
Launched 1851.

Dimensions 101.0' x 25.3' x 16.1'

The *Graf Von Schliefen* of Rostok was en route from Liverpool to Halifax, Nova Scotia with a cargo of 390 tons of salt and ten tons of soap in August of 1868. Her Captain, William Stogomaester, brought her through the North Channel and sailed, with a favourable west south west wind, towards the south end of Tiree. As he sailed north, his ship started to settle in the water and, on inspection, they found three feet of water in the hold, they had sprung a leak. Despite the strenuous efforts of the crew on the pumps, she continued to settle deeper and deeper as the water gained and eventually one of the two pumps clogged completely. The captain, concerned that they might founder, called his senior crewmen together and, after a short deliberation, they agreed that they should head for the nearest land and beach the ship. Around 9pm on the 8th land was sighted. They had lost their way in the excitement of their predicament and did not know until later that it was Iona. On the south side of the island, near the village of Iona itself, they spotted a sloping sandy beach and immediately steered the sinking ship towards it. As the ship approached the shore it grounded on a reef called Sgeir Rhua, and stuck fast. However the ship was only 150 yards from the shore and the crew were easily able to launch their boat and pull to the shore.

during salvage, and now lie alongside the ship in 15 metres on the shingle seabed at the base of the slope. The remainder of the wreckage is spread up the slope reaching 5 or 6 metres at the shallowest part of the site. The site is not subject to any current but could be exposed to strong winds from the south or east.

GUY MANNERING

**1160t. Three masted wooden sailing ship.
Launched 1850.**

As the twenty nine crew members of the *Guy Mannering* under the command of Captain Charles Brown completed the final preparations for their voyage to New York they could not have imagined the terrifying ordeal they were about to face. With a cargo of cotton and grain for her New York owner, Robert L Taylor, and six passengers aboard they left Liverpool on 2nd December, 1865 and for a week the voyage went well. By this time they were well into the Atlantic crossing but here their luck was to change. The weather deteriorated dramatically and for the next three horrendous weeks the ship was buffeted by ferocious winds and swept by huge seas. The passengers joined the exhausted crew manning the pumps and replacing the continually shifting cargo but the ship, with her sails and rigging torn to ribbons, was slowly but surely swept back towards the Scottish coast. As she tossed helplessly in the wild waters off Skerryvore on the 30th December the passengers and crew were relieved when another New York ship, the *J P Wheeler*, spotted them and signalled that she would come alongside and attempt to take them off their disabled ship. Their hopes were dashed when, in the fading light and spray, the two ships lost sight of each other and the people aboard the *Guy Mannering* were abandoned again to the mercy of the wind and waves sweeping them inexorably towards the rocky west cost of Iona.

The captain tried as best he could to steer his ship towards the one sandy bay on the west coast of the island but, with most of the small population of the island watching and waiting to help in the rescue, the *Guy Mannering* struck on a rock about a quarter of a mile offshore from Camus Cul an Taibh about 3pm on the 31st and immediately began to break up in the pounding surf. Within 30 minutes of striking the ship broke her back. The unfortunate passengers and crew were left with little alternative but to trust their lives to chance and to attempt the swim through the boiling surf to the shore. The brave islanders formed human chains from the shore into the surf to help the survivors reach

safety, nineteen of the thirty six people aboard managed to somehow reach the shore, the remainder were drowned in the huge breakers or crushed among the wreckage of the disintegrating ship which had disappeared from view within a few hours of going aground. The terrible wreck of the *Guy Mannering* and the bravery of the islanders who tried to save the shipwreck victims has entered into the local folklore of the island. The rock on which the ship went aground is known locally as Brown's Rock after the unfortunate captain of the ship.

The wreck of the **Harmonie,** Loch Gortan.

HARMONIE

322nt. Wooden barque.
Built in Raumo.
Launched 1860.

The Norwegian barque *Harmonie* was homeward bound in ballast from Liverpool when she was disabled in near hurricane winds and was driven ashore on Gorten beach, Coll late at night on 26th January, 1890. The villagers of Gorten awoke to find the ship high up on the beach but unfortunately were unable to render any assistance as the storm still raged and the huge waves were breaking over the stranded ship. They could see the terrified crew huddled for shelter at the forecastle head but could only watch and hope that the ship could stand up to the pounding until the tide receded. Two of the men from the ship attempted to make the shore in a small boat but it was quickly overturned and one of then was drowned. The other managed to reach the shore by clinging to one of the oars until he floated within reach of the waiting islanders. The remaining nine crewmen including Captain Christainsen were able to walk ashore at low tide, cold and exhausted but otherwise unhurt.

The rotting remains of the *Harmonie* are still visible, lying half buried in the sands of Loch Gorten. She dries out at low tide and is only partially submerged at high tide, as can be seen from the photograph on the opposite page, taken in 1994.

HISPANIA

644nt. Steel steamship.
Built by Antwerp Engineering Co, Belgium.
Launched 1912.

Dimensions 236.8' x 37.3' x 16.2'

Throughout history there are many hundreds of examples of a captain of a sinking ship choosing to go down with his vessel. Whether this is an act of the ultimate heroism and love for the ship or whether it was to avoid the wrath of the owners of the ship, which in past times was often not insured, can only be a matter for conjecture. There is no doubt that, as ships have become more reliable and as insurance of shipping has become universal, in recent times there are only a few examples of a skipper choosing to die with his ship. Captain Ivan Dahn of the Swedish steamship *Hispania* was one such example.

SS *Hispania*.

The *Hispania* was owned by Rederi A/B Svenska Lloyd and was registered in Gothenburg. Her final voyage began when she left Liverpool, loaded with a full cargo of steel, asbestos and rubber, bound for Varberg in Sweden on Friday 17th December, 1954. The weather was poor as she steamed north through the Irish Sea and the North Channel so Captain Dahn decided to take a route which would give them some protection from the weather by sailing between the islands of the Scottish west coast. Early evening the following day Mull was sighted and they steamed north into the Lynn of Lorne and then north west into the Sound of Mull.

It was very dark and the visibility was almost nil with the storm still raging, driving the rain and sleet into the faces of the *Hispania's* crew. Around 9pm, as they approached Tobermory, disaster struck. The ship ran onto Sgeir Mor, a reef close to the Mull shore, and shuddered to a halt. The first officer ordered the engines to full astern and after a short time the ship eased backwards off the reef but she was doomed. She started to list heavily to port and was taking in water rapidly. After running out the starboard anchor to avoid being swept away in the strong tides of the Sound the twenty one crewmen calmly launched two lifeboats but could not convince Captain Dahn to come with them. By this time the storm had abated and they rowed around for about an hour until, with a sudden lurch, probably as a result of a bulkhead giving way, the ship plunged beneath the surface. The last time the crew saw the brave captain he was standing on the bridge, his hand raised to his forehead in a defiant salute. The crew rowed across the Sound and landed safely on the Morven shore.

The Wreck Today

The *Hispania's* cargo was salvaged in the 1950s and in 1957 a wire sweep was carried out but otherwise she is still intact and as she sank in December 1954. She sits upright, with a slight list to starboard, in 30 metres of water in position 56°34.928'N, 005°59.216'W (GPS). She lies just inshore of the red channel marker but is normally buoyed and therefore very easily located. Her bow points due west towards the Mull shore. Depths on the deck range from 15-20 metres with of course the holds and engine room much deeper.

She is a spectacular wreck with almost every square inch of her metal surface covered in sealife and the almost inevitable good visibility making her one of

the best scenic wreck dives in Scotland. The ship, although one of the most dived wrecks in Scotland, is still virtually intact with companionways, handrails, doors all still in place. Only the wooden structures have rotted away and any brass fittings have of course disappeared but otherwise, a swim through her bridge or into the cavernous holds or engineroom is almost like a walk round a ship afloat.

The sheltered waters of the Sound of Mull make an ideal dive location and therefore there are few hazards beyond the normal dangers of a dive on an intact wreck. The current which sweeps through the Sound is the only exception making a dive at slack water the best choice.

HURLFORD

178nt. Steel steamship.
Build by Murdoch & Murray, Port Glasgow.
Launched Aug 1905.
(ex ABINGTON)

Dimensions 155.3' x 25.6' x 11.1'

The details of the loss of the *Hurlford*, lost at Roan Bogha, at the west end of Gunna Sound on 29th April, 1917 while outward bound from Glasgow under Admiralty orders are not available due to wartime censorship but it is easy to see how a ship could run aground on this isolated rock which just breaks the surface at low tide and rises sharply from relatively deep water all round.

The wreck, which is well broken, lies on the north east side of the rock in position 56°32.343'N, 006°40.083'W (GPS). She lies on a white shingle seabed, with her bow facing north west, at the base of the rock in 15-23 metres of water. There is still a substantial amount of wreckage spread over a wide area with her huge boiler as the main feature. The remains of the engine, winches and other recognisable items from the ship provide an interesting site for the diver to explore. There have been reports that the *Hurlford* lies on the west side of the reef and part of the wreckage consists of an intact clipper bow section. As stated, when visiting the site the authors found the wreckage on the north east side of the rock and the wreck explored did not have a clipper bow. However, during the search for the wreck we did locate the single blade of a propeller from another ship. It is therefore possible that there are two wrecks on the rock. The second would almost certainly be the *Saint Clair*, lost on Roan Bogha in September 1878, although the reports of wreckage with a clipper bow would appear to be inaccurate as neither the Saint Clair or the *Hurlford* had this distinctive feature.

This site is very exposed and is subject to strong tidal flows making calm conditions, slack water and good boat cover essential for a safe visit.

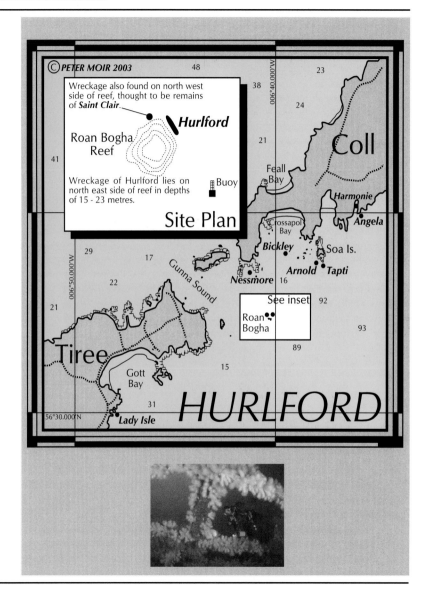

INGRID

2607gt. Steamship.
Built by McDougall Duluth Co., USA
Launched 1920.

Dimensions   251.0' x 43.7' x 25.8'

The Norwegian steamship *Ingrid,* owned by A/S I.A.Hamres Red, was en route from the Tyne to Hampton Roads and Cuba when she ran aground off Rubha Port Bhoisd, Tiree on 19th January, 1942. Due to wartime reporting restrictions details are vague but she was clearly well out of position as the captain first reported her ashore close to Barra Head when he sent out his SOS message at 9:10am that morning. Within thirty minutes further messages indicated that the crew were planning to take to the boats and only when they reached the shore did they find out that they were in fact on Tiree, not Barra. Reports over the next few days advised that the ship was breaking up in the terrible weather. When she was finally boarded on February 2nd the sea was reported to be boiling through her bottom, the engine room tidal and her rudder and propeller gone. Salvage was hopeless and she was abandoned as a total wreck.

The *Ingrid* ashore off Meall Mhor, Tiree.

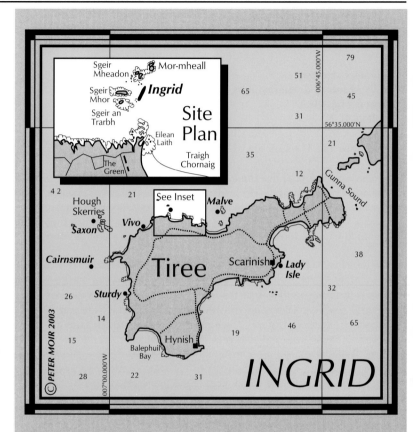

The Wreck Today

The *Ingrid* was heavily salvaged and has been further pounded by the swell at this exposed site. Her remains lie in shallow water at Sgeir Mhor in position 56°32.065'N, 006°56.003'W (GPS). The seabed here is around 6 metres and the wreckage is spread over a wide area with her boiler in the centre of the site. As the wreck is shallow it is heavily overgrown with kelp and subject to heavy swell when the wind is from the west. In calm conditions it is a pleasant shallow dive with lots of gullies and crevices to explore.

HMS JASON

810dt. Torpedo Gun Boat.
Built by Naval Construction & Armament Co., Barrow.
Launched May 1892.

Dimensions 230.0' x 27.0' x 12.5'

HMS *Jason* was an 'Alarm Class' torpedo gunboat built with an armament of two 4.7 inch guns, four three pounders and three eighteen inch torpedo tubes. Her 3,500 horse power engines gave her a top speed of nineteen knots. In 1908 or 1909 she was converted for use as a minesweeper and it is presumably in this duty that she was off the west coast of Mull in April of 1917. However on the 7th day of that month she was tragically lost when she herself struck a mine and sank midway between Mull and Coll with the loss of all hands. Her official complement was eighty five men. There is a wreck charted in the area but no precise location has ever been traced.

JOHN PRESTON

116nt. Wooden schooner.
Built at Port Dinorwic.
Launched 1855.

The details of the loss of the *John Preston* in December 1882 are not known but the wreck provides an interesting shallower dive in the Sound of Mull after a dive on one of the deeper more intact wrecks in the Sound.

The remains of the *John Preston* lie precariously on a sand/shingle ledge at the top of a dramatic underwater cliff. The site is approximately half a mile west of Lochaline Pier. Between the pier and the site a spectacular underwater cliff lies only a few metres from the shore dropping to depths well in excess of 50 metres. The wreck itself, as you would expect, has almost entirely disappeared but the remains of the cargo, piles and piles of slates, are still scattered across the seabed giving the wreck its local nickname - The Slate Wreck. There is still one large piece of wooden hull remaining and many bits and pieces of metallic structure scattered around.

The wreck lies in position 56°31.983'N, 005°48.198'W (GPS) in depths from 14-16 metres. The wreckage reaches to the edge of the cliff which then plunges below into the darkness. The site is generally sheltered from the worst of the currents in the Sound but is subject to gentle tidal flows which make a drift along the cliff face and excellent way to complete the exploration of the site.

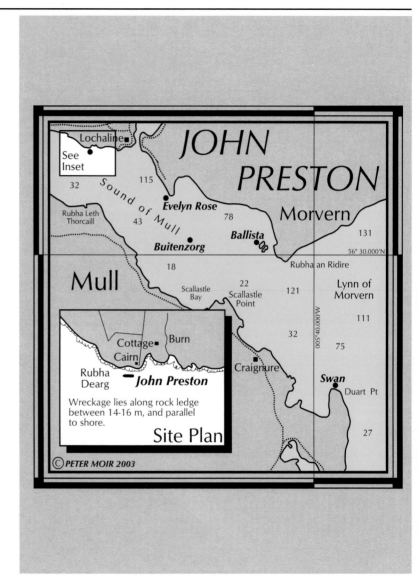

Wreckage lies along rock ledge between 14-16 m, and parallel to shore.

Site Plan

© PETER MOIR 2003

LABRADOR

2998nt. Steel steamship.
Built by Harland and Wolff, Belfast.
Launched 1891.

Dimensions 401.0' x 47.2' x 28.3'

There can be few remoter places in the British Isles to be shipwrecked than at Mackenzie's Rock near Skerryvore. It lies nearly fifteen miles from the nearest landfall at Hynish on Tiree and some sixty miles into the Atlantic from the Scottish mainland. For an ocean going liner to run aground and sink there with no loss of life is nothing short of a miracle, but this is exactly what happened to the Dominion Line steamship *Labrador* on 1st March, 1899.

The *Labrador's* voyage from St John's, New Brunswick for Liverpool was unremarkable for most of the trip but, as Captain Erskine's ship reached the eastern Atlantic, the weather closed in and, unable to take the sun for the next three days, he had to navigate as best he could by dead reckoning. During the night of the 1st of March and the early hours of the following morning he imagined himself to be somewhere off the north of Ireland but he was in fact some sixty miles off course to the north and heading, at full speed, straight for Skerryvore.

As the sixty two passengers were waking up and preparing for their last day aboard ship, they were disturbed by a slight shudder around 7am, but most dismissed it and continued with their preparations for the day. Slowly the alarm spread round the ship as they learned that she had run aground and that preparations were being made to disembark the passengers into the ship's boats. There was no great alarm but, by the time the boats had been launched, it was clear that the ship was badly damaged. The grain which formed the majority of her cargo was bursting through the decks evidently swelling as it was soaked by the inrush of sea water through the torn hull. Most of the passengers and crew escaped with only a few belongings but at least they were off the doomed ship.

Their plight would have been very serious if the weather had been bad but luckily the sea was fairly calm. A second even more fortuitous piece of luck was that, shortly after they left the *Labrador*, the Norwegian steamer *Viking* arrived on the scene and picked up all of the passengers and crew except one boatload who had already headed off for Skerryvore. Only after boarding the *Viking* did they learn how lucky they were. The *Viking* had also had problems with the weather and was well behind schedule and some four miles off course. If she had been on her planned route and time she would have been nowhere near Skerryvore. Even then, she nearly steamed past the stricken ship and was only attracted to her assistance when one sharp eyed crew member on the *Viking* spotted steam coming from the whistle of the *Labrador*. The engines on

the *Labrador* had stopped as the fires were extinguished by the rising water in the ship and there was insufficient steam to sound the alarm on the whistle but the white plume of steam was visible against the characteristic black of the funnel of the Dominion Line.

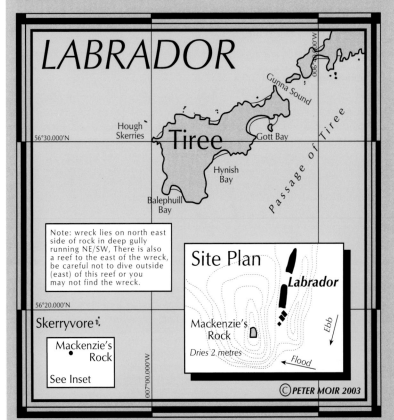

Over the next few days items of floating wreckage littered the surrounding sea and many items came ashore on Coll, Tiree and Mull. Only a few of the 153 mail bags aboard were recovered. The ship itself soon disappeared below water level and by the 6th March, had parted amidships and became a total wreck. She was later heavily salvaged for scrap.

The Wreck Today

This is one of the classic wreck sites of Scotland. It is certainly one of the remotest. The location of MacKenzie's Rock itself, lying three miles south west of the majestic lighthouse at Skerryvore, is the first challenge. At low tide the rock is just visible on the horizon from Skerryvore. At high tide the rock is best located using GPS although the swell, which is almost a continual feature of the site, may well result on waves breaking on the rock even at high tide. The wreck itself lies on the north east side of the rock in position 56°17.466'N, 007°10.047'W (GPS). The wreckage is vast. Her huge boilers and condenser lie within 50 metres of the rock in around 16 metres and the wreckage spreads out, towards the north east, from there. The stern steering gear is located in the centre of the wreck, obviously swept there by the huge forces of the sea which pounds the rock for most of the year. As the wreckage spreads further from the rock it is concentrated in a deep gully which descends to around 28 metres before the wreckage finally runs out. Note depths to the east of this gully rise to around 18 metres before descending again to depth. We suggest you commence the dive in shallows to west of the above position and work your way east, down the rock shelf into the gully.

The sealife on the rocks and seabed around the wreck and on much of the wreck itself is incredible with anemones and sponges of every variety, size, and colour imaginable. On many parts of the site an orange carpet of dead man's fingers totally obscure the rocks below. Huge wrasse and pollock patrol the wreckage and the many gigantic boulders and gullies which are a feature of the undulating seabed. All in all it is an incredible dive site. It is also a site that can only be visited in perfect weather conditions and with detailed advanced planning. The rock is totally exposed and subject to strong tidal flows and heavy swell. Good boat cover, using at least two boats, and use of surface marker buoys at all times are essential for a safe visit but it is worth the effort.

LADY ISLE

96gt. Iron steamlighter.
Built by R Dunster, Donchaster.
Launched 1941.

The little steamlighter *Lady Isle* ran aground as she attempted to enter the tight little harbour at Scarinish on 10th August, 1956. The crew abandoned her immediately and scrambled ashore. It was initially expected that she would be easily refloated as she sat upright in a fairly sheltered position. However a report at Lloyds more than a month later revealed that when pumps were put on board to make an attempt to empty her on 25th September they were not adequate for the job. While another set of pumps was sent for a close examination revealed that the little ship was more severely damaged than originally thought and she was abandoned as a wreck.

The remaining wreckage of the *Lady Isle*, which has clearly been the subject of heavy salvage at some point, lies between the two outermost rocks on the north side of the Scarinish harbour entrance. She lies in around 6 metres of water and covers most of the kelp infested seabed between the two rocks. Little recognisable remains apart from metal plates and girders.

SS *Lady Isle* aground off Scarinish Harbour.

MALVE

1488nt. Steel steamship.
Built by Port Arthur SB Co., Ontario.
Launched 1917.
 (ex MONIQUE VIEJEUX ex ROUBAIX ex WARFISH)

Dimensions 251.7' x 43.2' x 26.2'

Communications surrounding the loss of the Finnish steamship *Malve* on the rocks at Balephetrish Bay, Tiree were very confused and for a time it was believed that four men had lost their lives. Thankfully no one died but the ship was to become a total loss.

The story of the wreck begins with a message picked up by Malin Head Wireless station a 2:56am on St Valentine's Day, 1931. It stated that the ship was ashore at the south end of Coll but one hour later it was confirmed that she was actually ashore on Tiree. She had been on a voyage from Tallin to Manchester with a cargo of 2000 tons of paper pulp and timber when she went ashore. The weather had been atrocious with driving snow and gale force winds reducing visibility to almost nil and making navigation impossible. Captain Boxberg knew that he had run aground at low tide and, after an inspection revealed no apparent major damage, he hoped that his ship would come off safely at high tide so he and his crew stayed aboard while the trawlers *River Clyde*, *Dhoon* and *Caldew* which by now had arrived on the scene, stood by to provide emergency assistance if required.

The captain had guessed right as, after ballast water was pumped out and 50 tons of cargo shifted from hold 3 to hold 4, the ship did indeed refloat with the rising tide and was able to anchor in the bay awaiting a detailed examination for damage the following day. By 5am on the morning of the 15th the wind was rising and unfortunately, the gale force winds pushed her towards the shore again - this time she was doomed. The captain got up steam but the ship was unable to move ahead as she was surrounded by shallow reefs and eventually she went hard aground and stuck fast. Realising the danger of the position, as his ship almost immediately began to fill with water; Captain Boxberg put most

of his crew ashore in the ship's boat remaining on board himself with two others. The two trawlers, which had left the scene when the *Malve* refloated in fact radioed that they thought the captain and his two shipmates might indeed have been drowned as she went ashore for the second time but thankfully this was not the case. However, as the ship began to break up, the captain finally ordered his remaining crew to abandon ship and the three men

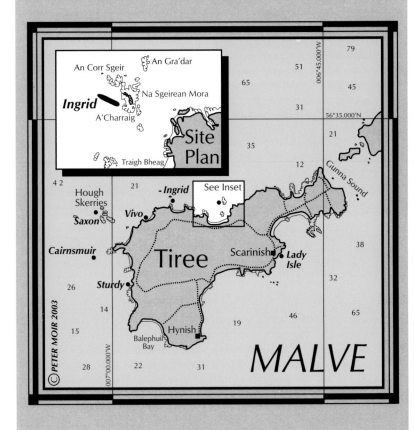

made their way to the shore in the last lifeboat. Despite a series of attempts to refloat her over the next few days the *Malve* stayed hard aground and became a total wreck.

The remains of the *Malve*, which has been heavily salvaged, lie on the rocks called Na Sgeirean Mora on the north side of Balephetrish Bay in position 56°31.952'N, 006°52.252'W (GPS). The wreckage is scattered over a wide area on the south side of the reef in shallow water up to 7 metres deep. Little recognisable remains although her propeller shaft is clearly visible and parts of her engine machinery are also reported to still be in position close to the reef. The site is very exposed from the west and north but otherwise is free from problems.

MINNIE KNAPP

184nt. Wooden brig.
Built in USA.
(ex HYDRA)

Dimensions 100.0' x 18.5' x 12.0'

The circumstances surrounding the loss of the brig *Minnie Knapp* are suspicious to say the least. The first indication of foul play occurred when the owner, Mr Samual Keith of Belfast, took the unusual step of insuring his ship, normally used only in coastal trading, against total loss. In addition he insured her for a sum well in excess of the value of the ship.

The *Minnie Knapp* left Glenarm in County Antrim with a cargo of 350 tons of limestone on 1st June, 1881. This cargo had her laden to her absolute limit and she rode very low in the water as she sailed to Belfast to pick up a last crewman before setting off on her planned trip to Newcastle-upon-Tyne. She left Belfast

Lough on 3rd July under the command of William Caldwell and headed north with a stated intention of sailing through the Minch and north round the top of Scotland. By the 7th, the vessel was in Tobermory and, after a couple of days anchored there, apparently because of contrary winds, they set off north again.

It was from then on that the actions of William Caldwell became suspicious. He steered his ship towards the treacherous channel between Rhum and Canna instead of out into the Minch and spent the next thirty six hours tacking back and forth between the two islands. He stated later at the enquiry into the ship's loss that the wind and tides were against him but it seems unlikely that, even with contrary winds, he would have been unable to make any headway in this time. Even when it was obvious that they were going to run aground, he failed to use his anchors to stop them, later stating that he was expecting a strong wind to spring up from the south that day and that this would surely have resulted in the loss of a vessel anchored close to the rocks at Canna. Eventually, around 10am on Friday 10th the ship did run aground close to the Canna shore. She came off within 15 minutes but was damaged and making water. At first the voyage north continued as the water inflow was not deemed serious and the crew were able to keep it under control with the pumps but, the following day, Caldwell decided to return to Ireland for repairs. By late in the evening of the 12th, as they sailed down the west coast of Mull, the water was reported to be gaining and it was decided that the ship would need to be run ashore. The crew, now exhausted from their hours at the pumps, were put into a small boat while Caldwell stayed aboard to guide the ship ashore. Again Caldwell's actions defy logic as, on a calm June day with light winds, he ran the ship ashore, not on one of the beaches on the west of Mull or Iona but on a barren rocky stretch of coast at the north west end of Iona beneath high cliffs making it certain that the ship would neither be refloated or even easily examined. Interestingly Caldwell chose to run his ship ashore in the exact gully that had been the site of the loss of another Belfast ship, the *Troubadour*, in January 1880. Inevitably the *Minnie Knapp* became total loss.

At the subsequent enquiry, while it was not directly stated that Caldwell had wrecked his ship on purpose, it was clearly implied that the actions taken during the unusual voyage were either the actions of a completely incompetent seaman or of someone intent in wrecking his ship in the remotest location he could find.

NESSMORE

2216nt. Iron steamship.
Built by Barrow Shipbuilding Co.
Launched 1882.

Dimensions 340.0' x 40.4' x 24.2'

It is difficult to imagine how a large steamship en route from Montreal to Liverpool could end up wrecked on the east side of Coll in Crossapol Bay but that is exactly what happened to the *Nessmore* on the 20th November, 1895. The *Nessmore*, which was owned in Liverpool by the Nessmore Company Ltd, had sailed from Montreal on November 6th with a general cargo and 520 cattle aboard. The captain, Amos Hawkett, commanded a crew of thirty six and he also had nineteen cattlemen aboard to take care of the livestock on the voyage.

The trip went badly, as they ran into a series of gales crossing the Atlantic, and he was first forced to change his intended route round the north of Ireland to the longer trip round the south then, on the 18th, back again as yet another storm, this time with hurricane force from the south east, battered his ship. He ran north before the wind to give his crew and the terrified cattle some respite from the incessant pounding of the gigantic waves but tragically, due to the dreadful weather, he began to lose track of the exact location of his ship. The next day the log showed that they had travelled 162 miles but, of course, this could not take into account accurately the extra distance covered as a result of the extra impetus of the driving wind.

Over the next twenty four hours, the captain attempted to navigate his ship in terrible conditions with driving rain and very limited visibility. At one point they had a brief glimpse of the flashing light of a lighthouse. They believed they were somewhere off the north west of Ireland and concluded that the light was Fanad Point Light but they were badly out in their reckoning and it seems likely that it was, in fact, Dubh Artach. With lead soundings being made every few minutes, the captain continued to steer the ship and, when land was sighted two miles off the starboard bow, he turned north west to head for deeper water, and intended to wait out the storm. The soundings confirmed that the water was

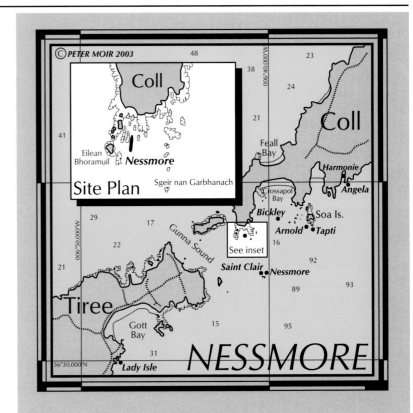

indeed getting deeper and he eventually ordered engines stopped thinking that he would drift safely north west into the Atlantic until he could get some visibility to see where he was headed. The night was so dark and the visibility so poor that it was impossible even to judge exactly in which direction they were drifting. At 10pm on the evening of the 20th, the seabed suddenly shoaled and Captain Hawkett ordered engines started and he again steered a course towards the north west expecting this would take him into deeper water but, almost immediately, breakers were spotted ahead and shortly afterwards, despite reversing engines, the ship ran gently aground. The engines were kept in reverse for a few minutes but this only succeeded in pulling the stern round until the propeller fouled on the submerged rocks and was smashed to pieces. Within an hour there was ten feet of water in the holds and the ship was doomed.

The crew made it safely to the shore in their boats and over the next few days first the cattle, then some of the cargo, were brought ashore but the vessel, lying among the rocks with a severe list to starboard, was clearly a total wreck. The position of the wreck made even removing the cargo very difficult and indeed one of the salvage vessels, the *Hyaena* went aground during the operation but thankfully got off later without severe damage. The wreck itself was later heavily salvaged by James Gush of Greenock and again in more modern times by local diver Chris Oldfield.

The wreck of the *Nessmore* lies among the shallow reefs east of Eilean Bhoramuil in position 56°33.594'N, 006°41.587'W (GPS). The exact location is on the east side of a rock which is charted as drying at 1.7 metres. Very little remains due to heavy salvage activity. The remaining plates and girders lie along the side of the reef half buried in the white sand in around 6 metres. The site is very sheltered except from a south east direction.

NEVADA II

3499nt. Steel steamship.
Built by Bremer Vulkan-Vegesak.
Launched 1918.
(ex ROVUMA)

Dimensions 420.2' x 57.9' x 28.1'

Rationing during both World wars caused many hardships, particularly on remote islands like Coll where even during peacetime many items, regarded as necessities by people living on the mainland, are often in short supply.

Luxury items like cigarettes became almost impossible to obtain except at exorbitant prices on the black market. The wreck of a huge ship crammed full of a varied general cargo of NAAFI stores, including millions of cigarettes, was like a gift from heaven and the islanders on Coll certainly took advantage of their windfall when the *Nevada* was wrecked there on 17th July, 1942.

The *Nevada* herself was originally a German ship but she was handed over to France as part of the country's war reparations at the end of the First World War. She served all over the world between the wars, finally under the ownership of the Companie Generale Transatlantique, and came over to the British when France fell in the early years of the Second World War. At this time she added 'II' to her name to avoid confusion with another British ship named *Nevada*. She was assigned to the management of the famous Paddy Henderson Shipping Company who sailed her in a number of convoys carrying cargoes to and from Britain.

In July of 1942 she left London bound for Bathurst in West Africa with a varied general cargo of NAAFI stores including the cigarettes and many other items - shoes, soap, Brylcream, vehicles, wheelbarrows, clothes, tools, foodstuffs and cloth. She headed for Oban and the convoy assembly point in the Lynne of Lorne and on the 19th she was off the west coast of Coll when she was enveloped in a dense fog. Due to an error in navigation she ran ashore in the poor visibility on the north side of Rubha Mor on the north west coast of the island. She wedged solidly on the rocks and almost immediately took on a severe list to port but all her crew were able to scramble safely ashore.

Over the next few weeks the combined efforts of the salvage teams and the islanders, and indeed some of the RAF crewmen stationed on the island, to salvage the cargo, either legally or illegally, have become a legend on the island. The *Nevada* herself, when examined by the salvage team was found to be afloat at the stern but with her two forward holds partially flooded. At first it was hoped that she might be pulled off after offloading some of the cargo from her forward holds but, on 22nd July, the weather deteriorated and over the next couple of days she pounded on the rocks further damaging her hull and she settled by the stern. The ship was written off as a total loss and the salvage competition began. By day the official salvors worked to load the supplies onto small coasters but by night the locals swooped down to help supplement the meagre supplies available on the island due to the shortages of the war.

Despite the activities of the islanders, which never reached the legendary heights of their neighbours on Eriskay on the wreck of the SS *Politician*, thousands of tons of supplies were saved from the sunken cargo ship over the next few weeks before she was abandoned.

The wreck of the *Nevada* lies close to the shore almost parallel to the north side of Rubha Mor in position 56°41.434'N, 006°29.579'W (GPS).

The remains of her bow are in the shallows close to the surface among the rocks and deep kelp. The ship, which is very broken due to subsequent heavy salvage, tumbles down the underwater rocky slope and cliff reaching a depth of around 16 metres on the white coral/shingle seabed at the stern. Here the remains of her stern steering gear rise dramatically above the seabed reaching 10 metres towards the surface.

Her intact boilers are the largest recognisable feature but there are still huge amounts of wreckage to explore. Much of her cargo, including vehicle parts, corrugated asbestos sheeting and drums of cement can be seen scattered among the wreckage and half buried in the shingle. There are virtually no hazards at the site as it is not subject to any significant tidal movement. The site is however very exposed to wind and swell from the west and north which would make it unsafe in rough weather.

© PETER MOIR 2003

Site Plan

Nevada II

Eilean Eileraig

Rubha Mor

Traigh Bhousd

Wreck lies hard in to north side of point, in depths of 4-16 metres.

See Inset

Cairns of Coll

Saint Brandan

Eilean Mor

Isle of Coll

Hogh Bay

Ballyhaugh

Arinagour

General Consul Ellissejeffe

Feall Bay

Harmonie

Angela

NEVADA II

OSTENDE

2718nt. Steel steamship.
Built by Swan Hunter, Newcastle.
Launched September 1903.
(ex EHRENFELS)

Dimensions 375.1' x 50.5' x 27.4'

The captain of the Belgian ship *Ostende* could not be certain what caused the damage to his ship as he did not see any signs of a mine or a torpedo. He was 9.5 miles west of Skerryvore Lighthouse, en route from New York to Liverpool with a general cargo of war supplies, on the night of the 16/17th of January, 1943 when, at 12:51am, the quiet of the night was shattered by an explosion near the bow of his ship and immediately she began to take in water. Within a short time number 1 hold was eighteen feet deep in water and, although the bulkhead between number 1 and number 2 hold seemed to be secure, the captain began a race to save his ship, planning to beach her at Scarnish on Tiree.

The wireless operators ashore listened to a series of dramatic messages over the next few hours as the captain fought to save his ship but thankfully, after a change of plan during the night, the message came through that she was beached in Loch na Lathaich near Bunessan on the south west coast of Mull. By the time the ship came to a halt in the shallow, sheltered loch the bulkhead between holds 1 and 2 had finally given way flooding number 2 hold. If the captain had not reached shallow water when he did his ship would almost certainly have foundered. As it was, she settled on a gently sloping sandy seabed with her bow in 4 fathoms and her stern in 6 fathoms of water.

SS *Ostende* as *Ehrenfels*.

The *Ostende* seemed to have been saved but unfortunately this was not the end of her story. Salvage tugs and small coasters were dispatched to the scene and began offloading cargo from number 1 hold to allow access to the damaged area of her hull. They planned to repair her where she lay and then tow her off. On the night of the 20th the drifter *Lydia Long* tied up alongside the *Ostende* and the men aboard both ships cleared up after they stopped work for the day. That night the villagers of Bunessan and the sleeping workers were awakened by a series of enormous explosions. The *Ostende* had somehow caught fire destroying her cargo, which included over 500 tons of bombs and artillery shells which exploded tearing the stranded ship apart. In the morning daylight revealed the dreadful damage. The twisted hull of the *Ostende* was almost totally submerged with only the forecastle and bridge sections visible above the surface. Two of her forty eight crew had been killed in the explosions. The *Lydia Long* was gone too but luckily her crew were safe. Divers inspected the wreck and described her as an unrecognisable mass of scrap and distorted plates. Incredibly, large amounts of her cargo did manage to survive the fire and explosions. This cargo was removed over the next few weeks by a salvage team before the ship was finally abandoned.

The Wreck Today

The *Ostende* has clearly been heavily salvaged in the post war years as almost nothing remains at the wreck site which is in position 56°19.344'N, 006°15.885'W. This puts her in the south west corner of the loch. The seabed here is sandy and the water is approximately 10 metres deep. The only signs of the *Ostende* are hundreds of brass shell casings which still litter the site. The Navy have visited the site a number of times to clear live ammunition and have been known to move on dive parties from the site. Otherwise the loch provides very easy diving as it is sheltered and not subject to any tidal movement.

PELICAN

409nt. Iron steamship.
Built by Pike & Co., Cork.
Launched 1859.

Dimensions 205.5' x 28.2' x 15.7'

The *Pelican* was originally built for the City of Cork Steam Packet Co., and served them for thirty eight years before being purchased by David MacBrayne. She was introduced on the Company's Scottish west coast routes, with even the odd trip to Iceland, where she gained a reputation as a fast and reliable ship. Towards the end of her career she was used as a coal hulk, first at Portree, then latterly at Tobermory.

On the evening of the 5th December, 1895 she was lying at her usual mooring in Tobermory Bay. In the early hours of the following morning a gale broke. The old ship's anchor chain parted in the rough weather and she drifted helplessly

SS *Pelican.*

across the bay and went aground on the west shore of Calve Island. The tide was at its peak when she went aground and as it receded, she gradually took on a list to starboard. She eventually slipped off the rocks and immediately sank in deep water close the shore.

The wreck of the *Pelican* sits upright on a mud and silt seabed in around 20-24 metres in position 56°36.953'N, 006°02.579'W (GPS). The hull of the ship is intact but little else remains as her engines were removed prior to her use as a coal hulk. Her wooden decking is also completely gone leaving only the shell of the ship to explore. The silty seabed causes visibility to reduce quickly but otherwise the wreck is free from hazards, lying in a very sheltered position close to the shore of Calve Island.

RAVENSHEUGH

1116nt. Iron steamship.
Built by Palmers, Newcastle.
Launched 1870.

Dimensions 263.0' x 35.2' x 22.4'

The Glasgow steamer *Ravensheugh*, owned by Robertson Mackie & Co, was lost four miles off Skerryvore on 29th October, 1911 after hitting a large submerged object presumed to be a derelict vessel. Initially after the collision, Captain Daniels believed that he could take his ship to Tobermory for repairs and, after taking the precaution of swinging one of the boats out on its davits to allow a rapid escape if necessary, he set course for the Sound of Mull. However, within a couple of hours and in an increasing breeze, it was obvious that they would not make it to Tobermory. In fact the ship was rapidly settling in the water and starting to list badly. Nine of the crew lowered one of the prepared lifeboats and, expecting the remaining ten men aboard to launch the second boat, cast off from the sinking ship. Unfortunately it seems that the crew aboard could not lower the second boat, probably due to the steadily increasing list and, as the men in the lifeboat were quickly swept away from the *Ravensheugh* into the night, they could only watch as she settled further and eventually they saw the masthead light disappear beneath the waves.

For the next ten hours the men in the lifeboat were swept north at the mercy of the wind and waves. At one point they spotted a trawler but could not attract the crew's attention. Eventually, around 3pm in the afternoon, they sighted land and managed to reach the shore on the small island of Gighay which lies a few miles north east of Barra. Their ordeal was not quite at an end. As they set about erecting a shelter from the gear and sail of the lifeboat they spotted a yacht moored in the Sound of Barra. When they returned to their lifeboat, intent on rowing out to the yacht, they found that it had broken adrift in the continuing gale and had blown out to sea. Luckily, after a night ashore, they managed to attract the attention of the crew of the yacht who took them aboard and brought them to Oban. At last their ordeal was at an end.

ROBERT LIMBRICK

103nt. Steel trawler.
Built by Hall Russell & Co, Aberdeen.
Launched March 1942.
(ex STAR OF FREEDOM)

Dimensions 126.2' x 23.7'

The storm which hit the Scottish west coast on the 5th February, 1957 was the worst in living memory with hurricane force winds gusting to 120 mph. On land many roads were blocked by fallen trees, communications were cut as telephone lines came down and there was widespread damage to buildings across the country. For the two Milford Haven trawlers caught off the west coast of Mull in mountainous seas it was a living nightmare. They kept in continuous radio contact as they headed towards the relative shelter of the Sound of Mull but they could not see each other, as the stinging spray, ripped from the crests of the huge breakers by the howling wind, reduced visibility to almost nil.

The skippers of the trawlers, the *Westcar* and the *Robert Limbrick*, were friends and encouraged each other through the night but it was clear that to attempt to enter the Sound in the dark was too dangerous and they concluded that they would have to ride it out in open water until daybreak. Suddenly, William Robson, skipper of the *Westcar* was shaken by a shout from the radio - " Mayday! Mayday! Mayday! *Robert Limbrick* hard aground." He heard an order to get out the rubber dinghy then ominous silence.

The *Robert Limbrick* aground.

The position of the unfortunate crewmen aboard can only be imagined as she was swept by huge waves beating against the exposed west coast of Mull. The next morning two local men from Dervaig who had been listening to the drama unfold on the radio, found the remains of the trawler smashed among the rocks at Quinish Point but there was no sign of the crew. All twelve crew members perished that night. Their bodies were washed ashore along the west coast of Mull over the next few days. The trawler was obviously a total wreck. Examination of the wreckage revealed that the propeller blades were stripped from the shaft but this almost certainly happened when she ran aground. The bridge telegraph indicated engine stopped but no mechanical fault could be found. It was concluded that the loss of the ship was entirely due to the horrendous weather conditions that night.

RONDO

2363gt. Steel steamship.
Built by Tampa Shipbuilding & Drydock Co., Florida.
Launched 1917.
(ex LAURIE ex LITHOPOLIS ex WAR WONDER 1)

Dimensions 264.0' x 42.0' x 21.2'

The *Rondo* was built in the US in the last frantic months of World War 1. She had been ordered under the cover of the Cunard Steamship Company to avoid contravening America's neutral status but before she was complete America had entered the war and the disguise had become unnecessary. She had been named *War Wonder 1* but was immediately renamed *Lithopolis*. She did not complete fitting out till September 1918 and effectively missed the closing action of the war. She was renamed *Laurie* in 1930 and finally *Rondo* in 1934.

In January 1935 the *Rondo*, now under Norwegian ownership, was in Glasgow and left for Dunstan in ballast intending to sail north round the top of Scotland and down the east coast to her Northumberland port destination where she was due to pick up a cargo for Oslo. As she sailed north and into the Sound of Mull on the 25th the weather was atrocious and she was forced to anchor in Aros Bay near Tobermory for shelter in a blinding snowstorm. As the crew settled down for an uncomfortable night, the anchor chain parted and she started to drift east down the Sound driven by the strong winds and the tide. The crew were powerless to guide the helpless ship in the darkness and could only hope that they would be lucky but this was not to be the case. The *Rondo* was swept onto Dearg Sgeir near Eileanan Glas almost demolishing the small lighthouse as she crashed ashore and stuck fast, high and dry on the rock.

The twenty two crew were in no danger but fired distress flares to attract the attention of nearby ships. As the new day dawned the *Rondo* was sitting securely astride the small rock and preparations began for a salvage attempt. The crew remained aboard for two weeks hoping that something could be done to save her but eventually she was abandoned to be broken up where she lay. This activity was well under way when she finally slipped off the rock and sank; bow first, in the deep water close to the island.

The Wreck Today

The steep rocky cliff down which the *Rondo* plunged makes this one of the area's most dramatic wrecks. She sits almost vertical, on her bow which crashed into the seabed 50 metres below the surface, while her rudder post, is often visible from the boat only a few metres below the surface. She lies in position 56°32.306'N, 005°54.749'W (GPS) very close to the north shore of Dearg Sgeir. The hull is all that remains lying against the steep rocky cliff but the metal

"head for the lighthouse"

of the ship is completely covered in a colourful mass of orange, white and green plumose anemones and dead men fingers plus a multitude of other encrusting sealife. The wreck is always patrolled by shoals of curious wrasse and huge saithe and pollock making it more like a dive on a tropical reef than on a Scottish wreck.

The wreck itself is only a shell but the diver can swim down inside the hull emerging to more broken wreckage beyond 30 metres and down into the gloom to the crushed bow at 50 metres. On the way back to the surface a swim outside and under the wreck shows the colourful sealife at its best.

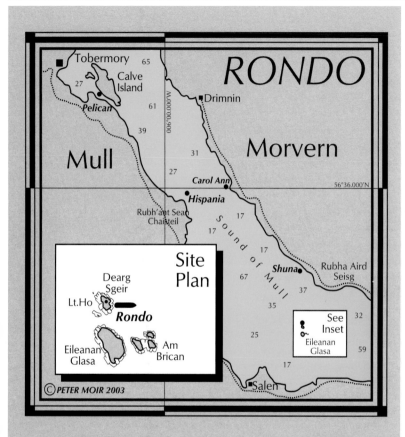

The site is swept by very strong currents making diving at slack water almost essential. Inside the wreck the diver is sheltered from the current but can be easily swept way if great care is not taken when emerging from the wreckage, either to head for the surface or to explore the outside of the wreck.

SAINT BRANDAN

154nt. Steel Steamship.
Built by Scott and Son, Bowling.
Launched November 1924.

Dimensions 145.0' x 23,8' x 10.1'

The Glasgow steamship *Saint Brandan* was bound from Talisker, Skye with a cargo of 200 tons of grain for her home port under the command of Captain Duguld MacDonald. On Saturday 20th October, 1928 she was caught in a ferocious gale off the Cairns of Coll and, in terrible conditions with Captain MacDonald unable to keep his vessel under control, she ran aground on a reef north of Rubha Mor on the north west tip of the island. With mountainous seas crashing into the grounded vessel, she was immediately abandoned by her captain and nine crew. They managed to launch two boats and disembark safely but then had to endure a dangerous three hours struggle to try to reach the shore. The crewmen quickly became exhausted but luckily they were spotted by the crew of the Fleetwood trawler *City of York* which was fishing nearby and were picked up to be taken to safety in Tobermory where they boarded the *Cygnet* to be taken to Oban. The *Saint Brandan*, which was initially caught amidships between two rocks, was reported to have turned over around 11am on the 20th and to have sunk in nine fathoms. She became a total wreck although some kind of salvage operation was attempted by the Liverpool and Glasgow Salvage Association. Perhaps they were attracted by the reports in the Daily Telegraph of the day of £8,000 worth of whisky aboard. In any event the attempt was abandoned on the 31st of October. The remaining wreckage is reported to lie in shallow water among rocks in the middle of the bay north of Rubha Mor peninsula.

SAINT CLAIR

69nt. Iron steamship.
Built by Birrell & Co., Dumbarton.
Launched April 1876.

Dimensions 84.1' x 20.0' x 8.0'

McCallum's steamer *Saint Clair* had a short but adventurous five year career. Her first brush with disaster happened only two and a half years after her launch when she capsized while alongside Salen Pier, Mull on 25th September, 1878. Tragically a woman and a child drowned in this incident but the ship was successfully raised. She continued in service until October 1880 when, on the 22nd of that month, she ran aground on Roan Bogha, Gunna Sound while en route from Tiree to Barra and quickly foundered in deep water near the rock. The crew managed to escape in their boat before she went down but the ship was a total loss.

There have been various reports on the location of the wreck of the *Saint Clair* around Roan Bogha but when the authors visited the site the only substantial wreckage located was from the SS *Hurlford*. However a blade of a small propeller was located on the north west side of the rock which could possibly be from the *Saint Clair*.

SS *Saint Clair.*

The steam trawler *Saxon* barely visible above the Hough Skerries.

SAXON

93nt. Steam trawler.
Built by Smith's Dockyard, South Shields.
Launched 1907.

Dimensions 120.3' x 21.6' x 11.6'

The hundreds of hidden rocks that make up the Hough Skerries cover a vast area off the west of Tiree and have been the final resting place of a good number of ships over the years. The Fleetwood trawler *Saxon* became the latest victim when she ran onto the south end of the rocks on 21st August, 1931. Skipper Christy and his eleven crew immediately realised that their ship was lost and they took to their boat. After a number of hours heavy rowing in the strong tides between the rocks and the Tiree coast they finally made it ashore and walked to Kilkenneth to raise the alarm.

The following day the skipper and the chief officer walked along the shore nearest the skerries and reported the *Saxon* almost submerged with only the funnel and part of the forecastle above sea level and lying with a heavy list to port. The weather continued bad for the next few days and it was only on the 25th that they managed to get a boat out to have a close look at the wreck. By this time she was well broken up and she was abandoned as a total wreck.

SHUNA

880nt. Steel steamship.
Built by A Vuijk & Zonen, Holland.
Launched 1909.

Dimensions 240.9' x 35.2' x 16.5'

Unusually for the time of year, as the Scandanavian Shipping Company's steamship *Shuna* steamed north up the Scottish west coast on her outward voyage carrying coal from Glasgow to Gothenburg in Sweden on 8th May, 1913, she ran into a bad storm. Captain Elsper was relieved to reach the relative calm and safety of the Sound of Mull but even here the visibility was poor with driving rain and sea spray. As he sailed past Craignure just after 9pm that Thursday night the visibility deteriorated even further as daylight began to fade. Just after 10pm, the ship ran onto Grey Rock and, although she did not stay aground, she quickly began to take in water. The captain decided to try to make for Tobermory but it was soon obvious that this would be impossible as the pumps were evidently failing to cope with the inrush of water. He decided to run his ship ashore on the Morvern coast hoping to repair her and refloat her later.

As the storm continued to lash his ship, he steamed at full speed towards land, managing to beach her safely north west of Rubha Aird Seisg where he dropped both anchors to the seaward side to be used later to pull her off. The bow was high and dry on the shore but huge waves smashed the side of the ship and were breaking over the bridge. Later, as the weather subsided somewhat, the captain dispatched the mate for Tobermory to summon assistance and the crew settled down to wait for help. The *Shuna* was gradually settling into the water and by 5am it was obvious that she was going to go down. The crew were forced to abandon ship and reached the shore safely in the ship's boats. They secured their ship to the shore with a sturdy hawser but this last futile effort to save her was to no avail. They could only watch helplessly as she settled further and finally, around 10am, the hatches blew off, the hawser snapped and she slipped beneath the surface. The crew rowed safely back to Tobermory which they reached around midday.

The *Shuna* was the last large wreck to be located in the Sound of Mull but by the time the location became known to sports divers she had been stripped clean of almost every single item of non ferrous metal. However she still makes an excellent dive. She sits upright in 30-32 metres of water, parallel to the shore, on a gently sloping seabed with the deck 16-20 metres from surface. Her deck structures are almost completely destroyed but her four holds, engine room and raised forecastle still give a clear picture of her former layout. The holds are still full of coal but it is possible to descend into

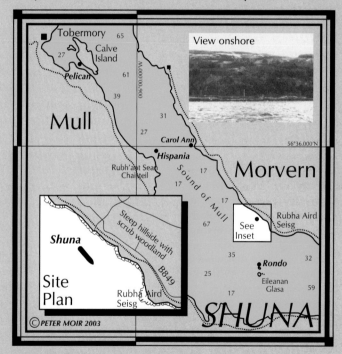

the engine room area and some other areas below deck level. The wreck lies at 55°33.413'N, 005°54.842'W (GPS), and is only 200 metres from the Morvern shore. It can be dived from the shore but it is a fairly long swim and not to be recommended. Unlike most of the other wrecks in the Sound of Mull, due to her relatively sheltered position in the bay, she is not subject to the strong tides of the area although some gentle current is possible.

SSAFA

**139nt. Steel motor trawler.
Built by Goole Shipbuilding
Company.
Launched January 1958.**

Dimensions 138.8' x 28.5'

The Fleetwood trawler *SSAFA* ran aground during a gale in Friesland Bay, Coll on Tuesday 17th January, 1961 to become the latest in a long line of trawlers from that port which have been lost off the Scottish west coast. The first indication of a problem was a mayday message received by Oban Radio at 6:36am GMT that morning. Within minutes a number of vessels were heading for her position to render assistance but Skipper Harry Pook, after a quick investigation below, cancelled the mayday one hour later as it was clear they were in no immediate danger. With the *SSAFA's* sister ship *Princess Ann* and the Mallaig lifeboat, which could not approach the wreck due to the *SSAFA's* position close to the shore among jagged rocks, standing by, they waited for the tide to rise hoping to refloat her at high water. Twelve of the crew were pulled ashore through the surf by the island lifesaving team and were now safely aboard the lifeboat leaving the skipper and three

others on the *SSAFA* to attempt to pull her off. However as the tide rose and the *SSAFA* gradually took on a severe list to port, it was obvious that they were not going to succeed and the skipper and his three colleagues reluctantly abandoned their vessel to be picked up by the lifeboat which then returned to Mallaig. Weather reports the day after she went ashore described sea conditions in the area as terrible with huge waves pounding the grounded trawler. The last sting in the tail of the story of the *SSAFA* came as the Clyde salvage vessel *Plantagenet* made her way from the scene later in the week. She too ran aground near Skye in a seven knot tide but luckily she survived, although she had to be towed back to the Clyde by one of her own tugs.

The motor trawler **SSAFA**.

HMS *STURDY*

905dt. Steel destroyer.
Built by Scotts, Greenock.
Launched June 1919.

Dimensions 276.0' x 26.7' x 10.9'

HMS *Sturdy*, an 'S' class destroyer, had entered service just after the end of the Great War and had served well until the outbreak of the Second World War in 1939. Fourteen months after Britain declared war on Germany *Sturdy* left Dublin for a regular patrol in the Western Atlantic with Lt. Commander Cooper in charge. Four hours later she was ashore, in dense fog, on the western shores of Tiree, near Sandaig. She ran onto the rocks at speed causing severe damage to the bow of the ship which was badly bent at the forecastle bulkhead.

Some of the sailors on board believed that they had been torpedoed and jumped into the sea in panic and in an attempt to save themselves. Tragically five men were lost as a result. One man did make it ashore and raced to the nearby house of Lachie McDonald to raise the alarm. Another local man, Captain Donald Sinclair, quickly went down to the beach close to the grounded ship and shouted to the men aboard to remain calm and remain aboard as they were in no danger. This action probably saved many lives as they were later all safely rescued. The graves of the men lost are in the little cemetery at Balemartine on the island. The *Sturdy* was almost completely removed during subsequent salvage operations. The track used by the salvage teams is still apparent running down to the shore from the village of Sandaig and some small items of wreckage are visible ashore. The major item of underwater wreckage is reported to be her boiler lying in shallow water just off the shore.

MV *Tapti*.

TAPTI

4411nt. Steel motor vessel.
Built by C Connell & Co., Glasgow.
Launched October 1945.

Dimensions 415.6' x 55.2' x 33.9'

The short voyage from the Mersey to the Tyne was to be the precursor to a long uncomfortable winter trip to India. However, January is often the worst weather month on the Scottish west coast. As Captain Coney navigated the *Tapti* north towards the Minch on the 17th of that month in 1951, the ship was caught in a typical January gale with strong south west winds driving sheets of heavy rain across her decks. The sixty crew, mainly hardened seamen from China and India, were sent scuttling for shelter as the downpour reduced visibility to almost nil. The British officers on the evening watch strained to see ahead as the rain rattled against the windows of the bridge, but they could see nothing except inky blackness outside.

Without warning there was a tremendous crash as the ship ran aground and she shuddered to a sudden halt. The ship shook as the captain tried in vain to free her and she listed first one way then the other before the swell from the south swung her stern ashore and aground high on the rocks. She finally settled with a heavy list to starboard and the crew set about preparations to abandon her in case she started to go down.

All that night they kept in continuous wireless contact with Malin Head Radio as a fleet of rescue vessels headed towards their position. By morning Mallaig and Barra lifeboats, two frigates and two trawlers were standing by but could do little as the ship settled deeper in the water. Eventually, as the list reached a precarious sixty degrees, the captain ordered the crew to leave the ship and they scrambled down the nets which had been thrown over the side and into the waiting lifeboats. No one was hurt and they were all taken safely to Tobermory leaving their ship behind on the rocky islet of Eilean Soa. Four days later during Saturday night the *Tapti*, pounded by yet another severe gale, slipped off the rocks and sank in deep water.

The MV *Tapti* aground.

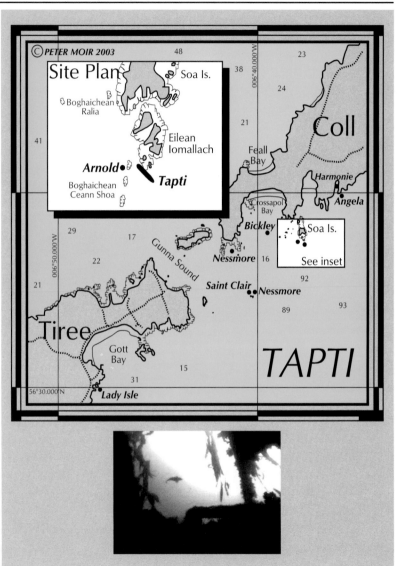

The Wreck Today

The *Tapti* was a large ship and despite the obvious attentions of salvage teams over the years remains an impressive wreck. She lies south of Eilean Iomallach in position 56°33.664'N, 006°37.845'W (GPS) in depths from 10 to 25 metres. Her stern is nearest the shore and in the shallowest part of the site with the bow bearing south east. Large pieces of wreckage are strewn across a rock then sandy seabed with many still recognisable features along the entire length of the ship. Her bow is the most impressive aspect of the wreck. The bow section is separated from the rest of the wreckage and points to the surface rising nearly 15 metres directly from the seabed. The impressive wreckage and the masses of colourful encrusting sealife make this a memorable dive site. There is very little current in the area but the site is exposed from the south and can therefore be subject to heavy swell if the wind is from that direction.

TEUNIKA

114nt. Motor vessel.
Built by E J Smit, Westerbroek.
Launched 1936.
 (ex WILHELMINA ex VELOCITAS ex WILLEM ex MERKEN)

Dimensions 112.0' x 21.6' x 8.3'

At 08.08 GMT on 16th May, 1969 the radio at Oban Radio crackled into life with a mayday message from the MV *Teunika*, in trouble with her engine out and making water off the west coast of Mull giving her position as 10 miles north west of Tobermory. The MV *Claymore* set out from Tobermory to her rescue and other ships too raced to the scene. Forty minutes later the first to arrive was the trawler *Corena* who immediately sent a short radio message cancelling the mayday, giving their position as 12 miles west of Tobermory. She had taken the *Teunika* in tow and they were heading for the Sound of Mull. It seemed that everything was going to work out well but less than 40 minutes later another message arrived at Oban from the *Corena* - the *Teunika* had sunk eleven miles west of Tobermory and the crew were safely aboard the *Corena*.

The Mallaig lifeboat gave the position of the loss as 253 degrees two and a half miles from Calaich Point. A wreck is charted in position 55°36.875'N, 006°21.915W which is close to the position given by the lifeboat, this may prove to the wreck of the *Teunika*.

THESIS

151nt. Iron steamship.
Built by McIlwaine, Lewis & Co., Belfast.
Launched January 1887.

Dimensions 167.0' x 25.0' x 11.7'

Details of the loss of the Belfast steamship *Thesis* are very vague as contemporary reports are unusually brief and lack any explanation of her loss. She was en route from Middlesbrough to Belfast with a cargo of pig iron in October 1889. She had sailed north round Scotland and, as she turned south, she presumably passed through the Minch before taking a route close to the mainland and through the Sound of Mull. As she reached the south end of the Sound, towards midnight on Tuesday 15th, the night was calm and apparently clear.

Newspaper reports then indicate that she "ran onto a reef at Inninmore Point. " It is not clear where the grounding took place but it seems likely that she had struck on the small island of Eilean Rubha an Ridire. The crew of eleven managed to get ashore safely but the *Thesis* was doomed. She sank in deep water some four hours later near the Morven shore at Rubha an Ridire.

The Wreck Today

The wreck of the *Thesis* lies on a steeply sloping shingle seabed in position 56°29.933'N, 005°41.466'W (GPS) only fifty metres from the rocky shoreline. The bow points to the shore and lies in just over 20 metres while the stern lies in 35 metres with a depth of around 30-32 metres on the wreck at the stern. The wreck itself is basically only the hull of the ship as all superstructure and decking have disappeared. Many of the hull plates have also fallen away and lie scattered on the seabed on either side of the wreck.

The state of the wreck makes it possible to have a spectacular dive in the often excellent visibility. A diver can swim the entire length of the vessel below deck level with the many holes in the ship's sides allowing light to penetrate inside the hull and the diver to peer out at the shoals of fish that patrol the wreck

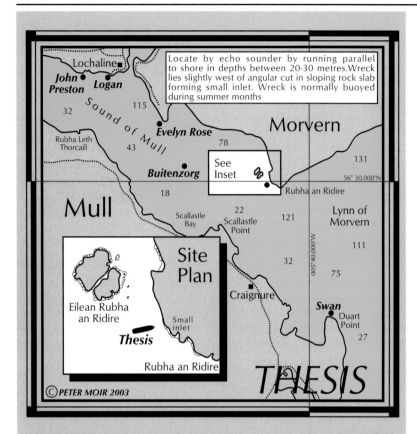

Locate by echo sounder by running parallel to shore in depths between 20-30 metres. Wreck lies slightly west of angular cut in sloping rock slab forming small inlet. Wreck is normally buoyed during summer months

Lochaline
John Preston
Logan
32
115
Sound of Mull
Rubha Leth Thorcaill
43
Evelyn Rose
78
Morvern
Buitenzorg
See Inset
56° 30.000'N
18
Rubha an Ridire
Mull
22
Scallastle Bay
Scallastle Point
121
Lynn of Morvern
131
111
32
75
5.000'W
Site Plan
Eilean Rubha an Ridire
Small inlet
Craignure
Swan
Duart Point
27
Thesis
Rubha an Ridire
© PETER MOIR 2003
THESIS

and even when the current drops or at slack water it is still recommended for the experienced only as it can turn from slack to a strong run in the time it takes to complete a dive. When the tide is strong the dive described above is the only one possible as otherwise the diver is liable to be swept off the wreck or at least will spend an uncomfortable time clinging to the wreck to avoid being swept away.

TOBERMORY GALLEON

800t. Spanish Armada Ship.

There is no doubt that the most famous shipwreck in the region is the " Tobermory Galleon." The story of the ship, its arrival in Tobermory, its loss and subsequent attempts to salvage her "treasure" have become almost legend, to the extent that it is sometimes difficult to ascertain what is fact and what is fiction. Even the actual name of the ship now lying deep in the mud in Tobermory Bay is subject to speculation and to this day has never been definitively established.

The story of the wreck begins with the English rout of the Spanish Armada in the English Channel in 1588. After the battle the fleet was scattered and many of them chose to sail for home round the north of Scotland, rather than risk returning through the Channel. The sailors and the defeated soldiers of King Philip's army had to suffer a horrendous voyage through the stormy winter seas round Scotland and the west of Ireland before reaching their homeland. Around the rugged coastline along the route lie the wrecks of many of the ships which didn't make it home at all.

One of the Spanish ships arrived at Tobermory in late September or early October 1588 to renew her sails which had been reduced to tatters as a result of the attentions of both the English warships and the wild Scottish weather. The local landowner, McLean of Duart, promised the Spaniards help in return for their assistance in his fight with his rival, McDonald of Islay. This resulted in a series of successful and bloody raids on McDonald's properties on Canna,

at all times. As you descend and manoeuvre round the boiler and the remains of the engines, shafts of light pierce the darkness through empty portholes. Emerging into the stern hold and then on down towards stern itself the light fades slightly but generally is still good even on the seabed at 35 metres beneath the back end of the ship.

The Sound of Mull is well known for its strong currents and the wreck of the *Thesis* is probably the most affected as the tides whips round the headland at Rubha an Ridire. At some states of the tide the wreck will be undiveable

Rhum, Eigg, Muck and Ardnamurchan. Later McLean was declared a rebel for these attacks in which many McDonalds were massacred at the hands of the Spanish soldiers under his command.

In November 1588 the ship was still lying anchored in the Bay. The cause of the explosion that destroyed the ship and most of its crew is again subject to much speculation but there is no doubt that the gunpowder aboard ignited and the ship blew up, caught fire and sank in the middle of Tobermory Bay leaving only fifty to sixty Spaniards alive. Potential causes of the explosion range from simple accident to sabotage either by McLean himself or by English secret agents and even include a local legend that the gunpowder was ignited by sparks from the fur of a fairy cat sent to terrorise the Spaniards by a witch from Lochaber.

From the day the ship went down the legend of the Tobermory Treasure began. There have been dozens of attempts to salvage the wreck in the four hundred years since she sank but few have even found the remains and none have had much success in locating anything of value. Records of early explorations are scant but the first serious attempt seems to have been by Archibald Miller between 1680 and 1683. He reports seeing bells, anchors, plates and one "great gun" which he describes in some detail as well as a number of smaller guns many of which were brought to the surface despite the very crude equipment available to these early salvors. The next serious expedition was a two year effort by Captain Jacob Rowe between 1729 and 1731 but, although he cleared a lot of wreckage in the stern section area of the ship, he found nothing of value. The names of the people who have attempted to find the treasure over the years read like a " Who's who" of diving - James Gush from Greenock - he failed to find anything although his son did manage one gold coin on a later attempt - Commander Crabb in 1950 - Wharton Williams of HMS *Edinburgh* fame - all to no avail. In fact, the actual location of anything that has survived the years of salvage and lies buried deep in the mud of the Bay, is now completely lost.

As to the name of the ship there have been many suggestions - for many years *Admiralta de Florencia* was the most likely - but latest evidence is more or less conclusive and indicates that the ship was the *Santa Maria de Gracia y San Juan Bautista* - an 800 ton ship built in Ragusa (Dubrovnic) commanded by Don Diego Tellez Henriquez.

All that remains of the *Vivo's* engine.

VIVO

754nt. Iron steamship.
Built by T & W Smith, North Shields.
Launched July 1883.

Dimensions 240.9' x 34.3' x 13.6'

The Newcastle steamship *Vivo* was en route from her home port to Dublin with a cargo of 1500 tons of coal for her owners, R.B. Fenwick & Co., when she encountered dense fog while off Tiree on 12th December, 1890. Lost in almost nil visibility, she eventually ran ashore near Balevullin at Traigh Bail-a-Mhuilinn. The weather was calm at the time she went ashore and the crew were easily able to make their way ashore but the ship was destined to be a total loss although it is almost certain that much of her cargo was salved and the ship herself was probably substantially dismantled where she lay.

The Wreck Today

The only item that remains on the wreck site is a portion of the engines with one massive crankshaft lying in the shallows at position 56°31.348'N, 006°57.516'W (GPS) which is on the south side of the beautiful sandy bay at Balevullin. At low tide this small piece of wreckage is visible above water. At high water it makes an enjoyable short snorkel with the rusting old engine silhouetted against the gleaming white sand of the bay. It is very exposed from the west and the north.

MULL, COLL AND TIREE

Listed below are a selection of 65 smaller vessels wrecked within this area. This list is included as a basis for further research. Names suffixed by (S) denote extensive salvage work or total removal subsequent to date of loss.

NAME	BUILT	TONNAGE	HULL	TYPE	LOST	CAUSE	LOCATION
Adamton	1904	1494nt	S	SS	08.04.1916	T	10mls SW Tiree
Adventure	-	206nt	W	Bg	15.02.1847	S	Mull
Aid	-	88nt	W	Sr	27.08.1847	S	Tobermory, Mull
Annie Melling	1906	221gt	-	Str	11.08.1922	C	Near Tobermory
Aranda	1890	1838gt	I	SS	05.08.1916	M	Off Skerryvore
Chieftan	1860	85gt	I	PS	20.08.1861	S	Arinagour, Coll
Clara R	1866	212nt	W	Bg	15.01.1887	S	Scallasdale, Mull
Crane	1902	68nt	I	SS	25.02.1908	S	The Stirks, Sound of Mull
Dean Swift	1840	22nt	W	Sk	17.03.1854	F	Off Tobermory
Defender	1903	68nt	S	Str	14.01.1909	S	Skerryvore
Defiance	-	34t	W	Sr	31.12.1863	s	Friesland Rk, Coll
Diamond	1867	34nt	I	SS	11.09.1884	S	Hynish, Tiree
Diligence	1764	82bn	W	Bgn	23.11.1795	S	NW Mull
Duke of Argyll (S)	1852	100gt	I	PS	12.01.1858	S	Sound of Mull
Eli	1931	4332gt	S	MV	10.09.1940	Gfr	Off Skerryvore
Emildor	-	-	-	Str	14.01.1925	S	Arinagour, Coll
Fisher Queen	-	-	W	MFV	00.00.1973	S	SW Coll
Francis Yates	1839	183nt	W	Bg	03.10.1860	S	Coll
Glenarm	-	-	I	SS	24.12.1895	S	Scallasdale, Mull
Glenlyon	1900	66gt	S	SS	13.04.1931	S	Balephetrish Bay,Tiree
Golden Gleam	1949	27nt	W	MFV	27.10.1954	S	Sound of Mull
Hero	1876	152nt	W	Bn	15.09.1878	S	Grey Island, Sound of Mull
Hurra	1868	399nt	W	Bk	04.03.1884	S	Ardlanach Pt, Mull
Hyena(S)	-	-	I	SS	02.12.1895	S	Eilean Bhoramuil,Tiree
Industry	1865	90nt	W	Sr	08.02.1889	S	Craignure, Mull
James	1838	37gt	W	Sk	11.12.1869	s	Scarnish, Tiree
Japonica	-	-	-	Tr	11.08.1913	S	Gott Bay, Tiree
Jessie	1854	58nt	W	Sr	30.11.1888	F	Loch Sunart
Johanna	-	-	W	MV	29.04.1968	S	Near Lochaline

NAME	BUILT	TONNAGE	HULL	TYPE	LOST	CAUSE	LOCATION
Katherine Ellen	-	-	W	Sr	23.09.1879	S	Craignure, Mull
Kingston Beryl	1928	356gt	S	SS	25.12.1943	M	Off Skerryvore
Kitty	-	-	W	S	16.04.1847	F	Off Tobermory
Lady o'the Lake	1877	33nt	S	SS	16.03.1900	S	Calve Island, Mull
Laristan(S)	1927	3863nt	S	SS	19.01.1942	S	Beist Bay, Tiree
Logan	1921	99gt	S	SS	15.12.1961	F	Near Lochaline Pier
Macduff	1892	67nt	S	SS	20.07.1908	F	Ardmore Pt, Mull
Maid of Lorne	1893	42nt	I	Sltr	17.04.1896	S	Eilean Ura, Iona
Maister	1802	322bn	W	S	13.12.1822	S	West coast, Tiree
Mandale	-	-	W	Bk	19.08.1850	S	Breacheaha, Coll
Margaret Wetherley		211gt	S	Str	05.02.1943	S	Sound of Mull
Mary Clark	1834	29nt	W	S	27.08.1847	S	Tobermory
Mary Smethurst	1882	96nt	W	Sr	29.12.1908	S	Tobermory
Mayflower	-	8nt	W	Sk	22.06.1872	F	4miles north of Coll
Menai	1856	77nt	W	Sr	08.04.1896	S	Scallasdale, Mull
Michael John	1857	66nt	W	Sr	24.01.1868	S	Crossapol, Coll
Nancy	1873	232bn	W	Bgn	08.02.1885	S	Dubh Sgeir, Tiree
New Blessing	1865	158nt	W	Bn	12.12.1883	S	Duart Point, Mull
Nydalen	1920	625t	S	SS	31.03.1940	S	1ml S Arinagour
Ocean Tide	1917	227gt	S	Str	15.01.1942	S	West coast of Tiree
Pecten	1927	7468gt	S	SS	25.08.1940	T	15 miles W of Skerryvore
Peggy	-	-	W	S	15.01.1835	S	Tiree
Protesilaus	1910	9577gt	S	SS	13.09.1940	S	5 miles NW of Skerryvore
Regina	1865	378bn	W	Bk	08.10.1872	S	Hynish, Tiree
Rhine	1816	121nt	W	Sr	14.01.1860	S	Coll
Richard Crofts (S)			S	Str	20.02.1953	S	Cornaig, Coll
Richard Thomson	1862	99nt	W	Bn	02.02.1873	F	South of Coll
Riddha	1902	701t	S	SS	01.12.1902	S	Cornaigbeg Pt, Tiree
Robert Norras(S)	-	-	W	Sr	23.09.1879	S	Craignure, Mull
Saint Anthony	1899	115gt	S	SS	03.09.1931	S	Balephetrish Bay,Tiree
Scarinish	1898	31nt	W	K	11.11.1917	S	Calve Island, Mull
Seal	1892	44nt	S	SS	26.09.1893	C	2miles W of Lochaline
Siber	1878	323nt	W	Sr	22.04.1883	S	Skerryvore
Sultan	1856	399t	W	Bk	15.12.1873	S	Crossapol, Coll
Troubadour	1862	133nt	W	Bn	30.12.1879	S	Iona
Wharfinger	1892	57nt	S	SS	21.01.1911	F	Off Lochaline, Sound of Mull

BIBLIOGRAPHY

BOOKS

Blackburn	Dive Islay Wrecks	Bucknall 1986
Buchanan & Fairgray	Kintyre/Gigha Dive Guide	Buchanan/Fairgray 1994
College	Ships of the Royal Navy - Vol.1	Greenhill 1987
College	Ships of the Royal Navy - Vol.2	Greenhill 1987
Dewer	Collision at Sea - How	Brown 1989
Drummond	HM U-Boat	Allen 1958
Duckworth & Langmuir	Clyde and Other Coastal Steamers	Brown 1939
Duckworth & Langmuir	Clyde River and Other Steamers	Brown 1937
Duckworth & Langmuir	West Highland Steamers	Tilling 1935
Elliot	Armarda Britain	David & Charles 1987
Hannan	Fifty Years of Naval Tugs	Maritime Books
Hocking	Dictionary of Disasters at Sea	London Exchange 1989
HMSO	British Vessels Lost at Sea 1914-18	Stephens 1977
HMSO	British Vessels Lost at Sea 1939-45	Stephens 1983
Larn	Shipwreck Index of GB - Vol. 4	Lloyds Register
Larn	Shipwrecks of GB and Ireland	David & Charles 1981
Macdonald	Dive Scotlands Greatest Wrecks	Mainstream 1993
McDonald	The Clyde Puffer	David and Charles 1977
McLeay	Tobermory Treasure	Conway 1986
Martin	Full Fathom Five	Chatto & Windus 1975
Munro	Scottish Lighthouses	Thule Press 1979
National Maritime Museum	Sipbuilding Monograph	N M M
Navy Records Society	Old Scots Navy	Navy Records Soc. 1914
Paterson	The Light in the Glens	House of Lochar 1996
Preston	Days at the Coast	Stenlake 1994
Rohwer	Axis Submarine Successes	Stephens 1983
Sawyer & Mitchell	Liberty Ships	Lloyds Press 1985
Tennant	GB Merchant Ships Sunk by U-Boat	Starling Press 1990
Thompson	Cook, Welton & Gemmell	Hutton Press 1999
Williamson	Clyde Passenger Steamers	Maclehose 1904
Whittaker	Off Scotland	C-ANNE Publishing 1998
Young	Britain's Sea War	Stephens 1989
Zanelli	Shipwrecks Around Britain	Kaye & Ward 1978
Zanelli	Unknown Shipwrecks Around Britain	Kaye & Ward 1974

NEWSPAPERS

Argyllshire Herald
Campbeltown Courier
Daily Record
Glasgow Herald
Glasgow Evening News
Greenock Advertiser
Greenock Telegraph
Lloyds Shipping Gazette
Oban Times
Scotsman

PERIODICALS

Diver Magazine
Scottish Diver
Scots Magazine
Sea Breezes

ARCHIVE MATERIAL AND OTHER SOURCES

Board of Trade Enquiry Reports
Glasgow Chamber of Commerce Archives
House of Commons: British Session Papers Wreck Returns
Hyrdographic Department, Royal Navy
Janes Fighting Ships
Lloyds Register of Shipping
Lloyds Register of Yachts
Northern Lighthouse Board
Royal National Lifeboat Institute

ballan wrasse

deco again!

plumose anemone

inside the stern - Ospray II

Riant

shade and colour - Criscilla

looking out - Benghazi

boiler - San Sebastian

under the stern - C

sub
Argyll